Extreme Politics

Extreme Politics

*Nationalism, Violence, and
the End of Eastern Europe*

CHARLES KING

OXFORD
UNIVERSITY PRESS
2010

OXFORD
UNIVERSITY PRESS

Oxford University Press, Inc., publishes works that further
Oxford University's objective of excellence
in research, scholarship, and education.

Oxford New York
Auckland Cape Town Dar es Salaam Hong Kong Karachi
Kuala Lumpur Madrid Melbourne Mexico City Nairobi
New Delhi Shanghai Taipei Toronto

With offices in
Argentina Austria Brazil Chile Czech Republic France Greece
Guatemala Hungary Italy Japan Poland Portugal Singapore
South Korea Switzerland Thailand Turkey Ukraine Vietnam

Copyright © 2010 by Oxford University Press, Inc.

Published by Oxford University Press, Inc.
198 Madison Avenue, New York, New York 10016

www.oup.com

Oxford is a registered trademark of Oxford University Press

Library of Congress Cataloging-in-Publication Data

King, Charles, 1967–
Nationalism, violence, and the end of Eastern Europe / Charles King.
   p. cm.
Includes bibliographical references and index.
ISBN 978-0-19-537037-9; 978-0-19-537038-6 (pbk.)
1. Ethnic conflict—Europe, Eastern. 2. Political violence—Europe, Eastern.
3. Nationalism—Europe, Eastern. 4. Europe, Eastern—Ethnic relations—Political aspects.
5. Europe, Eastern—Politics and government—1989– I. Title.
JN96.A38M55 2010
305.800947—dc22   2009038940

Printed in the United States of America
on acid-free paper

For
Archie Brown

Acknowledgments

I am grateful to several journal and book editors for allowing me to present my ideas in their forums. Some of the essays in this volume were published in an earlier form, and portions are reproduced here by permission. The original publications were "Nations and Nationalism in British Political Studies," in Jack Hayward, Brian Barry, and Archie Brown, eds., *The British Study of Politics in the Twentieth Century* (London and Oxford: The British Academy and Oxford University Press, 1999), copyright © 1999 The British Academy; "The Micropolitics of Social Violence," *World Politics* 56, no. 3 (2004), copyright © 2004 The Johns Hopkins University Press; "Post-postcommunism: Transition, Comparison, and the End of 'Eastern Europe,'" *World Politics* 53, no. 1 (2000), copyright © 2000 The Johns Hopkins University Press; "The Benefits of Ethnic War: Understanding Eurasia's Unrecognized States," *World Politics* 53, no. 4 (2001), copyright © 2001 The Johns Hopkins University Press; "Diaspora Politics: Ethnic Linkages, Foreign Policy, and Security in Eurasia," *International Security* 24, no. 3 (2000), coauthored with Neil J. Melvin, copyright © 2000 by the President and Fellows of Harvard College and the Massachusetts Institute of Technology; and "Migration and Ethnicity in Eastern Europe and Eurasia," in Zoltan D. Barany and Robert G. Moser, eds., *Ethnic Politics after Communism* (Ithaca, N.Y.: Cornell University Press, 2005), copyright © 2005 by Cornell University. Portions of chapter 1 appeared as "Scots to Chechens: How Ethnic Is Ethnic Conflict?" *Harvard International Review* (Winter 2007), and one section of chapter 6 appeared in earlier form as "The Kosovo Precedent," *Newsnet: The Newsletter of the American Association for the Advancement of Slavic Studies* (May 2008). A roundtable that I organized at the 2006 annual meeting of the

American Historical Association contributed to my thinking about the "loser nationalisms" as addressed in chapter 3. I thank my copanelists Nina Silber, Mrinalini Sinha, Timothy Snyder, Ronald G. Suny, and Larry Wolff for their stimulating presentations.

For advice, helpful conversations, and healthy debates, I thank Zoltan Barany, Erica Benner, Michael Brown, Rogers Brubaker, Sally Cummings, Chip Gagnon, Zvi Gitelman, Katherine Graney, Marc Howard, Nelson Kasfir, David Landau, the late Joseph Lepgold, Sean Lynn-Jones, Neil J. Melvin, Rob Moser, Razmik Panossian, Andrew Wilson, Christianne Hardy Wohlforth, William Wohlforth, and two reviewers for Oxford University Press. At the press, David McBride was a stellar editor and an encouraging voice for this project.

I have benefited from the help of several research assistants over the years. They were Jennifer Garrard, Drew Peterson, Jeanette Rébert, Felicia Roşu, Matthew Schmidt, and Adam Tolnay. Georgetown University—in particular, the Edmund A. Walsh School of Foreign Service, its Center for Eurasian, Russian, and East European Studies, and the Department of Government—has provided a wonderfully collegial home since 1996. I thank in particular the Honorable Robert Gallucci, former dean of the School of Foreign Service, for his leadership and support. My friends in the City of Alexandria Pipes and Drums have helped me revel in and guffaw at the absurdities of national myths. As always, my beloved Maggie Paxson has been there with deep intelligence, insight, love, and tea.

This book is dedicated to Professor Archie Brown, my doctoral supervisor at Oxford, whose intellectual verve and good-natured guidance have inspired generations of political scientists in the United Kingdom, the United States, Russia, and beyond.

Contents

Abbreviations

CIS	Commonwealth of Independent States
EU	European Union
GUAM	Georgia, Ukraine, Azerbaijan, Moldova—officially known as the GUAM Organization for Democracy and Economic Development
IDP	internally displaced person
IOM	International Organization for Migration
KLA	Kosovo Liberation Army
NATO	North Atlantic Treaty Organization
OSCE	Organization for Security and Cooperation in Europe
SNP	Scottish National Party
UN	United Nations

Extreme Politics

I

Introduction

Every autumn at local parks throughout the United States, thousands of Scots come together to have an ethnic conflict. Kilt-clad chieftains from the major clans—the MacGregors and Campbells, the McDonalds and Wallaces—march with tartan banners held high. Bagpipers parade back and forth, drones erect and chanters skirling. Warriors whoop and terriers yelp as they descend on the soccer field or baseball diamond. Occasionally, someone denounces the English. Then, one of the clans receives a trophy for being the fiercest, and everyone decamps to the beer tent.

These are the peculiar rituals of Scottish Highland games, a growing form of weekend entertainment for Americans of Celtic heritage (and many who have no family connection at all). Two centuries ago, however, the Scots would have seemed less quaint. Thousands of people were killed in interclan feuding. Highlanders staged bloody rebellions against English rule. The British Crown and feudal lords responded with what would now be called ethnic cleansing, forcibly removing Highland farmers in a sweeping campaign known as the Clearances. "Till the Highlanders lost their ferocity, with their arms, they suffered from each other all that malignity could dictate, or precipitance could act," wrote Samuel Johnson during a tour of the region in 1773. "Every provocation was revenged with blood, and no man that ventured into a numerous company . . . was sure of returning without a wound."[1] Scottish nationalism still exists; in the early 2000s, in fact, it seems to be on the rise. But as you stand in line at a municipal park in Virginia or Pennsylvania, waiting for a sample of Scotch whisky or a lunch of meat pie and shortbread, all surrounded by gentle enthusiasts trussed up in sporrans and plaids, Scotland's ancient enmities and nationalist struggles seem a universe away.

Why do some social conflicts appear to endure across the centuries, while others become the purview of suburbanites who happen to spend their weekends puffing on bagpipes? What do we know about nationalism as an idea and as a species of social mobilization? Is the experience of western Europe fundamentally different from that of the old communist east, where nationalism and ethnic disputes were some of the dominant themes of the 1990s? Could being a Serb or a Chechen, in other words, ever become the same thing as being a Scot?

Many of these questions were of critical importance to scholars and foreign policy practitioners in the immediate post–cold war period, the long decade that stretched from the fall of the Berlin wall on November 9, 1989, to the terrorist attacks on New York and Washington on September 11, 2001—that dreamlike era from 11/9 to 9/11, lodged between the cold war and the "war on terror."[2] The upsurge in nationalist animosity, the sentiments of blood and belonging, and the horrors of genocide and ethnic cleansing seemed to define politics and social life after the end of superpower competition. These new ills were held responsible for everything from the violent breakup of Yugoslavia to the sluggishness of political reform across parts of the old eastern bloc. Many of the great debates of the 1990s—over recognition of the newly independent states of eastern Europe and Eurasia, Western intervention in Bosnia and Kosovo, the genocide in Rwanda, the fate of East Timor, and the role of the United Nations and regional organizations as arbiters in substate disputes— were bound up with matters of cultural identity, nationality, and conflict. Today, similar issues are said to be among the critical drivers of international politics, from sectarian clashes between Sunni and Shi'a in Iraq to the plight of civilians in Darfur.

Writing on these issues has been a growth industry over the last two decades. Yet there has been a fundamental disconnect between popular understanding of the origins and evolution of violent politics, particularly politics with an ethnic tinge, and the work of scholars and analysts who seek to understand the basic mechanisms of contention. When new insights appear, they too often remain the purview of small groups of specialists, trained to speak to one another but rarely venturing to make the latest findings available to a wider readership, both within their own disciplines and beyond.

To take one example, it is often said that the 1990s witnessed a vast upsurge in interethnic disputes. Explanations for this phenomenon have included the end of the cold war, the demise of communism, and the machinations of thuggish politicians seeking to preserve their livelihoods and reputations in a time of uncertainty and social change. Yet the empirical evidence points in exactly the opposite direction: toward a decrease in the level of armed conflict, including that associated with ethnicity and nationalism, after 1989.[3] Devastating wars occurred in the Balkans, the Caucasus, and elsewhere, but on a global scale, the 1990s were a period of relative peace compared with what had come before. In 1992, Boutros Boutros-Ghali, then secretary-general of the United Nations, argued that the end of the cold war provided a historic opportunity for countries to realize the original collective security aims of the organization's founders:

> In these past months a conviction has grown, among nations large and small, that an opportunity has been regained to achieve the great objectives of the [UN] Charter—a United Nations capable of maintaining international peace and security, of securing justice and human rights and promoting, in the words of the Charter, "social progress and better standards of life in larger freedom." This opportunity must not be squandered. The Organization must never again be crippled as it was in the era that has now passed.[4]

That vision has been frequently criticized as utopian, especially given the devastating violence that was descending on Bosnia even as the secretary-general outlined his agenda for the future. But by and large, the idea was not far-fetched: that the end of proxy wars, fueled by the ambitions of great powers and marketed with the rhetoric of capitalism and communism, would signal a diminution in conflict worldwide. In fact, for a brief moment, it was more of a reality than is often recognized today.

What did we learn in that era, the historical hiatus between the cold war and the war on terror? This book examines the history and theory of what might be called extreme politics—nationalism, social violence, and large-scale social change. It aims to provide fresh insights into these phenomena and, in the process, to help interpret a now voluminous set of scholarly literatures for non-specialists. It is intended both for professional social scientists and for readers who, although desiring to know something about why people kill one another en masse, may not wish to trawl through the often formidable research that has revealed important features of the origins and evolution of violent confrontation. The book is both an introduction to some of the major issues in the study of nations, nationalism, and violent change and a critical contemporary history of academic approaches to these subjects.

This book draws many of its examples from eastern Europe and Eurasia, and the chapters in the second half of the book focus explicitly on this region and its problems after the end of communism in 1989 and the collapse of the

Soviet Union at the end of 1991. In part, this is a result of personal interest; my own area of expertise is the postcommunist world, even though I have ventured beyond it as a political scientist and historian. But eastern Europe and Eurasia in the 1990s became something of a large-scale natural testing ground, a place where dominant theories of the state, social violence, and regime-level change could be refined or rejected.

Moreover, the region—as a region—seemed to dissipate as the decade progressed. What had once been a distinct piece of real estate, defined by a common ideology, political structure, and foreign policy, became nearly unrecognizable by the turn of the twenty-first century. Much of central Europe and the eastern Balkans were part of the EU and NATO, with consolidated democracies and variegated foreign policies that sometimes sought to split the difference between Brussels and Washington. Russia, after a decade of crisis and fitful democratization, had reemerged as a regionally confident and globally ambitious power. The small wars and ethnic conflicts of the 1990s—from Bosnia to Azerbaijan to Tajikistan—had subsided; many remained only shakily resolved, if at all, but the chaotic politics and social discord that had accompanied the end of communism in the Balkans and Eurasia seemed to be a thing of the past. Democracy and authoritarianism, strife and concord, and reform and reaction were all present in a part of the world that had, years earlier, seemed a politically homogeneous place: the outer and inner empires of the old Soviet Union.

Through a series of linked essays, this book tries to make sense of these monumental changes and put them in the broader context of scholarly theorizing about nations, ethnic groups, and violence in general. It also attempts to bring together several distinct scholarly conversations, ways of writing and doing research that usually take place in the echo chamber of individual disciplines, and to pull into the present the distant debates and controversies that are often lost in the quest to be cutting-edge. The subjects covered here—from the politics of ethnic diasporas, to the nature of civil war, to the problem of who gets recognized as an independent country—necessarily lie at the frontiers of different scholarly fields. It is for that reason that, with some notable exceptions, issues that have been monumentally important on the ground have tended to be marginal to mainstream debates within political science. The essays in this book might thus be seen as a set of early reports from the borderlands—the fractured frontier zones not only of Europe and Eurasia but also of the intriguing boundaries of comparative politics, international relations, security studies, and, to a degree, history.

Historians criticize political scientists for being overly "presentist," defining phenomena with little appreciation for their historical contingency and context. In most instances, political scientists are guilty as charged, if for no other reason than that they tend to bracket contingency as a way of focusing the mind on the question of causality—an area in which historians, for their part, have sometimes been known to play fast and loose. Scholars of nationalism, ethnic politics, and social violence can also be overly presentist in a different sense: failing to understand the debates within their own or cognate disciplines that animated scholars in decades past and that, mutatis mutandis, cover many of the same issues that scholars in the 1990s came to see as new and unexplored. Just as policy makers were prone to see the alleged upsurge in nationalist violence as novel, so, too, scholars tended to write as if they had discovered a wholly new social phenomenon—nationalism—or at least one to which earlier generations had paid little heed. As the chapters that follow show, there is much to be gained from bringing historical sensibility—a sense of the history of scholarship itself—to our work. That is part of what being methodologically rigorous ought to mean: knowing something about the earlier conversations and controversies that have shaped the methods, categories of analysis, and intellectual fashions that researchers take for granted today.

Chapter 2 examines a peculiar feature of the most influential writings on nations and nationalism: that they themselves seem to have a national origin, as the products of thinkers who were born or made their careers in the United Kingdom. That fact may well have been responsible for the growth of nationalism studies as a field. The particular intellectual climate in British political studies, such as a respect for methodological eclecticism and historically grounded research, made British writers uniquely attuned to the importance of nationalism when many of their American colleagues were inclined to dismiss it as a derivative of backwardness. When nationalism irrupted onto scholarly and policy agendas in the 1990s, it was to this long tradition of British theorizing that people in the United States and elsewhere naturally turned—but in ways that may not be helpful in creating robust theories of nationalist phenomena.

Chapter 3 begins with the observation that the history of nationalism is not necessarily written by the winners but that it is almost always written about them. Historians and social scientists have focused their attention largely on those who are able to craft coherent narratives of national belonging, appeal to the masses, build states, and get those states recognized by some legitimizing international institution. Yet in many instances, nationalist ideas never take the form of nationalist movements. In others, clan, class, or countryside remains the principal form of social organization and obligation. What are the limits of contingency when it comes to the origins, development, and ends of nationalism? Why do some nationalisms endure and others effervesce, becoming pet projects of nostalgic émigrés and disgruntled exiles? This chapter offers a conceptual framework for understanding failed nationalisms while contributing to comparative theorizing on the evolution of nationalist ideologies, political movements, and state building.

Chapter 4 focuses on the study of social violence, particularly those instances of violence that are said to be fueled by national or ethnic identity. The debates of the 1990s over the causes of and responses to violence of this type—from civil wars to ethnic cleansing—were important. But in general, there were few links to older theoretical traditions. This chapter offers an analytical history of "ethnic conflict" research and shows how theorizing about mass violence has begun to turn back toward its origins in problems of social order, state-society relations, and group mobilization. New work in the field breaks down the intellectual wall that has grown up between the study of something called "ethnic conflict" or "nationalist conflict" and a long line of work on collective action in political sociology and other fields. This new micropolitical turn in the field entails uncovering the precise mechanisms via which individuals and groups exchange the benefits of stability for the risky behavior associated with mass killing.

Chapter 5 turns to eastern Europe's recent past and how scholars have sought to understand the complexities of postcommunism. Two decades after the end of European and Eurasian communism, the once vitriolic debates between "area studies" and "the disciplines" have largely disappeared. Access to archives, survey data, and political elites has allowed east European countries to be treated as normal arenas of research. Recent work by both younger and established scholars has made real contributions, not only to the understanding of postcommunism but also to broader research questions about the political economy of reform, federalism, transitional justice, and nationalism and interethnic relations. Today, one of the key issues for students of postcommunism is explaining the highly variable paths that east European and Eurasian states have taken since 1989. Compared with the relative homogeneity of outcomes in earlier transitions in other regions, the record in the east looks more diverse: some successful transitions and consolidations, several stalled transitions, a few transitions followed by a return to authoritarian politics, and some transitions that never got off the ground. This chapter offers conceptual routes into the postcommunist world by focusing on the institutions of the communist state, the institutional dimensions of ethnic solidarity and mobilization, and the emerging patterns of interinstitutional bargaining in the first years of postcommunism.

Chapter 6 examines the phenomenon of substate violence in the postcommunist world, particularly the array of unrecognized states that emerged after the end of the Soviet Union and the waning of several full-scale wars on the post-Soviet periphery. Within international relations, discussions about how civil wars end have concentrated mainly on the qualities of the belligerents (ethnicity, commitment to the cause) or on the strategic environment of decision making (security dilemmas). Work in sociology and development economics, however, has highlighted the importance of war economies and the functional role of violence. This chapter combines these approaches by examining the mechanisms through which the chaos of war becomes transformed into networks of profit, and through which these in turn become hardened into the institutions of quasi states. By examining such places as South Ossetia and Nagorno-Karabakh, this article develops a framework for thinking about the process of state making in the former Soviet space and its relationship to questions of violence and national identity. A later section analyzes the impact of Kosovo's declaration of independence in February 2008, the precursor to the brief Russia-Georgia war of the following August.

Chapter 7, written in its original form with Neil J. Melvin, expands the discussion of nationalism and ethnicity from a domestic context to an international one. How does ethnicity matter in international affairs? Are ethnic diasporas—dispersed cultural groups tied to a distinct homeland—a source of insecurity, or can nation-states instrumentalize "their" diasporas without threatening neighboring countries? This chapter addresses these questions through a comparative analysis of three transborder ethnic groups in post-Soviet Eurasia (Russians, Ukrainians, and Kazakhs) and the policies that their respective kin-states have pursued toward them since 1991. Nationalism in the new states of Eurasia and eastern Europe has been blamed for ethnic discrimination at home and assertiveness abroad. But the issue of transborder ethnic populations becomes a foreign policy priority only under specific circumstances. Often, wrangling among domestic interest groups, resource scarcity, and competing state priorities matter more than rhetorical appeals to defend ethnic kin in determining whether governments seek to mobilize support for coethnics in other countries.

Chapter 8 considers another aspect of transstate ethnicity: the movement of people across international frontiers. States normally worry about keeping people out; empires tend to be concerned with keeping them in. But the distinction between these two problems can disappear when empires are in the process of remaking themselves into modern states—when the structures of power remain weak, lines of authority unclear, and territorial boundaries of the polity uncertain. In eastern Europe and Eurasia, the demographic changes of the 1990s—from refugee flight to labor migration—continue to alter the social landscape in profound ways. The causes and consequences of these changes are poorly understood, however. The postcommunist world provides a stellar setting in which to study the impact of population movements on social structures and political behavior, particularly interethnic relations and ethnic politics. This chapter uses two case studies—on the so-called status law governing Hungary's relationship with ethnic Hungarians abroad and on the vexed issue of human trafficking, particularly the migration of sex workers—to illustrate how ethnicity and institutions interact when people seek to move across frontiers.

Chapter 9 concludes with an examination of cliophilia—the overuse and misuse of history in east European and Eurasian studies. Rather than dismissing historical analysis, this chapter calls for a more nuanced use of historical evidence by political scientists, as well as more attention to problems of causation and comparison among historians. In the study of nationalism and ethnic relations in particular, we might benefit from honing an appreciation for the controversies and scholarly traditions that have animated our fields in the past. In the quest to be new and different, we sometimes redraw lines of debate that were fought over or erased by older generations. The future of the field depends on the degree to which we are able to build on, not just repeat, the research programs of previous eras.

In 1964, the historian and political essayist Hugh Seton-Watson published his *Nationalism and Communism*, a series of articles that surveyed the postwar landscape in central and eastern Europe and assessed the evolution of politics in the region since the consolidation of communist rule.[5] Seton-Watson had been present at the creation of the communist world, just as his father, the eminent historian R. W. Seton-Watson, had been present at the birth of its predecessor, the shaky democracies and authoritarian polities sired by the First World War. The themes that Seton-Watson fils addressed seem in many ways foreign today. His era was one in which revolutionary change was a given and in which Europe was divided into clear blocs, each claiming a right to govern based on morality and the exigencies of security. The seventeen years covered by his book—the period from 1946 to 1963—had seen a wholesale change of political regime across Europe's eastern half. Yet both East and West seemed more fractious than was often alleged by elites on both sides of the cold war divide. Soviet-Yugoslav unity was at an end. Hungary had rebelled, unsuccessfully, against the Soviet Union. Tensions were rising between the Soviet Union and China. The movement toward west European unity was stagnating, bogged down by contention among the Atlanticist, pan-European, and intensely national orientations of the region's constituent states.

Some of those themes seem quaint today, and others are still very much a part of the international scene. The postcommunist world, like the communist one of Seton-Watson's time, witnessed a series of rolling revolutions two decades ago. Nationalism has remained a potent force, one that is only occasionally corralled by affirmations of European unity. The project of building a pan-European political, economic, and security order is far more advanced than in Seton-Watson's day, but divisions remain over basic questions of foreign policy and future development, from the recognition of Kosovo, to relations with a revived Russia, to the next waves of enlargement (if any) of the EU and NATO. For Seton-Watson, the stability of the postwar order was threatened by interbloc and intrabloc dissension, nationalism, and the persistence of the robust neo-Victorian virtues of industrialism and militarism that he attributed to the Soviet state—a formidable challenge to the "fin-tailed cars, waist-high culture, [and] angry young men" that seemed to characterize the flaccid West.[6]

In short, Seton-Watson believed that the period of relative stability that followed the revolutionary changes of the late 1940s was a fantasy. The further we recede from the equally revolutionary changes of the late 1980s and 1990s, the more we may come to believe the same thing. The seeming stability ushered in by the anticommunist revolutions, the violent demise of the communist federations, and the rapid expansion of Western political and military institutions may likewise be more an interlude than a postscript—one that bears some resemblance to earlier interregna, from 1919 to 1939 and from the late 1940s to the early 1960s. The essays in this book are a partial record of the odd politics of the fleeting postcommunist era, a time that has already given way to new forms of political life across Europe and Eurasia.

PART I

Theory and Comparison

2

The National Origins of
Nationalism Studies

One remarkable fact in the literature on nations and nationalism is that, over the last half century, the most influential studies of nationalist politics are those of authors tied by birth or education to a single country: the United Kingdom. The works of Hugh Seton-Watson, Elie Kedourie, Ernest Gellner, and Anthony D. Smith continue to be the major guideposts in a dense thicket of scholarly work on the subject.[1] Despite a long line of studies of nationalism by American historians and a growing interest in ethnicity among American social scientists after the 1960s, the most-cited works in the field have long been those by authors who have made their careers within British universities. In the 1990s, with renewed attention focused on the nation-state and its discontents, these authors and their compatriots were discovered by a new generation of political scientists, international relations specialists, sociologists, and journalists. Britain has also been important in the development of a sense of professional camaraderie among scholars with an interest in nationalist phenomena. The Association for the Study of Ethnicity and Nationalism, founded under Smith's aegis at the London School of Economics and Political Science (LSE), is the English-speaking world's major professional organization devoted to the comparative study of ethnic, racial, and nationalist politics. Two of the most important journals in the field, *Ethnic and Racial Studies* (established in 1978) and *Nations and Nationalism* (established in 1995), are both edited in Britain, the former at the University of Surrey and the latter at the LSE.

American scholars educated in the tradition of Carlton Hayes, Hans Kohn, and Boyd Shafer—much read by American historians but less frequently by political scientists—would probably object to the suggestion that Britons have played a leading role in the study of nationalism.[2] The claim seems even more peculiar in light of the upsurge in new research on national identity and ethnonational mobilization by United States–based historians, political scientists, and sociologists since the mid-1960s. Karl Deutsch, Louis L. Snyder, Walker Connor, Ted Robert Gurr, Donald Horowitz, and other U.S. researchers have become mainstays in the literature on nationalism and the comparative study of ethnic politics.[3] However, the study of nationalism does have discernible national origins, and those origins have marked the field in important ways. British writers on nationalism have come from disparate disciplines and arrived at substantially different conclusions about the origin of nationalist sentiment, the conduct of nationalist politics, and the future of the nation-state. But among the major contributors to the field, there is a particular sensitivity to the power of nationalism and its fundamental connections to other topics of concern to students of politics, from the bases of social identity to party politics to the causes of violent conflict. Focusing on the national idea at a time when it was largely outside the interest of their political science colleagues in the United States, British scholars carved out a distinct field of study located at the nexus of the humanities and the social sciences.

The literature on nationalism, even that generated by scholars working in a single country, is gargantuan. Nearly every major British historian, political scientist, sociologist, and political theorist, whether writing on political interactions within states or between them or on the normative principles by which such interactions ought to be governed, has touched on the question of nationality. Furthermore, the intellectual openness of British social science has meant that the study of nationalism, like the study of other sociopolitical phenomena, has been a truly multidisciplinary endeavor; research in the field continues to draw on the expertise of historians, sociologists, linguists, and anthropologists, in addition to political scientists.

This chapter explores some of the major trends in the British study of nationalism and relates them to broader substantive and methodological concerns within the social sciences. British scholars have made profound contributions to our understanding of nations and nationalism and have aided in the development of a distinct, multidisciplinary field dedicated to research on ethnic and national phenomena. At the same time, however, the future of multidisciplinary scholarship in this area is by no means clear. The defining features of British political studies, including a respect for methodological eclecticism and historically grounded research, have made British writers uniquely attuned to the importance of nationalism at times when many of their American colleagues dismissed it as the residuum of retarded modernization. The chapter concludes with reflections on future directions for research and proposals for thinking about the study of nationalism and its relationship to broader debates within political science.

Intellectual Traditions and the Study of Nationalism

In terms of methodology and approach, political scientists may sit at "separate tables," as Gabriel Almond once wrote, but they also sit on separate continents.[4] The study of politics in Britain and America has long borne a national stamp. It is one of the few academic fields whose intellectual fissures have developed mainly along national lines. In the United States, the discipline of political science has evolved in the direction of ever greater methodological self-consciousness; the specification of variables, the stress on falsifiable hypotheses, the generation of testable inferences, and the elaboration of deductive theories of political behavior have become standard components of political science education and scholarship. These developments have not been without their critics, and there is today as little consensus as in the past about what constitutes the truly dominant paradigm within American political science. However, mainstream political science, as represented in flagship journals such as the *American Political Science Review* and *International Organization*, remains dominated by scholars for whom a theory's generality is a virtue superior to its empirical accuracy.

In Britain, however, there has long been a tension within political studies between a Whiggish traditionalism and the growth of a sense of skeptical professionalism: between scholarship informed by the descriptive or normative concerns of history, law, and moral philosophy, and research influenced by the methods and agendas of political scientists in the United States and, perhaps, parts of continental Europe.[5] The differences between American and British approaches can certainly be overstated; over the last two decades, there has been a degree of convergence between methods and research agendas on both sides of the Atlantic. But for the development of scholarship on nationalism, the relative lack of consensus about the scope and methods of political science in Britain was critical, for it was precisely the unsettled nature of the discipline that facilitated the growth of a distinct, multidisciplinary field defined more by its object of study than by its disciplinary pedigree. The pluralism of opinions on the meaning of political science was a catalyst for the development of a professional community of scholars reflecting and writing on the origins of nations and the conduct of nationalist politics.

In British higher education, the relatively permeable boundaries between the various social sciences have generally allowed a greater degree of communication across disciplines than in the United States, where the growth of a reasonably well-defined discipline of political science, with its own agendas and professional standards, has tended to discourage the development of autonomous areas of research outside the concerns of the discipline's mainstream. Today, graduate students are socialized in a particular professional tradition, "trained" as political scientists, at the same time that they are introduced to a body of knowledge associated with the established specializations—American politics, comparative politics, international relations, political theory—in which they choose to concentrate. The chief criterion against which their work is judged tends to be the degree to which it contributes to the theoretical questions at the cutting edge of the established subfield or of the discipline as a whole; the potential contribution to the literature on a particular region, period, or theme is generally of secondary concern. In this respect, what Michael Oakeshott called in a different context the "sovereignty of technique" defines American approaches to the study of politics.[6]

The enthusiasm for such a program in Britain has generally been more muted, informed by a suspicion that political science, to paraphrase Alfred Cobban, may be merely a label for avoiding the adjective without achieving the noun.[7] The unsettled nature of disciplinary boundaries in the United Kingdom has meant that research tends to be evaluated according to rather different criteria than in the United States. Empirical accuracy, originality, style of argumentation, and contribution to existing research on a distinct region, period, or theme (the same criteria that might inform the work of, say, a historian or legal scholar) have been paramount. The object of research, rather than the discipline in which research is conducted, has been the major determinant of professional loyalties and standards of scholarship. Before his delivery of the Conway Memorial Lecture in 1932, Harold Laski, then professor of political science at the LSE, was introduced by the chair with the observation: "He has the training and outlook of the historian. Schemes and projects that lack a basis in history are no more than an exercise of fantasy in a world of dreams."[8] One can imagine a similarly complimentary introduction for a British politics professor today, but more than a few American political scientists would consider such remarks at best a mild insult.

One result of these differing professional traditions was the relegation of studies of nationalism to the periphery of American political science and, concomitantly, their unusual growth within political studies in the United Kingdom. Until the 1970s, many American political scientists were prone to view nationalism as an atavistic sentiment that would eventually disappear as societies became more variegated and economies more modern. Seeing nationalist movements as either echoes of a premodern past (as in residual ethnic attachments in

Western democracies) or as masks for the process of modernization itself (as in the nationalism of postcolonial states), mainstream political scientists tended to ignore the power of the national idea and leave its elucidation to departments of history. When political scientists did turn their attention to questions of ethnicity or nationalism, it was most often in the context of racial, ethnic, or regional politics in the United States. Historians, for this reason, were responsible for the bulk of the scholarship produced in the United States on nations and nationalism after the First World War. Carlton Hayes's graduate seminar at Columbia University trained generations of prominent scholars, and Hayes's own writings, especially his *The Historical Evolution of Modern Nationalism*, remain part of the core literature for American historians of nations and nationalist ideology.[9] The hegemony of historians was not, of course, complete. Karl Deutsch in political science, Rupert Emerson in international relations, Joshua A. Fishman in linguistics, and Leonard W. Doob in psychology were early advocates of bringing the techniques of social science to bear on contemporary nationalist phenomena.[10] In the main, however, the study of nationalism remained outside the professional interest of most American social scientists, and political scientists in particular, through the late 1960s.

Doubts about the power of nationality were also to be found in Britain, of course. Both Harold Laski and G. D. H. Cole were convinced that the nation-state was, by the middle of the twentieth century, already an outmoded form of political association. E. H. Carr adopted the infelicitous title *Nationalism and After* for his speculations on sovereignty and international order after the Second World War.[11] But since the study of nationalism was never dominated by a single academic discipline, much less the relatively nebulous discipline of politics, there was no academic mainstream from which it could be marginalized. The methodological pluralism of political studies meant that the object of research, rather than the boundaries of the discipline, defined the field of study. Likewise, the stress among British political scientists on empiricism and historically informed research was especially suited to the study of a phenomenon whose manifestations were both complex and particularistic.

The study of nationalism in Britain has thus been marked by a kind of providential antiprofessionalism. Intellectuals with interests and expertise difficult to corral within a single academic category have dominated the field, and their eclectic interests have placed them at various times at the nexus of politics and philosophy, history and anthropology, or sociology and cultural commentary. Gellner, who ended his career as the first director of the Center for the Study of Nationalism at the Central European University in Prague, also occupied posts at various stages as a professor of social anthropology and as lecturer in sociology and in philosophy; his academic corpus (leaving aside his numerous essays and reflections on contemporary events) touches on subjects ranging from linguistic philosophy to the religious beliefs of the Berbers.[12] The same point could be made about any number of other scholars who have made important contributions to the field.

Beyond the sociology of academic research, three other factors have made British scholars particularly sensitive to the power of nationalism. First, the personal biographies of British writers themselves are important. The study of nationalism has always had a certain *Mitteleuropäische* disposition. Gellner and Eric Hobsbawm (as well as their North American contemporaries Hans Kohn, Karl Deutsch, and Thomas Spira, the long-time editor of the *Canadian Review of Studies in Nationalism*) were born in various parts of the Habsburg empire or its successor states. Throughout Gellner's work in particular, the Habsburg experience remained a powerful symbol of the force of national passions and the tragedy of governments that failed to accommodate them. Hugh Seton-Watson, scion of a family whose name is synonymous with the historiography of the Habsburg, Romanov, and Ottoman lands, was himself both a student of and activist for the peoples of Europe's former continental empires.[13] John Plamenatz, who made a significant if largely unappreciated contribution to the debate on nationalism and individualism, was by birth a Montenegrin. C. A. Macartney, the great historian of nationalism in central Europe, was the grandson of a Bulgarian colonel.[14] Similar points could be made about Isaiah Berlin, J. L. Talmon, and others with central and east European connections.[15] It is not difficult to find in their writings an element of the personal, both in their appreciation for the ambiguities of national identity and in their reflections on the challenges of assimilation, especially for European Jews.[16] Born in one collapsing empire and educated in another, many of these thinkers were uniquely placed to recognize the enduring importance of nationality and particularly disinclined to dismiss it as a remnant of premodernity.

Second, the British study of nationalism has clearly had an important relationship to British politics and foreign policy. Scholarly work has been as much influenced by a practical concern for dealing with the manifestations of nationalism as by an academic interest in its origins. In the last century and a half, crises at home and abroad have attracted the attention of thinkers with a special interest in nationality and self-determination. The Greek crisis of the 1820s, the Bulgarian atrocities of the 1870s, the problem of Ireland, and the fate of India and other colonial possessions have all prompted serious debate among British political theorists and statesmen over the bases of nationality and the claim to national liberation.[17] The well-known study on nationalism commissioned by the Royal Institute of International Affairs, issued just three months before Hitler's invasion of Poland, addressed both rising nationalism on the continent and the problem of self-determination within colonial states; by 1939, both had become of considerable practical importance to British policy makers.[18] Gellner's later writings on nationalism were similarly concerned with the dangers of nationalism for postcommunist governments that ignored the sources and salience of mobilized ethnicity.[19] At the same time a colonial power, a multiethnic metropole, and the only Western democracy in the post–World War Two period to have fought a war in defense of its sovereign territory, Britain perhaps more than other developed states has experienced firsthand the power of the national idea.[20]

Third, the question of what exactly constitutes national identity in Britain itself has never been straightforward. As Richard Rose has reminded political scientists since the 1960s, the United Kingdom is a multinational state in which the territorial dimension of politics is fundamental.[21] British studies of nationalism have thus existed within the context of debates on the relationship between the unity of the kingdom and the competing national and subnational identities of its constituent parts. From early debates between Ernest Barker and Hamilton Fyfe over the meaning of "national character" to discussions in the 1980s and 1990s led by Tom Nairn, John Rex, Bhikhu Parekh, and others on the challenges of an increasingly multicultural Britain, questions of nationality have never been purely academic.[22]

The same could, of course, be said for North America and Australia, where the problems of forging unified national communities out of an array of linguistic, cultural, and religious groups have preoccupied sociologists and political scientists for decades. But in Britain, the problem has perhaps been more acute for one important reason: Britain has been at once an old, continuous European nation and a settler community. The political symbols and institutions of the state are part of a specific national tradition; the distinct cultures of the British Isles were blended in the eighteenth and early nineteenth centuries into a hybrid Britishness by the dual forces of war and Protestantism.[23] At the same time, because of the legacies of colonialism and the forces of globalization, Britain has also become a highly variegated and multiethnic state, where the bonds of national sentiment and the boundaries of the national community are increasingly indistinct, and where the relationship between Britishness and its various subordinate identities—Scottish, Welsh, Muslim, and many others—is decidedly problematic. Intellectual debates on the meaning of nationhood, the dilemmas of multiculturalism, and the link between nationality and territory have therefore been conducted in a political context in which the answers to these questions continue to have considerable practical relevance. Today as in the past, "What ish my nation?" as Macmorris asks in the third act of *Henry V*, has no uncontroversial response.

Up to now, I have spoken of the development of a relatively distinct and multidisciplinary field of nationalism studies in Britain, which was in part the result of the methodological dispositions of political studies itself, and in part the result of the personal backgrounds of the major scholars in the field and broader features of British academic and political life. The sections that follow analyze three overarching themes in this field: the ideology of the nation and the relevance of political ideas to nationalist politics, the sources of national identity and communal solidarity, and the legitimacy of claims about nationality and rights to self-determination.

The National Idea

One of the major lines of debate in the study of nationalism over the past century has been whether the content of nationalist thought is a legitimate and relevant subject of research. All nationalist ideologies offer at the same time an ontology, a philosophy of history, and a theory of political legitimacy. For nationalists, the world is composed of discrete nations, primordial *Urvölker* whose members share a number of ascriptive traits, among which might number physical appearance, cultural symbols, shared historical memories, and linguistic peculiarities. Each of these groups has an intimate historical connection to a particular piece of land, and the effort to assert and defend claims to this territory forms the motor of history. Disputes may arise between rival claimants to the same territory, but there is at the end of the day a fact of the matter to be uncovered: Either the cultural—if not genetic—antecedents of a modern nation occupied a given territory at a given point in history or they did not, and sifting through these contesting claims to uncover the truth is the task of historians, archaeologists, and ethnographers. Feelings of solidarity among members of the same nation are natural, for they are based on shared historical memories of the struggle for self-definition and self-determination. Political boundaries that mirror the demographic boundaries of the national group are normal and laudable; borders should be genuinely "inter-national," setting off one nation from another rather than merely demarcating the horizons of state authority. On this view, political movements that seek to remedy the divide between nations and states are therefore both predictable and praiseworthy.

These basic assumptions about the nature of nations and relations among them underlie all nationalist discourse. For scholars, though, the degree to which these assumptions are appropriate topics of research has proved to be controversial for two reasons. First, the question of nationalist discourse has defined the divide between scholars whose methods and assumptions draw on the traditions of intellectual history and those interested in the search for patterns of social and political behavior. Second, it has focused attention on the issue of the relative autonomy of the national idea: whether nationalism should be seen as sui generis or as an epiphenomenon of more fundamental political or economic processes.

The history-of-ideas approach, which seeks to locate nationalism at the nexus of political philosophy and everyday politics, has had a long tradition in Britain. Alfred Cobban, Elie Kedourie, and Isaiah Berlin were among the foremost chroniclers of the national idea, tracing its origins among German intellectuals at the end of the eighteenth century, its manifestations in eighteenth- and early-nineteenth-century western Europe, and its spread to the captive nations of east-central Europe by the end of the nineteenth century.[24] These writers share several conclusions about the origins and evolution of the national idea.

First, the terms *nation, nationality,* and *nationalism* are inherently protean, and any attempt to arrive at an overarching definition for these terms and their derivatives does violence to their essential embeddedness in the historical periods in which they appear. Second, the emergence of the idea of timeless national communities, in which individuals are thought to express their true individuality only as part of a culturally defined collective, emerged as a response to the rationalism and individualism of the Enlightenment. Nationalism as a political ideology, therefore, is fundamentally antirational, "an off-shoot," in Berlin's words, "of the romantic revolt."[25] Third, the national idea—in particular, the concept that sovereignty should lie with the people and that "the people" are coterminous with a culturally distinct nation—has historically played a major role as a catalyst for liberation. The sense that one's own personal struggle against cultural discrimination is part of a wider injustice visited upon one's nation by alien oppressors has been a powerful guarantor of liberty and a bulwark against tyranny. But fourth, when dislodged from the concept of democracy, nationalism can become an excuse for authoritarianism. As long as the nation remains defined as a community of rights-bearing individuals, nationalism can serve the benign purpose of unifying the community against external threats. Once the perceived interests of the collective are defined in opposition to the interests of its individual constituents, however, the nation becomes inimical to human liberty. The history of nationalism is therefore the history of competing definitions of the nation, with purveyors of nationalist ideologies offering their own rival versions of history, culture, and identity in the political marketplace.

This focus on the origins and manifestations of the national idea arose from the persistent belief among many scholars that nationalism is, above all, a state of mind, a corporate will that inspires large numbers of individuals within a national group and that lays claim to the allegiance of even more.[26] It is, in the colorful metaphor used by Kedourie, a type of "political bovarysme," a philosophy inspired by too little reason and too many romantic novels.[27] This view had an important impact on the research agendas of scholars concerned with nationalist politics. Since nationalism was seen as, at base, a mental state, the most that scholars could hope to do was trace its development over time and reveal the ways in which the seemingly natural division of humans into distinct national categories was the product of a historically contingent idea. Changeable and indistinct, the idea of the nation was not readily susceptible to anything other than a more or less descriptive account of its origins and evolution. As the British historian and politician Ramsay Muir asserted at the beginning of the last century, "[nationality] cannot be tested or analysed by formulae, such as the German professors love."[28]

But is the history of an idea ever really helpful in addressing the questions of most concern to social scientists? The inherent difficulties of tracking the evolution of any political idea, especially one as changeable as that of the nation, is only part of the problem. A more basic issue is whether elucidating the history of the concept could ever reveal anything valuable about the politics of nationalism itself. If nationalism is analyzed only as an idea (especially, as many twentieth-century writers concluded, as an idea whose time had come and gone), then there seems little hope of being able to address some of the key questions about nationalism as a political force: Given the array of possible forms of political association, why has the nation proved to be so persistent and universal? What is it about nationality as a source of group loyalty that sets it off from religion or class? Under what conditions do national allegiances trump all others? Within individual nations, why do some conceptions of national identity endure while others become quaint footnotes in the history of the respective national group? Examining the evolution of an idea can be useful as a reminder that no political concepts spring fully formed from the minds of political scientists but instead trail behind them a string of multiple and often mutually contradictory meanings. But once this fact is recognized, the history-of-ideas approach seems to offer little in the way of explanatory power.

The question of the utility of intellectual history to the study of nationalism lay at the heart of a long-running debate between Kedourie and Gellner. Kedourie's *Nationalism* masterfully traced the evolution of "nation" from eighteenth-century thinkers such as Immanuel Kant and Johann Gottfried Herder through to the creation of new European national states after the First World War. The book began as a series of lectures that the author prepared shortly after joining the Department of Government at the LSE, then headed by Michael Oakeshott. Kedourie approached the subject of nationalism primarily as a problem in the history of ideas. To treat it otherwise, he argued, was merely a species of economism; those who give in to the "sociological temptation" to seek general explanations for nationalist phenomena, treating nationalism as a development to be explained away by reference to economic or other social forces, misunderstand the autonomous character of the national idea and the variety of radically different forms that it has taken over the past two centuries. Like Molière's Monsieur Jourdain, who discovered that he had been speaking prose all his life, nationalist thinkers would surely be surprised to hear from social scientists that their doctrine of nationality was, in reality, "either an expression of bourgeois self-interest, or an industrial lubricant, or a reflection of deep subterranean movements slowly maturing through centuries and millennia."[29]

Kedourie's attack on social-scientific treatments of nationalism was aimed largely at Gellner, who had earlier questioned his view that Kant's concept of individual autonomy prefigured later nationalist views on the right to self-determination of culturally defined collectivities.[30] As Gellner argued, while Kedourie had shown that the nation is a logically contingent concept—that the national is in no sense natural—the corollary, that nationalism is also sociologically contingent, was nonsensical. If the nation were a more or less accidental creation of European thinkers, as Kedourie maintained, might not the appearance of culturally defined political units and the proliferation of feelings of connection and attachment to these units also be merely accidental? On the contrary, Gellner held, although the idea of the nation, like any political ideology, was certainly contingent on the backgrounds and intellectual predispositions of its authors, its spread and success as an organizing principle were the direct results of changes in social relations on the eve of industrialization. The shift from structurally defined, hierarchical, and static forms of social organization to culturally defined, egalitarian, and mobile societies during the process of modernization created a milieu in which ideas about the unity of the nation could take root.[31] An account of the tortuous path via which modern concepts of the nation have arrived on the political scene might be a useful corrective to the views of nationalists themselves, but such an enterprise cannot explain why those ideas and not others have proved so politically successful since the end of the eighteenth century.

The issue of the utility of intellectual history was only one strand in a much broader discussion about the determinants of nationalism and national identity, a discussion that Gellner once termed "the LSE debate."[32] In many ways, it exemplified the divide within British studies of nationalism between historians and social scientists, between an older tradition of seeing nationality primarily as an idea and a newer approach that sought general explanations for the social solidarity that characterized nationalist politics. Even among social scientists, however, questions about the sources of national sentiment and its relationship to the cohesion of cultural communities have proved no less controversial.

Identity, Solidarity, and the Reductionist Impulse

Beyond ideology, the question of the solidarity of national groups has also been central to discussions of nationalist politics. Why is it that, given the range of possible foci of human loyalty, groups coalesce around the particular array of common cultural symbols, linguistic peculiarities, and shared histories represented by the nation? And under what conditions does the nation eclipse other potential symbols of allegiance? The most familiar response to these questions, one often encountered in discussions about post–cold war ethnic conflicts, is the view that nationality is as fundamental a component of personal identity as kinship; as a result, it represents a uniquely powerful source of group solidarity and a potential mobilizational resource for political elites. On this view, nations, while perhaps not the timeless entities imagined by nationalists themselves, are nevertheless rooted in established patterns of belief and behavior that bind individuals into communal groups and mark them off from others. A collective name, a common language, shared history, common customs, and perhaps distinctive religious beliefs or a sense of allegiance to an ancestral homeland are the key manifestations of this collective identity. Modern nations, then, do not arise ex nihilo but are instead the direct heirs of long-standing reciprocal bonds within human communities.[33]

Although variants of this view—now often labeled primordialism or perennialism—have become commonplace in discussions of ethnicity and nationalism after the cold war, as an account of solidarity within ethnonational communities it suffers from several serious shortcomings, both empirical and methodological. In the first place, the assertion that modern nations have existed in an unbroken line from primordial cultural communities is contradicted by the manifest heterogeneity of populations and the fluid nature of personal identity before the advent of structured systems of mass education. Even today, nations are far less homogeneous than primordialist views allow; there is rarely an undisputed correspondence between the claims to a particular territory by nationalist groups and the willingness of neighboring populations to accede to them. Moreover, by reifying nationality and seeing it as the most salient of an entire portfolio of personal identities, primordialists cannot explain how nationalism might intersect with other forms of social mobilization tied to class, gender, or regional affiliation.

Of even more concern are primordialism's methodological difficulties. First, primordialist claims beg the question of the sources of communal cohesion and solidarity. Although this problem does not mean that primordialists have nothing interesting to say, it does mean that their ability to offer genuine explanation is severely limited. The problem arises from the fact that primordialists normally fail to make a distinction between solidarity (the ties of culture or custom that bind individuals into relatively cohesive social units) and collective action (the mobilization of these units toward a particular goal). The latter is simply assumed to be more likely in cases in which the former is present. Attempts to test the primordialist hypothesis that nationality is a perennial component of collective identities therefore reduce to tautologies: National solidarity is taken as given and used to explain group behavior, while cases of collective action—demonstrations, ethnonational violence, war, and the like—are in turn offered as evidence for the existence of group solidarity.[34]

A second problem is that, because they have no way of identifying solidary groups other than by pointing to cases of collective action, primordialists tend to choose their case studies on the dependent variable. They seek to explain nationalist sentiment by concentrating only on cases in which nationalist mobilization has taken place. The problem with this method is that, since such accounts tend overwhelmingly to focus on cases in which nationalists have succeeded in mobilizing individuals around a given set of ascriptive traits, primordialist arguments can do no more than assume (rather than demonstrate) that nationalism was a necessary outcome of the presence of those traits themselves. From the outset, then, primordialists violate two of the basic tenets of social-scientific methodology: proffering a hypothesis that is essentially unfalsifiable and then attempting to test the hypothesis by choosing cases on the dependent variable. The mere fact that primordialists assume the very thing that most students of nationalism want to explain—group solidarity—should lead one to look with skepticism on the usefulness of such treatments of nationalist phenomena.

Although the debate in Britain has normally been framed in a language less self-consciously scientific, the question of the roots of social solidarity within national groups has been basic to the study of nationalism. Early discussions about the utility of "national character" as an analytical tool, as well as the rebirth of studies of "political culture" in the 1970s and 1980s, centered on precisely the issue at stake in debates over the sources of national identity and their relationship to group solidarity: To what extent do culturally defined communities share identities, norms, and values that are useful in explaining political behavior?[35] Discussion has normally focused on two sets of issues.

First is the question of the reducibility of national identity, that is, the extent to which nationality and national solidarity arise only as epiphenomena of other social processes. The position of Anthony Smith, sometimes mistakenly equated with primordialism, combines an appreciation for the modernity of the national idea with a sensitivity to the enduring ethnic cores around which contemporary national groups have coalesced. On Smith's view, nations in the modern sense of the term—bounded sociopolitical groups with a single, over-arching sense of identity and community—are unquestionably of modern vintage. It was not until perhaps the French revolution that genuine nations appeared on the European scene; before then, localized identities or loyalty to particular political elites formed the bases of group solidarity.

But as Smith has argued, a recognition of the modernity of nations themselves, or at least the modernity of the concept of nationalism, does not preclude our acknowledging the existence of long-standing cultural and linguistic commonalities as the bedrock on which modern nations have formed. National identities and their attendant sense of communal solidarity are not immutable, but they are enduring; the trappings of nationalism, while themselves surely invented and manipulated by political and cultural elites, are embedded in pre-existing ethnic communities (or *ethnies*, in Smith's usage). The mobilizing power of nationalism can neither be reduced to its adherents' laboring under a false consciousness about their history and identity nor explained away by the observation, often made by nationalists themselves, that their awakening to a shared identity often results from external oppression. Rather, national appeals have historically been so powerful precisely because the modern versions of national identity rest on long-standing bonds of belonging, obligation, and commitment within relatively homogeneous cultural communities.

For Smith, as for Hans Kohn, recognizing the power of these enduring attachments need not lead one down the path of primordialism. Indeed, appreciating the ethnic origins of modern nations is primarily an effort to rescue primordialism's sensitivity to nationalists' own pronouncements about their identity and the sources of group solidarity, while jettisoning its propensity to take nationalists simply at their word. Nationality, then, is reducible neither to timeless bonds of blood and land nor to the cynical manipulation of national symbols by political elites. Rather, the mobilizing strength of nationality lies somewhere between the two, grounded in enduring ethnic attachments that have, in the modern era, become ever more politically salient.

Gellner, like Smith, was firmly opposed to the reductionist impulse. Nations were neither present instantiations of timeless social bonds nor ephemeral sources of identity whose exit from the historical stage would be hastened by the advance of modernity. The former view, which Gellner termed the "Dark

Gods" theory of nationalism, rested on a naively static conception of human society. The latter failed to appreciate the genuine sentiments of solidarity that bind individuals into distinct culturally defined communities:

> Those who oppose nationalism hope that Reason will prevail,
> aided perhaps by Student Exchange Schemes, the British Council,
> foreign holidays, re-written history textbooks and *au pair* girls.
> Those who favor nationalism, on the other hand, hope that a grey
> cosmopolitanism and a false bloodless ethos will not submerge the
> true sources of vitality, and they trust that the old Adam will out.[36]

Both views, Gellner noted, share a belief in the naturalness of national affiliation: One is born into a nation as one is born into a family. They differ only in their evaluation of this fact. For the nationalist, the natural character of national bonds imbues them with an authenticity that other allegiances will always lack. For the antinationalist, the fact that national sentiments are a natural part of human existence means only that individuals should work even harder to ensure the triumph of reason over their innate nationalist passions.

The relative malleability of these identities has been another question of pressing importance. One of the most enduring problems for students of nationalism, particularly those interested in the process of nation building in newly independent states, is the extent to which national myths can be self-consciously constructed. Under what conditions are national symbols most easily manipulated? How far can the historical record be stretched to accommodate the exigencies of nationalist history and communal identity? And how, if traditions really are invented, can they nevertheless become such powerful rallying points in times of political crisis? Nationalism may well involve getting history wrong, as Ernest Renan famously noted, but how far can nationalists continue getting it wrong before someone calls them to task?

There is clearly no easy answer to these questions, and most political scientists, whether in Britain or elsewhere, have focused mainly on debunking nationalist myths rather than attempting to explain their durability. The literature on the "invention" of nations and their cultural accoutrements is now immense, and political scientists have been as active as historians and cultural theorists in critiquing the ostensibly timeless character of nationalist mythology and revealing the ways in which national symbols have been forged (in both senses of the word) over the past two centuries.[37] Although such deconstructionist accounts of nationalism have shed considerable light on the apparent falsity of many nationalist claims, studies in this genre can sometimes suffer from the defect of telling us little that we did not already know. We know from Marx, for example, that national myths and symbols can be recycled and infused with meanings radically different from those with which they were originally imbued. Detailing still further instances of this phenomenon in the remotest corners of the globe seems to add little to our understanding.

More seriously, proponents of this approach often have trouble developing a sustainable research agenda, other than to discover still further fraudulent myths to expose. As a result, much of the deconstructionist literature on nationalism sometimes represents little more than antiquarianism, interesting for the bizarre nature of the cases it studies but unable to build on previous work to deepen our understanding of the evident power of nationalist myths. Indeed, in many ways the proliferation of deconstructionist studies in the 1980s and 1990s represented a return to the older history-of-ideas approach to nationalism. Since they were concerned primarily with confronting nationalist mythology and revealing the mutable definitions of the nation over time, such studies normally encountered the same problems faced by historians of ideas: Once all the myths have been debunked and the nation revealed as a social construct, we are still left with the question of why individuals and groups seem prepared to sacrifice blood and treasure in defense of an identity so patently ephemeral.

Concern over the persistent tug of national sentiment—even among liberal intellectuals who ought to know better—prompted British scholars to focus on yet another aspect of nationalism: the relationship between nationality and the demands of liberal individualism. How to reconcile feelings of communal solidarity, individual rights, and the supposed right to self-determination of national groups has been an enduring theme in British scholarship for the past century and a half. Its resurgence in the 1990s sparked renewed debate on the compatibility of communal sentiments, the requirements of the liberal conscience, and the imperatives of international order.

Liberalism and Self-Determination

The problems of explaining the origins of the national idea and the sources of national solidarity have been only part of the British study of nationalism. There is, in addition, a long tradition of speculation about to what extent the demands of nationalism should be accommodated by both political philosophers and policy makers. The concept of "liberal" or "civic" nationalism is often considered one of the great contributions of British political thought to this question. From David Hume, Lord Acton, and John Stuart Mill through John Plamenatz and Isaiah Berlin, to the upsurge in discussions of communitarianism, liberalism, and national self-determination in the 1980s and 1990s, the relationship between communal values and individual rights has been a perennial feature of studies of nationality in the United Kingdom.[38] Acknowledging individuals' need for a sense of community and connectedness while abjuring culturally exclusive definitions of the community, "civic" nationalists are often contrasted with their "ethnic" counterparts, for whom the collective will of the culturally defined nation is held to be superior to the wills of its individual constituents. In the case of civic nationalism, love of country and a sense of fellow feeling with one's compatriots are shields against alien oppression and tyranny at home. In the case of ethnic nationalism, by contrast, the nation takes on a more sinister character, endangering liberty by subjugating individual freedom to the demands of the communal group.

Of course, the picture has never been as clear as facile distinctions between civic and ethnic forms of the national idea would indicate. It is as easy to uncover a distinctive strand of ethnic exclusivism within British discussions of nationalism as it is to find more inclusive, civic conceptions of national identity.[39] What George Orwell called prodding "the nerve of nationalism"— the tendency for otherwise civically minded individuals to transform overnight into ethnic exclusivists, given the right circumstances—has never been far removed from debates about the nature of the British state, relations within the empire, and Britain's place in Europe.[40]

More important, among liberal intellectuals themselves there has long been a certain ambivalence about nationality. On the one hand, as Acton argued, when combined with a love of freedom, a strong national sentiment could advance the cause of human liberation. Nationality, if tempered by respect for the individual, could assist in throwing off foreign despotism, buttressing self-government, and guarding against the excessive powers of the state. If all members of a political community shared some traits of character, interest, and opinion, then the state's natural tendency toward centralization and absolutism could be checked.[41] If all that is meant by nationality is a sense of fellow feeling, a positive sentiment of connection with members of one's own national group, then the relationship between nationality and individual freedom seems unproblematic. On the other hand, if nationality refers to an array of special obligations that one owes to fellow countrymen beyond those that are owed to them in virtue of their being human, then the relationship becomes rather more troubling.

Liberals have therefore found themselves faced with a dilemma: Any theory that might encourage a people to prefer the tyranny of their own tribe to the kindness of strangers seems worthy of condemnation, but it is precisely this aversion to foreign rule that has frequently been a catalyst for liberation and democratization. Liberal critiques of nationalism have thus traditionally sprung as much from uneasiness as from principle: uneasiness about how to reconcile those special sentiments of camaraderie one might feel toward one's compatriots with the wider duties owed to the whole of humankind. Liberals feel instinctively, Mill wrote, that placing a fellow countryman in a special category of duty and loyalty is more worthy of savages than of civilized beings, but "grievous as are these things, yet so long as they exist, the question of nationality is practically of the very first importance."[42] In fact, Mill noted, the evils of nationalism notwithstanding, without some strong sense of cohesion, countries tended to fall under the spell of tyrants who impose unity at the expense of individual liberty. It was no accident that among both ancient and modern states the most powerful countries were those in which fellow feeling was strongest. There was thus good reason for believing that sentiments of sympathy and union among the inhabitants of a particular country, however unphilosophical, were a necessary precondition of liberty and good governance.[43]

These issues, which have occupied British philosophers and political theorists for some two centuries, have been of more than academic importance, for they have raised questions about the degree to which really existing national sentiments ought to be accommodated or, indeed, cultivated by state institutions. Discussions on this issue have normally proceeded in three directions. First has been the relationship between patriotism and nationalism. The former, associated with a love of country and a sense of community with one's compatriots, has frequently been contrasted with the culturally exclusive forms of nationalism found in parts of continental Europe. While devotion to preserving the traditions and institutions of one's country seems a precondition to continued independence and the rejection of foreign domination, calls for the union of all conationals into a single, culturally homogeneous state invites individuals to mortgage their freedom for the perceived good of the collective.[44] "If all the various peoples within a clear-cut unit of territory under a common rule suddenly begin to think of themselves as a common nation," wrote Bernard Crick in his classic *In Defence of Politics*, "no great harm is done. But if criteria of language or religion or race are accepted, then those who live just over the borders . . . must be brought into the fold."[45] Such feelings are not only potentially harmful to the political communities in which they arise but may also threaten international stability.

Second has been the question of the role of state institutions in fostering collective identity. Some sense of fellow feeling has generally been seen as essential to the smooth working of democracy, but there has been disagreement over whether such feelings arise spontaneously or only through state intervention. In other words, is multinationality to be prized within states, as Acton argued, or should the boundaries of statehood mirror insofar as possible those of the nationality? This issue became of increasing importance within Britain over the course of the twentieth century. Calls from the kingdom's constituent units for greater local autonomy—encapsulated in the debates about political devolution to Scotland and Wales, as well as the Troubles in Northern Ireland—called into question the future of a fully United Kingdom. At the same time, Britain's manifest ethnic heterogeneity and the greater attention paid to problems of interethnic discord, racial discrimination, and home-grown terrorism highlighted the problematic relationships among Britishness, Englishness, and the myriad identities of the country's South Asian, East Asian, and Afro-Caribbean communities. (In the late 1990s, Bernard Crick led the effort to devise a plan for national civic education as part of Britain's requirements for naturalized citizens, a plan implemented by Tony Blair's Labour government.)

Third, national self-determination as a principle of international politics has received considerable attention from British scholars, especially international relations specialists. The principle that national groups should be able to determine their own fate has been viewed as a largely progressive force when employed as a means for delivering oppressed peoples from tyrannical rule, but for all its positive components, the principle of self-determination has not generally been seen as absolute. As the experience of Versailles and the League of Nations illustrated, self-determination must be tempered by the practicalities of creating economically and politically viable states behind internationally defensible borders. In this regard, the meaning of self-determination has been understood in terms of process rather than outcome: Members of a national community should be able, insofar as is practicable, to determine their own fate, but the institutional form that such self-determination might take need not be a new, wholly independent state. There is no reason to believe that the only desirable expression of self-determination should be the nation-state, and indeed, given the heterogeneity of most existing states, complete self-determination would contradict the notion of state sovereignty. As Alfred Cobban argued in *The Nation State and National Self-Determination*, there may, in fact, be many other types of association through which communities can express their will to determine their own destiny.[46] Cultural autonomy, regional self-government, and the Commonwealth have all been offered as potential models for reconciling respect for nationality with the desire for political stability. The challenges of self-determination after the breakup of multinational federations in eastern Europe, as well as the increased salience of cultural identity in established democracies, gave renewed vigor to all these debates in the 1990s.

Each of these areas—the distinction between patriotism and nationalism, the role of government institutions in multicultural societies, and the place of self-determination as a principle of international politics—has illustrated the broad, multidisciplinary approach that British scholars have taken to the study of nationalism. Historians, political theorists, and legal experts have joined political scientists in tackling the major issues at the heart of nationalism and aided in the development of a distinct, problem-driven field of study influenced more by common research concerns than by common disciplinary affiliations. At each stage, the peculiarities of the British experience have helped account for the unusual vigor with which British intellectuals have tackled the most perplexing questions of nations and nationalism and the singular contribution of British thinkers to this scholarly field.

Conclusion

In terms of the sheer volume of new scholarship, few fields within political science have been as fertile in the last two decades as the study of nationalism and ethnonational politics. Doctoral dissertations, journal articles, monographs, edited volumes, and conferences on every facet of nationalism have proliferated at a remarkable rate. After the end of the cold war, the appearance of nearly two dozen new European and Eurasian states and the apparent upsurge in ethnonational disputes within and among them gave increased prominence to the study of nation building and nationalist territorial claims.

On one level, the results have been encouraging. We now know more than ever about the national idea: its historical origins, its various types in the developed and developing worlds, its relationship to gender and racism, and the contingent character of its manifestations. Generations of graduate students have written case studies of nationalism in every region of the world, and even the most insignificant nationalist movements have found their interpreters. It is a mark of the field's maturity that it has even generated its own array of conventional truths. That traditions are invented, that nationalism creates nations, that national communities are imagined, and that the nation is a gendered concept have become ideas that are repeatedly reaffirmed, reinterpreted, or rejected in countless new publications every year.

Despite the active engagement of a large scholarly community, however, the genuine explanation of nationalist phenomena has remained elusive. We know something (although perhaps not nearly enough) about the relationship between electoral systems and party formation, the paths from authoritarianism to democracy, and the advantages and disadvantages of parliamentary and presidential government. But we still know painfully little about why some Serbs and Croats found it preferable to push their societies toward social anarchy than spend another hour together in the same state. Indeed, the same questions that concerned scholars a century ago, in Britain or elsewhere, remain central to the study of nationalism today: Under what conditions do national claims prove a more powerful mobilizing force than appeals to class or other social categories? What is national identity, and how does it shape interactions among individuals? What kinds of institutions are most appropriate for reducing the chances that ethnonational tensions will escalate to violence? One need only compare the most recent books in the field with Frederick Hertz's insightful though largely unread *Nationality in History and Politics*, first published in 1944, if one needs convincing that the study of nationalism, like the study of politics more broadly, is still struggling to become a cumulative science.

It is an occupational hazard of studying nationalism that the more one knows about a particular instance of nationalist politics, the less one is willing to generalize to other cases. Studies of nationalism are particularly susceptible to the Zanzibar phenomenon; any generalization about the sources or conduct of nationalist politics drawn from a limited number of cases can always be met with the objection that "It isn't like that in Zanzibar."[47] But given that analyzing *n* cases of nationalism will always be inferior to studying *n* + 1, there are two practical things that can be done to ensure that the study of nations and nationalism retains its vitality in the century ahead.

First, there must be further serious discussion about what precisely the object and scope of the study of nationalism are meant to be. The political utility of the term *nation*, as James Mayall noted, has never been matched by its analytical clarity.[48] As a result, most studies begin by lamenting the paucity of serviceable definitions before proceeding to offer new, allegedly more adequate ones. But the proliferation of definitions, typologies, terms, and labels has more often clouded than clarified our understanding. It would be difficult to find within political science a field with more definitions and taxonomies, and fewer general theories, than the study of nationalism. Definitions and terms are often vague and ad hoc, arrived at with little thought given to the purpose that the definition is supposed to serve or to the plethora of typologies that have been devised before.[49]

Moreover, the types and categories into which nationalist movements and ideologies are separated are often unhelpful. It is common to find, for example, nationalist movements cavalierly divided into such categories as "colonial," "diaspora," "totalitarian," or "irredentist," a division that is patently nonsensical. Since each category is constructed according to a different criterion, the labels are useless in elucidating the essential dynamics of the nationalist movements placed under each rubric. The first tells us about where the nationalist movement takes place, the second about the geographical distribution of its target population, the third about the proclivities of its leadership, and the fourth about its political program.

Second, the focus on the vocabulary of theory building has deflected attention away from the need for further debate on the grammar of a theory itself. In other words, even though confusion about the terms to be used in describing nationalist phenomena has been a serious obstacle, even more problematic has been the almost complete absence of debate about what an adequate "theory of nationalism" might entail. Should it tell us something about political mobilization, about personal identity, or about the origins of ideology? Might it account for the power of political symbols, the determinants of voting behavior, or the foci of group solidarity? Or should it be expected, heroically, to do all the above? Understanding nationalism has not been nearly so difficult as agreeing on what a single "theory" of it—if there can ever be such a thing—might reasonably be expected to explain.

The British study of nationalism has made a valuable contribution to our understanding of the contingent character of nationalist ideology and the social bases of nationalist movements. British scholars have explored the mutable conceptions of the nation through history, the changing sources of group solidarity, and the relationship between demands for national self-determination and the exigencies of practical politics. Today, British political scientists are themselves divided about the most appropriate methods for studying nationalism. Some defend the eclecticism of the past, others call for more quantitative research, and still others argue for the elaboration of deductive theories of nationalist behavior. Like Anglicanism, the British study of nationalism has always been a broad church. The national origins of nationalism studies have been superseded by genuinely global scholarly networks and research programs. But the intellectual orientations, methods, and key research questions bequeathed by an older scholarly tradition continue to influence debates today. The central challenge in the future will be to create more truly comparative studies of nationalism, organized according to clear conceptions of the main aims of research itself.

3

Loser Nationalisms

How Certain Ideas of the Nation Succeed or Fail

"I write to you from the beautiful, passionate, ruined South," wrote Oscar Wilde in a letter to Julia Ward Howe in the summer of 1882. Traveling through the United States, delighting and infuriating audiences in one town after another, Wilde reported that he had bathed in the Gulf of Mexico, breathed in the scent of magnolias, and "engaged in Voodoo rites with the Negroes." But he especially enjoyed a visit to Beauvoir, a plantation on the Gulf of Mexico between New Orleans and Mobile. His host there was Jefferson Davis, the former president of the Confederate States. Davis was living in easy and obscure retirement, the cataclysmic conflict of the 1860s now two decades past. The old president was the forgotten chief of a failed nation, Wilde wrote, a nation that was now "living chiefly on credit and on the memory of some crushing defeat." Yet that, he concluded, was part of Davis's—and the South's—charm: "How fascinating all failures are!"[1]

Ernest Gellner famously observed that the class of nationalisms that "failed to bark" is far larger than the class of successful ones.[2] In some instances, nationalist ideas never manage to produce nationalist movements. Their purveyors become voices crying in the wilderness, curiosities and oddities left behind by more powerful, alternative visions of the nation. In other instances, it never occurs to anyone to try to make a nation at all, so that the obliging ties of family, clan, class, or territory remain the dominant forms of social organization and loyalty. But what are the boundaries of historical contingency when it comes to understanding the origins, development, and ends of particular forms of nationalism? Why do some nationalisms endure and others fade away, becoming the quaint obsessions of antiquarians, émigrés, and exiles?

The history of nationalism is not necessarily written by the winners, but it is almost always written about them. Historians and social scientists have dealt mainly with the nationalist ideologies that are able to create credible narratives of national belonging, appeal to the masses, build states, and then get those states recognized by a sizable number of other countries. Throughout the now extensive theoretical and comparative literature on nationalism, the normal method is—as a political scientist would say—to choose case studies on the dependent variable: to analyze inductively the causes of a particular phenomenon by selecting a set of cases in which the phenomenon has actually occurred. Such a method ignores the historical losers, consigning them to obscurity and eliminating them from theoretical consideration. By and large, they are thus unavailable as cases for enriching the discussion of where nationalist ideas come from, how they wend their way into the consciousness of populations, and under what conditions they produce polities that end up as legitimate parts of the international system.

This chapter discusses the literature on nationalism and the sources for many of our existing theories about the origins and development of nations and nationalist movements. It highlights the utility of studying failure, while also urging caution about the difficulties of defining what exactly failure—or, for that matter, success—might mean. Next, the chapter provides a brief tour through three nationalisms that might be said, in various ways, to have failed: the national desires and travails of the Confederate States of America, Scotland, and Circassia (a region of the northwest Caucasus located in what is today the Russian Federation). Finally, the chapter draws specific lessons from these cases and demonstrates how a greater appreciation for the causes of both national success and national failure might enhance our views of nationalism as an idea, a movement, and a form of social solidarity. The chapter does not offer a magical formula for predicting which nations are likely to succeed and which not. Rather, it proposes to add nuance to our understanding of what it means to be one of the "fascinating failures" that Oscar Wilde identified during his trip along the Gulf Coast.

Theorizing Failure

The comparative and theoretical literature on nationalism, in English and other languages, is vast. It stretches from the early work of French and British writers such as Ernest Renan and Hugh Seton-Watson, through the sociological approaches of Karl Deutsch, Ernest Gellner, Anthony Smith, and Rogers Brubaker, to the comparative historical treatments of Eric Hobsbawm and Liah

Greenfeld, and through deconstructionists like Benedict Anderson (see chapter 2). The range of questions that writers in these traditions address is massive—so massive, in fact, that the study of something called "nationalism" has become an entire academic industry, not a discrete research program. After all, it would be odd to expect that a single research question, set of hypotheses, or theory should account for the paintings of Jacques-Louis David, the music of Wagner and Smetana, the electoral behavior of Sinn Fein and United Russia, and the disintegration of Yugoslavia. Today, nationalism is a subject heading or shelf mark, like "democracy" or "Argentina," rather than a meaningful set of contending theories.

Overwhelmingly, however, these literatures have in common the fact that they derive their theories from (and often, in turn, test their hypotheses according to) cases in which nationalism, in various ways, succeeds. The archetypical case studies found in Hans Kohn's classic *The Idea of Nationalism* (1956)—the English, Irish, Italians, Poles, Germans, Hungarians, Greeks—are still among the forms of nationalism that, with some exceptions, inform thinking on the phenomenon as a whole. The field has been enriched, of course, by adding even further cases, and there is today scarcely a country, region, or ethnic group claiming the label of "nation"—from Kurds to Basques, from Xinjiang to Aceh—that has not found its interpreter. But the lure of success is profound, even as it impedes truly comparative work on the origins and development of particular forms of the national idea.

Early students of nationalism began with the belief that, to understand the real causes of nationalism as a phenomenon, theories should be most readily built out of the raw material of success. Alfred Cobban, writing in the 1940s, held that nationalism was important in a political sense only insofar as "the existence of linguistic and cultural affiliations between a number of tribal communities" received some form of "institutional embodiment." When those affiliations did not exist, or where they were not instantiated in political institutions, nationalism simply did not exist as a "political fact."[3] Kohn shared that view. His basic assumption was that nationalism as an idea presupposes the existence of a nationality, defined by certain "objective bonds" delimiting a "social group." For Kohn, nationalism was simply an idea that sometimes attached itself to an objective social reality. To ask why nationalism failed was to answer one's own question: It could fail as an idea only if there were no objective substrate to which it could profitably cling.[4] Karl Deutsch, writing in the 1960s, hailed from very different social-scientific traditions, the fields of sociology and sociolinguistics, yet his view of the origins of nationalism was remarkably consonant with those of historians like Cobban and Kohn. "National consciousness, like all consciousness, can only be consciousness of something which exists," Deutsch wrote.[5] All attempts to cultivate a sense of nationalism within a given population must link up with really existing sentiments, beliefs, communicative skills, experiences, or other traits shared by the members of that group.

From Ernest Gellner forward, that approach has been treated as a rather unsophisticated reading of nationalist phenomena. Indeed, one of Gellner's signature contributions to the field was to observe that nationalism depended less on any predefined and preexisting "nationality" than on the existence of the state. If nationalism as an idea and a movement was parasitic on anything at all, it was not on history, culture, or language, but rather on what Gellner called "a prior and assumed definition of the state."[6] More recently, Rogers Brubaker has argued for shifting the scholarly gaze even further away from the alleged preconditions for nationalist success. Scholars should focus their attention not on defining what nations are but rather on analyzing the process by which the quest for such a definition comes to matter in social life.[7]

Yet despite such warnings to proceed contrariwise, our thinking about the success or failure of nationalist ideas and movements has not really advanced much beyond the simple equation of a half century ago: no nationality, no nationalism. Indeed, even when scholars admit the basic constructedness of national identities, stories of imperial decline and state breakup are often written as if they were the inevitable outcome of successful nations struggling to breathe free—with little space given for groups who conceive of themselves and their concerns in terms other than national ones. On this view, as Jeremy King has noted, "the forebear to nationhood [is] not nonnational politics but nonpolitical ethnicity."[8]

There are twin teleologies at work in nationalism and its study. One is the implicit teleology woven into many national narratives, despite their plainly sine-wave record of success and failure. The other is the problem of presentism. If a nationalist ideology or movement has succeeded at the time the analyst is writing about it, the tendency is to see that nationalist phenomenon as, if not foreordained, then at least real and perhaps even legitimate. If the nationalism has clearly failed at the time the analyst is writing, the tendency is to see it as fatally flawed in some way. The problem is that—however much we may acknowledge the contingent nature of nationalist success—we are locked in a dialogue with the very nationalist ideologies we scrutinize. We sometimes implicitly accept the narrative that nationalists themselves use, which rests on the idea of perennial identities and destinies. Even in debunking national myths, we can end up strengthening the basic conceptual vocabulary and time line of nationalism: a line that stretches from ethnogenesis, through national consciousness, to the rise of nationalist movements embracing the whole population. That, in turn, perversely sustains the very language of over-determined success. As Timothy Snyder has written, "Refuting a myth is dancing with a skeleton: one finds it hard to disengage from the deceptively lithe embrace once the music has begun, and one soon realizes that one's own steps are what is keeping the old bones in motion."[9]

Studying failure keeps the discussion in the national frame, of course; failed nationalists, like their successful counterparts, still view the nation as timeless and its requirements as philosophically and morally prior to those of the village, the town, the region, the religion, or even the family. But taking failures seriously helps to shift the discussion away from presumed connections between the existence of ostensibly unconscious ethnonational communities and their inevitable transformation into politically aware movements. It causes us to focus, instead, on the contingent but identifiable features that cause some ideas of the nation to have purchase within their target communities and in the wider world.

Every successful nationalism is alike, but unsuccessful nationalisms fail in their own ways. Successful nationalist ideologies garner widespread appeal among their target populations. They transform nationalist movements into the accoutrements of statehood. They have their statehood recognized by an authoritative body that speaks on behalf of the international community. Nationalist ideologies might be said to fail if they miss any one of these criteria. They can have no appeal, for example, but somehow wind up, through little more than historical accident, with states. They can have appeal and build the accoutrements of statehood, but never achieve international recognition. Those that manage none of these things remain the quixotic project of a few nationalist intellectuals, with little resonance among their putative conationals or in the broader world. Those that manage them all become the nations and nationalisms that have formed the basis of our comparative theorizing: the French, Germans, British, Italians, Spanish, Russians, Chinese, Japanese, and a limited set of others.

These three criteria—mass appeal, state building, and recognition—are not exhaustive, but they do seem to constitute a minimal array of traits that coincide with the cases that exist at the top of a hierarchy of success and failure. They also usefully capture three of the dominant strands in writing about nations and nationalism. The mass appeal of the national idea is the subject of the oldest theoretical traditions in nationalism studies, stretching back at least to the beginning of serious social-scientific and historical engagement with the topic in the 1940s and 1950s. Nationalism as state-building strategy—that is, nationalism as a political and social force rather than a disembodied idea—has been the subject of an equally rich body of theorizing, particularly in sociology and political science. The legal and philosophical dimensions of nationalism form yet a third strand of theorizing: Under what conditions should new states be recognized, and what claims does the nation have on individual and group allegiance as against the claims of humanity in general? These three minimal criteria for nationalist success thus reflect the major debates within the extensive scholarly literature on nationalism as much as they accord with a common-sense view of what being a successful nationalist might entail.

If we accept these criteria for success, each of which can either exist or not exist, there are eight types of cases. Only one is really the domain of antiquarians: the type that has no mass appeal, generates no state, and is never recognized by anyone. Another type—the ideal type for nationalists themselves—manages to garner all three things, and it not surprising that this variety of nationalism has normally generated the most attention. But between these poles, there are many cases left to consider. Some of the possible paths of nationalist evolution are summarized in Table 3.1.

Nationalist typologies are legion, and one introduces yet another at one's peril. But this typology seeks to make sense of several scholarly discussions and provide a way of thinking about a host of different labels normally applied to both nationalisms of various stripes and to forms of state organization. The first category—which I label simply "nation-states"—points toward the nationalisms that succeed in gaining mass appeal, states, and recognition (although these three things need not be achieved in this order). The second consists of the polar opposite: nationalisms that remain the purview of committed enthusiasts, without ever gaining much traction among wider publics. These "antiquarian nationalisms," as I have labeled them, are real features of the international system; they can have punctuated success, in the sense that bands of nationalist entrepreneurs can certainly have a major impact on politics, for example, through the targeted use of disruptive violence. But they remain political oddities and the objects of individual obsession rather than bases of mass appeal.

The other categories map different combinations of these three basic criteria. "Unrecognized nation-states" manage to secure mass appeal and build real state institutions, yet lack the imprimatur of the international community. "Failed states" are those in which international recognition remains in place, yet the reality of external sovereignty is belied by the absence of mass commitment or functioning institutions on the ground. "Weak nation-states" are those in which, despite the good will of both domestic constituents and international supporters, functioning state institutions remain elusive. "Warlord states" manage to exercise some degree of real control over territory, perhaps even creating highly functional institutions of governance, yet their genuine appeal

TABLE 3.1. Types of Nationalist Success and Failure

Mass Appeal	Creation of Functioning State	International Recognition as Sovereign Nation-State	Label	Examples
Yes	Yes	Yes	Nation-states	Germany, Italy, France, Ireland, Israel
No	No	No	Antiquarian nationalism	Laz, Sorbs, Ruthenians, Circassians, "White Supremacists"
Yes	Yes	No	Unrecognized nation-states	Confederate States of America, Turkish Republic of Northern Cyprus, Abkhazia, Somaliland (1991–), Kosovo (1999–2008), Southern Sudan, Hezbollah-controlled southern Lebanon
No	No	Yes	Failed states	Somalia, Bosnia (1991–95), Afghanistan (after 1979), Iraq (after 2003)
Yes	No	Yes	Weak nation-states	Albania (1991–92, 1997), Georgia (1991–93)
No	Yes	No	Warlord states	Regions of China during the "warlord period" (1916–1928), regions of Afghanistan (1979–2001), regions of Iraq (2003–8)
No	Yes	Yes	Ernest Gellner's "state-nations"	Kazakhstan, Turkmenistan, Kingdom of Serbs, Croats, and Slovenes/Yugoslavia (1918–1941), Moldova
Yes	No	No	Nascent nation-states	Kosovo (1981–1999), Scotland (before 1999?)

to constituents and their ability to attract international legitimacy remain low. "State-nations," to borrow Gellner's term, are those in which the reality of recognized statehood precedes the creation of large-scale nationalist appeal, or to put it more bluntly, the latter may be a conscious creation of the former. "Nascent nation-states" are those that experience the first flush of nationalist sentiment and mobilization, while distinct state institutions and recognition remain only possibilities for the future.

There are caveats to this typology. Being a winner or a loser depends on where one slices into the historical narrative. Hungarian nationalism was a failure in 1848, something of a success in 1867, a kind of failure in 1920, and a success today. Croatian nationalism was a mitigated success in 1868, a qualified failure in 1918, an equally qualified success in 1941, a failure in 1945, and a resounding success in 1991. Scottish nationalism and Flemish nationalism were failures in the 1710s and the 1830s, respectively, but both may yet be successful by the 2010s. If they turn out to be so, they—like the Croatians and others—will no doubt interpret their good fortune as the end point of a thousand-year dream of national consciousness and independence, rather than an unpredictable oscillation between success and failure. But are there ways of thinking about nationalism in discrete periods that can help us imagine, in a systematic and comparative way, the common features of failure?

Loser Nationalisms

In several historiographical traditions, it is commonplace to acknowledge multiple strands of nationalist thought and sentiment. Russian nationalism is said to have had both a "Westernizing" face, one that sought to link Russia's fate to that of Europe, and a "Slavophile" face, which sought to highlight the commonalities linking Russia with the other Slavic nations of east-central Europe. Modern Turkish nationalism has had its "Turanian" strand, which looked for the ethnic origins of Turks in the steppes of Central Asia, and its Republican or neo-Ottomanist strands, which accented in various ways the civic or pan-Islamic dimensions of Turkishness.

Studies of individual nationalisms certainly admit plural visions of the nation in any particular tradition, even if the comparative literature has by and large tended to focus only on the winners. But there are two suspicious elements even in these more nuanced treatments of national history. First, is it really the case that only two or three visions of the nation ever emerge in particular cases, or are the various schools of nationalist discourse in part the post hoc creation of later historians? Second, even if we admit the multifarious nature of nationalism in any particular case, we are still left with the question of why one or more seemed to win out where others fell by the wayside. In other words, admitting the multivalent character of any particular nationalism leaves unexplored the truly difficult question: Why do some visions of the nation seem quaint today while others appear—even to committed cosmopolitans who ought to know better—supremely natural?

To explore these themes, the following sections go on a brief journey through three nationalisms that failed—but ones that failed in sometimes bizarre and unpredictable ways. The journey runs from the familiar to the exotic, from the American South to Scotland to Circassia, the region along the northeastern coast of the Black Sea: three regions of mountains and plains, of hollers, straths, and gorges, upland and lowland, where pockets of nationalist sentiment continued to exist even after the grandest schemes for making modern nations seemed to fall by the wayside.

As these cases show, concentrating on the failures can reveal something of the mechanisms through which particular views of the nation come to dominate otherwise fractious and divided societies, but also the ways in which the commitment of elites to a particular nationalist narrative can end up being a bet on the wrong historical horse. These cases do not necessarily lead toward a single theory of nationalist failure; such a thing is as chimerical as a general theory of nationalism. But they are illustrative of the ways in which historical contingency can be parsed and disaggregated, if scholars are willing to take seriously the alternative pathways via which the parade of modern nations might have admitted—save for a few discrete historical events—more entrants than we normally allow. There is no single feature all these failures share, and looking for one is a naive way of approaching a complicated and contested historical record. But one place to look is in the message of nationalism itself: the degree to which nationalist elites were able to craft a message that was able to stand up to its own innate contradictions. The bar to nationalist success is usually remarkably high; Gellner's barking dogs are by far the minority in a very large pack. But it may well be that the consistency and coherence of nationalist claims themselves offer a clue as to why some nationalisms, in distinct periods, end up as something other than nation-states.

Confederates: The Lost Cause

The failure of the Confederate States of America has a long and venerable history both as an object of historical research and as a focus of nationalist discourse. The weaknesses of Southern industrial capacity, inadequate military supply chains, antiquated social hierarchies, and the inherent contradictions of a slave-based social and economic system seeking independence for itself are part of the much-plowed terrain of Southern history. The narrative of noble defeat and the "lost cause" has formed part of the warp and weft of Southern history since Reconstruction, joining the pantheon of other grand and galvanizing narratives of loss in national histories, from the Alamo to Kosovo.

In a famous essay on Southern identity, the historian C. Vann Woodward examined the distinctive features of Southernness, settling on the ignoble trinity of poverty, failure, and pessimism as the defining traits of the South's historical experience.[10] Failure—the loss in the Civil War, the down-and-out legacies of Reconstruction, and the rearguard resistance against integration and civil rights—has been central to a particular, and particularly white, version of Southern identity for the last century and a half.[11] Over much of that period, Southern intellectuals repeatedly sought to define themselves and construct their culture in ways that both celebrated failure as a legacy of the past and literally hoisted its flag as a symbol of defiant resistance to the present. But the Confederate case raises searching questions about the limits of constructedness. What are the frontiers of the imagination when it comes to the nation? Are all national narratives ultimately the same? Can the choices of political and intellectual elites take nation building down roads that ultimately lead to failure?

In the case of the Confederacy, there was a continual tension between two forms of the national idea. On the one hand, the nation was conceived as rooted in the unique traditions of a distinct society, a society that stood in clear counterpoise to that of the North. That vision of the South had many components. Religion and religiosity played a role, as did traditions of chivalry, honor, and rank. Its precise character was a subject of much debate among Confederate intellectuals. Yet slavery, for many Confederate nationalists, lay at the base of this society, since it best encapsulated the organic and mutually dependent relationships that were held to undergird Southern society as a whole. The master-slave nexus—with the former having a paternal regard for the well-being of the latter, who in turn owed obedience and contentment—was a microscopic form of the bonds of duty and obligation that were seen as the quintessential features of Southern life. Moreover, slavery provided the bedrock for an entire social and economic system that allowed the best men to devote their time to leadership, authority, and governance. If the North was a land of greedy industrialists, radical abolitionists, and white workers toiling for meager wages, the South was an idealized society of men and women of different ranks and races, each conscious of their predestined role in the harmonious social firmament— some as obedient servants, others as wise stewards.[12] And that belief resonated well beyond the drawing rooms of Richmond and Atlanta, deep into the rank and file of Southern soldiery.[13]

On the other hand, Confederate nationalism underscored the idea of an essential continuity between 1776 and 1861—between the ideas and values that had animated the struggle for American independence from Britain and those that now inflamed the belief in the new Confederate States. The very system of government that had been put in place after the War of Independence relied on an explicit recognition of the unique prerogatives of the several states united. Now, the overweening power of the federal government threatened to backtrack on the fundamental compromises that had been accepted by the founders. The events of 1861 were thus not a departure from the ideals of 1776 but rather their apotheosis.

This dual narrative placed Confederates in a peculiar bind not faced by more clearly ethnicist visions of nationalism, including those European examples that Confederates themselves cited as inspirations. By turns civic, territorial, and racist, the Confederate vision was blurry and inconsistent. It was a nationalism that sought the continued subjugation of a sizable part of its own population. That population and its peculiar social status were nevertheless thought to be central to the national project. At the same time, the Confederate nation found itself vying for a political and philosophical heritage that was also claimed by its chief opponent in a brutal war. It was a movement of radical return, an ideology founded on recovering an allegedly foundational social hierarchy within a government that depended more and more on people— slaves, upland whites, industrialists—who shared few of the essential values that Confederate intellectuals hoped they would recover.[14] Few nationalisms have faced such serious—and self-imposed—obstacles. It was not simply military defeat but the convoluted and contradictory nature of the national narrative itself that made Confederate nationalism, as Wilde knew, both passionate and ultimately ruined.

Scots: Highland Dreams

Mark Twain famously remarked that the chief cause of the Civil War was Sir Walter Scott. Confederate nationalists and the southern public at large were avid consumers of Scott's novels. His romantic vision of chivalrous knights, demure but resourceful ladies, and a hierarchical and ordered society fit with the Confederacy's vision of its own recoverable past. To many Scots, however, Walter Scott is today at best an oddity and at worst an embarrassment. The monument to his memory towers over Edinburgh's new city, a blackened Gothic fantasy to a writer now largely unread. Scottish nationalism, too, has had fortunes no less variable than that of Scott himself, one of the chief creators of a particular way of being Scottish. On the one hand, Scottishness possesses one of the most instantly recognizable sets of "national" paraphernalia in the world, from sway-ing kilts to screeching bagpipes to bouncing terriers. One need only visit a St. Andrew's Society dinner in Inverness or Chicago to discover that the Scots are one of few nations whose members actually purchase their own tourist gear.

Yet for most of the last four centuries, Scottish nationalism as a political project has been a failure. Indeed, Scottish nationalism has rarely been reflected in movements, demonstrations, or calls to action but rather, as the journalist Andrew Marr has noted, in a certain "sullenness, an emptiness, at the centre of Scottish public life."[15] The Scottish Crown was united with that of England in 1609. The two parliaments were fused a century later, in 1707. Thereafter, peri-odic risings threatened the unity of the conjoined kingdom, but these were doomed affairs, led by one or another discontented claimant to the Scottish throne and intertwined with broader concerns: the machinations of French for-eign policy, the grievances of the Catholic minority in an overwhelmingly Protestant state, and the designs of Highland chieftains in a society in which their feudal privileges were quickly being eroded. Indeed, in one version of Scottish nationalism, it is defeat, rather than victory, that takes pride of place. The vanquishing of the son of the pretender to the Scottish throne, Prince Charles Edward Stuart, at the battle of Culloden in 1745 represented the last military threat to Scotland's place in the United Kingdom—and a Kosovo-like emblem of dashed defiance for the most romantic nationalists. That brand of Scottishness—Catholic, clannish, and Jacobite (that is, supporting a Stuart rather than a Hanoverian dynastic line)—had only a marginal presence after "the '45." It followed Bonnie Prince Charlie into exile in Europe and appears today only in the harmless chauvinism of nostalgic "Scottish-Americans."

Securing Scotland's place in the kingdom depended on at least two things. First, the political compromise of 1707 allowed a great degree of local autonomy for Scottish institutions, even as the parliamentary privileges Scotland had long enjoyed were eliminated. The idea of Scottish uniqueness—through legal codes, an educational system, and a separate church—remained in place after the end of self-governance. Second, the old clan chiefs in the Highlands were supplanted by—or in many cases turned into—landlords. That transformation, which took place within the course of a single generation, set the stage for the slow demo-graphic shifts that pushed farmers and small-scale cattle drovers from their homes and replaced them with the vast and profitable herds of sheep that would become emblematic of Highland life. It also shifted the weight of Scotland's economy even farther south, toward the Lowlands and Borders, which became intimately tied to the mills, kilns, and lathes of the north of England.

These two features of Scotland's full union with Britain also allowed the space for Britons to discover, in Scotland, their own local savages. The great oddity of the nineteenth century is that just as social and economic power in Scotland shifted to the Lowlands, the Highlands became popularized as the essence of Scottish identity. The kilt, the bagpipe, the fuzzy "Highland cow," Highland games, and just about every other element of allegedly Scottish national identity that one might believe in today were wholly manufactured in the nineteenth century—and many of them owe their origins to Walter Scott. He was the chief orchestrator—in every sense of that term—of George IV's famous visit to Edinburgh in 1822, the first visit of a British monarch to Scotland in more than a century.

It was a truly dazzling affair. Edinburgh burghers were wrapped in kilts and belted plaids, portraying themselves as chieftains of one or another ancient clan. At a celebratory dinner, the king was so moved by this display of Highland unity and loyalty that he offered a solemn toast to "the chieftains and clans of Scotland." J. G. Lockhart, Scott's biographer and a witness to these events, later wrote that "so completely had this hallucination taken possession, that nobody seems to have been startled at the time by language which thus distinctly conveyed his Majesty's impression that the marking and crowning glory of Scotland consisted in the Highland clans and their chieftains," not in the growing industrial and manufacturing power of the Lowlands.[16] A similar hallucination about the nature of Scottish identity would continue to inform popular British views of the north country, from the dress and deportment of Highland regiments to Queen Victoria's personal fascination with Scotland and its invented traditions.[17]

One of the deficiencies of Scottish nationalism as a political movement was the fact that it existed in so many different varieties. There was the Stuart and Jacobite variety, intent for a time on the restoration of a deposed monarch. There was the regionalism of the plebeian Lowlands, which was counterpoised to the clannish and aristocratic variety found in the Highlands. The Scottish church—the vaunted and conservative Kirk—understood that its historical privileges, at least since the early eighteenth century, could be best preserved within a union with England, but separatists within the Kirk itself found nationalism to be an antidote to church hierarchs, who were perceived as liberal innovators. Working-class nationalism, born in the factories and shipyards of Dundee and Glasgow, saw the defense of Scottishness as a route toward class liberation and even world revolution, while other progressive politicians found the all-union Labour Party as the best guarantor of the interests of the toiling masses. That party, in turn, periodically found the nationalist message to be a useful electoral tool, even when local support for home rule north of the border was minimal—as evidenced by the soggy failure of a referendum on home rule in 1979. By the 1990s, yet another strand of Scottish nationalism appeared in the form of a repackaged Scottish National Party (SNP), which proclaimed a multicultural, territorial vision of Scottishness as a subset of a broader project to build a common European identity.

Modern Scottish nationalism—the movement for devolution of power from London to Edinburgh and for the restoration of the Scottish parliament—thus had little to do with the mythic brand of Scottishness pioneered by Sir Walter Scott. The saltire-and-tartan form of nationhood became the bailiwick of dour romantics, the "members o' St. Andrew's Societies sleepin' soon, . . ./On regimental buttons or buckled shoon," as the poet Hugh MacDiarmid described them.[18] More recent Scottish nationalism has been a matter of practical politics. The first great political victory for the SNP, the most radical of local political parties, took place not in the rural and traditionally Gaelic-speaking Highlands but in the urban, Lowlands, and English-speaking south, through a by-election victory in a race for a British parliament seat in 1967. As the SNP continued to grow in power, it was in large part because of its out-lefting the left, especially as the Labour Party, the traditional winner in modern Scottish elections, eased away from its working-class roots in the 1980s and 1990s. When Scottish citizens voted for the restoration of the Edinburgh parliament in 1997, that vote signaled the emergence of a new, territorial, civic, and pro-European vision of Scottishness, not the shortbread-and-bagpipes variety most familiar to outsiders. Nationalism turned out to be compatible with one form of unionism if not another: the EU version rather than the older UK one.

The "ethnic" version of Scottishness has been so utterly manufactured—and in such an utterly self-conscious way—over the last century and a half that even modern proponents of an independent Scotland generally find it loathsome. Whereas Basque, Catalan, and Flemish nationalism cannot help but celebrate a particular culturally exclusive form of the ethnos—in these cases, one based on language—the Scottish variant has stressed inclusion, responsive governance, and social democracy as core values. That peculiar feature of modern Scottishness has helped to account for its persistent failure as a national project over the last four centuries but may yet point toward a peculiar kind of success in a territorially devolved Britain and a "regionalized" EU.

Circassians: The Uses of Misfortune

If one were to have traveled to the southern reaches of the Russian Empire in the nineteenth century, one might well have heard a Scottish accent lilting over the Eurasian steppe or echoing against the Caucasus Mountains. It might have belonged to one John Abercrombie, a man who was well known as the person to whom one could apply for a place to stay, introductions to local officials, and safe passage across the sometimes hostile steppe. (He is mentioned by several nineteenth-century travelers.)[19]

Yet despite his name, Abercrombie was not Scottish. He was Circassian, a member of the indigenous ethnic group then dominant in the northwestern Caucasus. The Circassians were a major obstacle to Russian imperial expansion in the region, but they were also a key target for the missionary zeal of Scottish Presbyterians, who established outposts among them in the early nineteenth century. The Scots translated portions of the Bible into local languages and held services at which Circassians were asked to convert from paganism or Islam, but they were also not beyond saving souls in a more clearly economical way: by purchasing children from Circassian parents and then raising them as Christians. Abercrombie was one such rescued child, and foreign travelers to the Russian Empire came to rely on this enterprising man with a Scottish brogue as their local guide and fixer.

Beyond the activities of missionaries, the Circassians were of considerable interest to strategists in western Europe. The "Circassian question"—the desire by some Circassian communities to remain independent of Russia and the proper policy of west European powers toward this issue—played a significant role through the first half of the century. Correspondents from major newspapers found their way to Circassia. British spies sought to meld the Circassians into a unified military force. Even the Circassian national flag—a stars-and-arrows design that today can be found flying across the northwest Caucasus and among the ethnic Circassian diaspora—was the handiwork of David Urquhart (a real Scot, as it turns out), who took on the highlanders' cause as his own and became their major publicist and intercessor in Europe.[20]

Those efforts came to little, however. Circassian nationalism ultimately fizzled. Looking back on their failed nationalist movement, two Circassian leaders tried to explain the situation in a letter to Queen Victoria in the 1860s: "During the Crimean war, we were accused by the Allied Powers of want of sincerity, not having participated with them against our common foe. This is true, but it was not the fault of our nation, as it proceeded from want of union and energy between our leaders."[21] The failure to unite had repercussions far beyond the failure of Circassian nationalism as an idea, for in the final stage of Russia's conquest of the Caucasus, virtually the entirety of the Circassian linguistic group was forced to flee their villages and traditional grazing lands. In a series of military campaigns from 1860 to 1864, the northwest Caucasus and the Black Sea coast were emptied of indigenous villagers. Crops were torched. Houses were destroyed. Columns of the displaced were marched either to the northern plains or toward the coast, where they were placed on ships and dispatched across the Black Sea to the Ottoman Empire. Entire Circassian tribal groups—perhaps as many as half a million people in all—were driven out, resettled, or killed en masse in a campaign that today might well be labeled genocide. "In the mountains . . . one can now find bears and wolves," wrote one contemporary observer, "but no highlanders."[22]

But Circassian nationalism had legs. The expulsions of the 1860s left many Circassians dead, to be sure, but it also created a vast new diaspora spread across modern-day Turkey, Jordan, and other parts of the Middle East—and in far-flung places such as Paterson, New Jersey. In these diaspora centers, Circassian intellectuals nurtured the same ideals of unity and resistance that had motivated their fathers and grandfathers, but they now had something that none of the earlier Circassian national leaders could claim: a tragic yet communal experience to which Circassians themselves could now appeal—the Russian-organized expulsions.

Circassian nationalism would continue to fail as a distinct political project. In the wake of the Russian revolutions of 1917, the diminished Circassian population in the old homeland (along with other north Caucasus peoples) established a briefly independent republic, which was soon crushed by the victorious Bolsheviks. Circassia, divided into a variety of autonomous republics, was absorbed into the Soviet Union, but the Soviet experience accentuated, rather than diminished, the sense of belonging to a single Circassian—or in the local language, Adyga—nation. Official dance troupes, folklore societies, and textbook histories underscored the sense of common identity among all Circassians, even if this identity was now held to be inseparable from the broader brotherhood of Soviet peoples.

When the Soviet Union collapsed in 1991, the Circassians made still further rumblings about renewing the old struggle. Few had the stomach for a real fight.[23] The region was largely Russian, rather than Circassian. It was divided among five autonomous administrative units, only one of which had a Circassian majority. The sense of separateness continued to be expressed mainly through music, dance, and other traditional cultural forms, rather than through politics. But with more and more diaspora Circassians now making the pilgrimage to the old homeland—and the 2014 Sochi Olympics casting light on what was once the Circassian coast—being Circassian may eventually mean more than waving the flag invented by an obsessive Scot. Indeed, Circassian intellectuals, popular songwriters, and Internet sites and chat rooms have even pioneered a particular way of labeling the events of the 1860s as genocide, known in the local language as the Istambulaqwa, "the flight to Istanbul." As some Circassians have begun to discover, demarcating and labeling discrete historical events can be a powerful tool of identity making in the present. The Istambulaqwa may yet join Appomattox and Culloden as symbols of grand defeats that have enabled some degree of nationalist success in a different historical era.

Conclusion

Southerners are today an antiquarian nation, Scots a nascent one, and Circassians perhaps somewhere in between. A century ago, we might have put them in rather different categories, even though none would have achieved the top-shelf label of successful nationalism. Writing history in the nationalist mode involves the application of philosophical necessity to an accumulation of historical accidents. Writing histories of nationalism can sometimes amount to the same thing. It is easy to succumb to the tyranny of presentism, to see the nations we find arrayed before us as the only ones available in the world. But there are a host of others. Some are the exclusive property of old men and women who will take the memory of their nation with them when they die. Others are the stuff of pop culture but not politics. Still others are the passions of distinct culturally defined nations that, however unsuccessful in the past, can find themselves suddenly catapulted into the position of state makers, with professors or playwrights becoming prime ministers virtually overnight.

The three nationalisms surveyed here—Confederate, Scots, and Circassian—were failures of a peculiar sort. The Confederates failed to create an independent state, and now only the most absurd politicians or reprehensible activists espouse all the elements that were once claimed as crucial to Southern identity. Yet the flag is still there, as is the popular memory of regional distinctiveness (even in parts of the United States that were not part of the old Confederacy). Scottish nationalism as it exists today is the product of a Victorian and largely English fascination with noble Highland savagery, grafted onto the labor movements of the 1960s and 1970s. Over the past three decades, it has been nurtured by the zeal for local governance that has swept across—and, indeed, has been encouraged by—the deepening and widening of the European Union. Circassian nationalism has likewise had its ups and downs. It failed in the 1860s, succeeded briefly after 1917, failed again in the early 1990s, yet has succeeded enormously as an idea and a sense of common identity among a global—and now increasingly aware and globally connected—diaspora.

The study of failure can enrich discussions of the major research questions that have animated the study of nationalism in at least four ways. First, it helps us focus our attention on causality rather than on typology. By unraveling why particular nationalisms fail—and fail in time-bound and peculiar ways—we can move beyond simply categorizing nationalisms by their alleged types (civic or ethnic, say) and ask why it is that, in certain times and at certain places, the nation as a project succeeds or fails. In other words, it helps us move beyond a simple deconstruction of the national idea and engage with contingency rather than simply stipulate it.

Second, it pushes us toward taking seriously the idea of alternative poles of allegiance. Nationalism as an idea and a movement can be a powerful form of group solidarity, but nationalism as a category of analysis can easily fall prey to uncritical groupism—assuming the prior existence of the very group whose solidarity we are trying to explain. Paying attention to failures can thus recast the question: not how does nationalism as a historical phenomenon arise, but rather under what conditions does the nation as one form of group solidarity trump all others?

Third, it helps us sort nationalism into its component parts: ideologies, social movements, state building, and the vexed matter of international recognition, all of which may have their own causes and dynamics. Frequently, scholars studying one of these phenomena end up claiming that they are studying nationalism as a whole, rather than one slender thread in a vast and knotted skein. Proceeding in this way can also help us sort out whether the social phenomena to which we give a "national" label are any different from similar phenomena that we choose to label differently. For example, might nationalist mobilization be appreciably different from mobilization around other poles such as class or political ideology, and if so, does such a difference matter for how we explain it?

In the end, studying failures can be a depressing business. Loser nationalisms involve stories that have, at best, melancholic endings, sometimes even grotesque and tragic ones. But they are part of the story of nationalism in the modern age. Our understanding of why people cheer, jeer, cry, or die at the sight of a colored banner waving in the breeze will be enriched when we begin to take the also-rans more seriously.

4

The Micropolitics of Social Violence

The Peloponnesian War was a contest between rival alliances, but it also involved what a political scientist might now call an internationalized substate conflict. In 427 BCE, a dispute erupted on Corcyra (Corfu), an island in the Ionian Sea. A small group of citizens conspired to sever the existing alliance between the Corcyraean city-state and Athens and restore the island's traditional link with Corinth. Soon, this pro-Corinth camp, the "oligarchs," ousted the pro-Athens "democrats." The coup was accompanied by shocking violence. Each side came to see the other as quintessentially different, even subhuman. When given a chance, they sought to wipe out anyone, women and children included, who might be identified as the enemy.

But the Corcyra affair, Thucydides says, had little to do with differences over foreign policy or with long-standing social cleavages. There was, instead, a certain utility to violence:

> Men were often killed on grounds of personal hatred or else by
> their debtors because of the money that they owed. . . . Leaders of
> parties . . . had programs which appeared admirable—on one side
> political equality for the masses, on the other the safe and sound
> government of the aristocracy—but in professing to serve the public
> interest they were seeking to win the prizes for themselves.[1]

"War," he concluded, "is a stern teacher." In times of social upheaval, the ability to wrap one's own ambitions in the mantle of justified violence may be the only thing that separates perpetrators from victims. The good pupils become the former; the poor ones become the latter.

Sorting through the confusing array of motives, interests, and post hoc rationalizations that accompany social violence has become a major subject for both scholars and policy practitioners. It was one of the central academic and foreign policy problems of the post–cold war period. Its attendant themes—ethnic conflict, peacekeeping, nation building—remain important today, although often under a different set of monikers: terrorism, counterinsurgency, postconflict reconstruction. Perhaps more than in any other field of research, comparative politics and international relations have found common ground in trying to understand why people kill each other in large groups outside the context of a declared interstate war.

The debates of the 1990s over the causes of and responses to substate violence were significant and wide-ranging.[2] There were empirical ones about whether civil wars were increasing in number and whether conflicts grounded in "identity" were more common than in the past. There were theoretical ones about the role of state structures, elite machinations, and rational calculations in group violence.[3] Others had a policy dimension, such as the efficacy of population transfers and partition, and when and how the United States or international organizations should intervene to halt civil wars and genocide.[4] New generations of graduate students were trained to think across the domestic-international divide. New journals and funded research programs flourished.

But in profound ways, these debates were also culs-de-sac—in a literal, not a pejorative, sense: They offered a route into a new research area but little place to go once one got there. There were too few connections to long traditions of theorizing about group mobilization and collective violence. Rather than linking up with these established literatures, much of the new research either began from scratch or focused mainly on how theories of international relations might be retooled to explain what appeared to be a new wave of ethnic conflict.[5] As a result, some of the discussions—over the role of external guarantors of peace agreements and the commitment problems of belligerents, for example—pushed the study of social violence into the same paradigm-level debates that have characterized the American study of international relations.

This chapter charts the changing nature of scholarship on social violence and civil war today. A new generation of research on large-scale social violence began to emerge in the late 1990s, both in mainstream political science and in the security studies subfield.[6] Much of this new research began to turn theoretical work on social violence back toward its roots in problems of social order, state-society relations, and mobilization. It resists the monocausal temptations of research drawn from a single theoretical paradigm, while nevertheless developing clear and sometimes elegant models of collective violence. Most important, it seeks to break down the intellectual wall that grew up in the 1990s between the study of something called "ethnic conflict" or "nationalist violence" and a long line of work on collective action in political sociology and cognate fields. In the end, the social sciences, and political science in particular, have now moved squarely into an era that reconsiders older approaches to some of the most brutal and tragic manifestations of political power.

The first section that follows examines how scholars have normally divided up the existing literature on social violence, particularly on ethnic conflict. This division tends to mischaracterize scholarly traditions in the field and can have undesirable consequences for how research programs are structured. The second section considers the original contributions of several new works in the field, particularly with respect to the reflexive nature of both violent and nonviolent mobilization and the role of formal civic associations as inhibitors of violence. The third section draws out the common theoretical and methodological positions in this work and in related scholarship. This expanding body of literature represents what might be called a micropolitical turn in the study of social violence: a concern with uncovering the precise mechanisms via which individuals and groups go about trading in the benefits of stability for the inherently risky behavior associated with violence—and how, as Thucydides knew, they often do it at the expense of people whom they previously called friends and neighbors. The fourth section assesses what such a turn might mean for research methods and theory making in comparative politics and international relations as a whole.

The Genealogy of "Ethnic Conflict" Research

In the now considerable literature on ethnic conflict, writers usually identify at least four theoretical positions, which might be labeled essentialism, instrumentalism, institutionalism, and constructivism.[7] Essentialism claims that social identities—religious, linguistic, ethnic—are key to explaining the onset and duration of violent conflict. These identities are durable, if not perennial, and disputes that involve identity might be expected to be more contentious than those over political power, natural resources, or ideology. Instrumentalism holds that identities themselves are less important than the particular political ends they serve. Since identities can be manipulated by political elites, research should concentrate on how they are wielded, not on their content. Institutionalism focuses attention on the formal and informal constraints that channel social identities and either facilitate or inhibit group confrontation.

Constructivism examines the process by which identities are formed. Any social identity is made, not begotten, and the perpetration of a violent act can itself be an intrinsic part of the process of transforming a latent identity into one that is politically salient.

The critiques are as well rehearsed as the ideal-typical approaches themselves. Essentialism posits the timeless existence of what are plainly protean identities and simply assumes, rather than explains, the link between who one is and what one does. Instrumentalism attributes too much power to the machinations of unscrupulous elites and portrays the masses as pawns in a vast mobilizational conspiracy. Institutionalism rarely shows precisely how institutional constraints are meant to work and, in any case, has little to say about where social institutions come from in the first place. Constructivism is intuitively right that social identities can be shaped, but it rarely offers an account of why identities take the shape they do (and why this fact should even matter in explaining mobilization and violence).

This is the standard way in which the now substantial political science literature on ethnic conflict, civil wars, and related themes characterizes its own past. There is nothing inherently wrong with dividing up previous scholarship in this way, of course. Marking off any "school" usually tucks diverse thinkers into procrustean beds, and it is possible to find scholars who have argued versions of each of these positions (although poor Clifford Geertz was ritually and unfairly cited, until his death in 2006, as the only living essentialist).[8] But this quadripartite vision of the past is scholarly genealogy as fictive kinship. It impels researchers to frame their work in response to an intellectual ancestry that is either wholly phantom or ancillary to the core concerns of the study of social violence. It is problematic in three major senses.

First, it uncritically fuses the literature on nationalism with literatures on ethnicity and collective violence. Many of the signature conflicts of the 1990s—Bosnia, Kosovo, Chechnya, and others—involved protagonists who self-consciously used the "national" label in describing their goals and grievances. That usage was a reflection of the indigenous way of speaking about social identities in eastern Europe and Eurasia; "nationalities," especially in the communist period, were what in any other context would simply be called ethnic groups. But this language had an effect on scholarship. If nationalities were coming to blows, the natural place to look for explanations seemed to be the literature on nationalism. This inclination was reinforced in the vocabulary adopted by journalists, politicians, and others outside academia to describe the major post–cold war conflicts and their belligerents: Slobodan Milošević was an "ultranationalist," while the Rwandan genocide was about "ethnic groups," and the Iraqi civil war involved "sectarians" and "militants."

The problem is that the classic literature on nationalism actually talks across, not directly to, the phenomena of social mobilization and collective violence. Many of the greats—Ernest Gellner, Anthony Smith, and Benedict Anderson, for example—were concerned mainly with the emergence of the nation as an idea, the development of modern national identities out of the congeries of clan, religious, and local identities that preceded them (see chapter 2). Their work has more to do with how movements that embodied the national idea arose after the eighteenth century, and less with the complex interaction of state institutions, competing social affiliations, and individual desires that are usually at play in modern ethnocultural movements, much less the even more complex dimensions of social violence.

The misuse of the nationalism literature also explains why "identity" has been such a frequent theme in recent research on ethnic conflict. By linking up with a literature that privileges the national idea, social scientists have naturally focused on the quality of belief and self-conception as a key variable in explaining mobilization and violence. Indeed, for their many putative differences, the four major schools of thought identified here are all, at base, about the nature of identity, whether primordial, manipulatable, constrainable, or mutable. An almost obsessive concern with this variable also led to an overstatement of the differences between older, allegedly ideological conflicts of the cold war period and the supposedly "identity-based" conflicts and "new wars" that came later.[9]

Second, this quadripartite view of the field casts as mutually exclusive a set of theoretical approaches that have never been genuinely at odds. Even if we allow that major writers on nationalism and ethnicity might fit into one or another of these camps, differences between them are really about the questions they ask, not the answers they propose. Benedict Anderson, for example, has been concerned with exploring the "modular" nature of the national idea, particularly its export from Europe to other parts of the world in the nineteenth and twentieth centuries. But he might just as well be cast as an institutionalist, insofar as he has stressed the role of censuses, cartography, and other formal conventions in cementing particular conceptions of the nation. Likewise, Donald Horowitz, in his influential *Ethnic Groups in Conflict*, was interested in elucidating the political pathways for managing conflict and avoiding violence in multiethnic settings. It should be no surprise, then, that he stresses the design of political institutions, even though he might equally be labeled a constructivist when it comes to the question of where identities come from.[10]

Imagining the theoretical landscape in this way—as a set of clear antagonists battling over the same conceptual terrain—fit remarkably well with the American tradition of international relations, the subdiscipline that witnessed an upsurge in writing on nationalism and intrastate violence in the 1990s.

Ernest Gellner and Anthony Smith, for example, had carried on a long debate about whether nationalism was based on universal, durable sentiments or on the exigencies of modernization, a debate that fit, with some necessary trimming, into the mold of the neorealist versus liberal institutionalist dispute in international relations. Benedict Anderson had argued that identities could be shaped in unexpected ways and that their content could, in turn, have causal power, something that might be cast as constructivism *avant la lettre*. As with most fictive kinships, however, this is a backward projection of current desires onto an otherwise unconnected past. The danger is that representing our scholarly heritage in this way can end up promoting the same paradigm-level debates that have bedeviled American approaches to the study of international relations.[11]

Third, this vision of the field marginalizes the scholarly literatures that are, in fact, most potentially helpful: work on social mobilization and violence in general. It is now common for scholars to embrace the constructivist view that no social identities are primordial, not even ethnic ones. Yet in the literature on ethnic conflict and civil wars, one frequently finds citations to classic work on the origins of ethnonational identity, ethnic political parties, ethnic voting behavior, ethnic minorities policy, ethnicity and economic development, and related topics. The implication is that the study of something we call "nationalism" or "ethnic conflict" falls naturally within this intellectual family. However, many of the research problems that have intrigued students of ethnic conflict and civil wars over the last few decades are already well represented in other literatures.

The relationship between identities and interests; the relative power of institutions, resources, and opportunities in facilitating mobilization; the function of atrocities and extreme violence; and the role of political entrepreneurs have been vigorous subjects of debate in cognate fields, from political sociology to anthropology and history.[12] Since the 1960s, scholars in these fields have developed progressively more nuanced approaches to the study of social mobilization and collective violence. Early studies that focused on the imponderable workings of "the crowd" were supplanted by macrolevel structural explanations.[13] These, in turn, gave way to greater appreciation for microlevel studies of opportunities, resources, framing, and social networks.[14] Today, running parallel to—and thus largely unconnected with—the literature on ethnic conflict and civil war are exciting projects for bringing together macrolevel and microlevel approaches, structure and intentionality, under a single "contentious politics" rubric.[15] Yet it was rather rare to find any of this work cited in the research on collective violence that emerged in the 1990s and early 2000s. By focusing on the adjective rather than the noun, scholars of "ethnic conflict" have by and large cut themselves off from the literatures of which they should naturally be a part.

Having an appreciation for this alternative intellectual genealogy is important. It admits a whole body of scholarship that has normally been sidelined. It situates the study of ethnic conflict within a tradition that, unlike the study of nationalism, asks the same kinds of social-scientific questions that are of most interest to scholars in the field today. And it allows for the emergence of a real consensus on basic concepts and analytical tools that paradigmatic debates between essentialists and constructivists do not. To illustrate how new approaches might be brought to bear on the study on mobilization and violence, the next section considers in detail three influential books, one on popular protest in the late Soviet Union, another on communal violence in India, and finally a broadly comparative study that draws much of its original empirical material from the Greek civil war, along with other work that seeks to ground our understanding of violent contention in the microrealities of social interaction. As this research shows, linking up with these older intellectual traditions can lead in profitable directions.

The Soviet Union, India, and Greece in Comparative Perspective

It is tempting to think of collective violence as anomalous, episodic, and irrational. The predominant image is one of a crowd running amok, consumed by the elemental passions of the group, lost in a bewildering mix of hatred, fear, and exhilaration. That may well describe a particular type of violence—the kind known in some southeast Asian societies as *amok*, whence the term in English—but it is hardly the norm. Violent episodes are, if not predictable, then certainly patterned forms of social interaction, even when they involve seemingly inscrutable bonds of culture and kinship. They have a certain life cycle that begins with precipitating events such as persistent prejudices or rumors, progresses through a brief burst of bloodletting, passes through a lull, and then rapidly escalates into a series of massive deadly attacks. De-escalation happens gradually, either because of an intervention by the forces of order or simple fatigue on the part of the perpetrators of violence.[16] That cycle seems to hold in many forms of mass violence, from street riots to massacres in the context of a civil war. Similar patterning can even be seen in two unusual types of collective violence, one in which the victim is single and the perpetrators multiple (lynchings) and another in which the perpetrator is single and the victims multiple (suicide terrorism).[17]

Some organization is usually involved in collective violence, but the picture of receptive masses whipped up by an unscrupulous leader is not quite true to life. As Donald Horowitz has pointed out, violence is in reality closer to a pick-up game.[18] It requires some minimally qualified activists to get things going. Beyond that, however, there are a host of other facilitating conditions that have little to do with the organizational skill or capacity of those who might have originally had an interest in fomenting disorder. There must be social norms that either allow for the prospect of violence or, more frequently, at some level condone it. Assuming that all rational people must condemn violence overlooks the relatively common condition of "the moral mass murder," instances in which social violence is generally approved, if not overtly supported.[19] There must also be a set of accepted social rules governing how the violent game is played: who is a legitimate target; the level of violence that can be meted out, from destruction of property to murder; and what counts as a sufficient condition for escalating from one level to the next.[20] And critically, as in a pickup game, there usually need to be lots of young men with nothing better to do. As Scott Straus has shown in his study of Rwandan *génocidaires* and John Gledhill in his analysis of antiopposition crackdowns in Romania, even in the midst of seemingly anarchic disorder, clear patterns emerge that can account for the level of social violence and how it is prosecuted.[21]

These factors are difficult to sort through, especially in contexts in which previous instances of violence produce echoes in the present. Violent behavior can become routinized, even ritualized, and putative root causes can become illusory.[22] The victims had it coming because of their past treachery. They were in collusion with the enemy. We just did it to them before they did it to us. All are common modes of justification, for the actual perpetrators as well as for the wider society of which they are a part. That violence begets violence is intuitively true—this is Thucydides' point about the Corcyra affair—and it is also a seductive aperçu. But it is also an unsatisfying place to end up. What precisely does the reflexivity of violence mean, and how can one even begin to study it without simply bracketing the past?

Mark Beissinger, in his influential *Nationalist Mobilization and the Collapse of the Soviet State*, points toward some answers. Beissinger assembled the most extensive list available of mobilizational episodes in the Soviet Union from the late 1980s through the early 1990s—marches, demonstrations, protests, strikes, riots, pogroms, civil wars—based on multiple-source coding of events reported in more than 150 Western and local newspapers and other periodicals: to be precise, from January 1987 through December 1992, 6,663 protest demonstrations and 2,177 incidents of mass violence, plus a few others from the preperestroika years. No other researcher has yet had at his disposal as detailed a catalogue of the accelerating street politics of the late Gorbachev period and the rising tide of popular unrest that attended the Soviet Union's demise.

The word *tide* is not just a metaphor. It is part of Beissinger's core argument: that the shape of protest activity in the late 1980s and early 1990s cannot be understood, much less modeled, without taking account of the reflexive power of mobilization itself. The organizers of demonstrations and even average participants were acting within a particular knowledge environment. They knew of mobilizational episodes and state responses in other parts of the Soviet Union. They were often in direct contact with, and emboldened by, activists from other republics and regions. Their calculus of costs and benefits, such as it was, was demonstrably influenced by their assessment of what had succeeded and failed in other circumstances. Any single protest was thus a wave in a much larger period of "tidal politics."

The very context in which individual events took place accounts for how the impossible came to be seen, in time, as inevitable: an uprising by the people in a political system that was self-defined as a people's democracy, interethnic violence within a country founded on the "friendship of peoples," and the swift disappearance of the world's largest state. The bounds of the politically imaginable expanded because, as Beissinger says, history "thickened" in the late Gorbachev era. Mobilizational events were chronologically clustered, a feature graphically clear from the data set. These individual events were not only the key arenas of contention between mobilized groups and the state but also the crucibles in which the solidarity that bound together those mobilized groups was formed.[23]

Structural features matter, of course, and the combination of resource endowments, formal political institutions, and political opportunities did have an effect on which ethnic groups or Soviet republics were likely to experience mobilization and at what period. Yet if any particular group lacked one of these structural advantages, there was always a ready and fungible substitute: the mere knowledge that other groups had already mobilized effectively. Otherwise structurally disadvantaged groups—with small populations, no clear history of grievances, and no institutional resources—experienced a rapid broadening of the bounds of their mobilizational horizons. Being poorly endowed, in the context of tidal politics, turns out not to be an obvious obstacle.

Having an appreciation for how actors themselves understood their environment helps to get at two of the most pressing questions about the nature of the Soviet collapse. First, why were some ethnic groups "early risers"—first-at-bat and successful mobilizers against the Soviet center—and others relatively passive until the center failed to hold? Second, why did some groups engage in almost universally peaceful protest, even in the face of extreme reactions by the state, while others turned to violence?

Before the breakup of the Soviet Union, the standard way of answering the first question was to point to the power of identity. The Soviet Union was, after all, a land of "captive nations," as the ideology of the West had it, which would sooner or later yearn to breathe free. At the highest level of abstraction, that was certainly true: The Soviet Union ended, and fifteen new countries, each one named for one of the fifteen constitutive republican nationalities of the Soviet federation, emerged on its ruins. But it is worth remembering that those who made this argument before the late 1980s were relatively few, and those who did almost universally bet on the wrong horse. The greatest threat to the Soviet system was thought to be the Muslims of Central Asia, the various ethnic populations that, in fact, turned out to have the lowest levels of mobilization.

The common response today, nearly two decades on, is to focus on structure, particularly the formal institutional resources upon which mobilized ethnic groups could draw—a republic-level parliament, party apparatus, and newspapers, among other things.[24] Structural conditions certainly mattered. All things being equal, having your own republic and being numerically larger, more urbanized, and less linguistically assimilated to Russian were good things for would-be mobilizers. Yet while these facilitating conditions might explain the onset of mobilization, they do not explain the fact of mobilization. For less well-endowed groups, there were certain benefits to backwardness. They could learn from the experience of the early risers, avoid costly mistakes, and engage in complex mobilizational activity in a short period. Over time, the "causal role of event-specific processes" grew, relative to the power of structural conditions.[25] Violence, too, was part of the mobilizational mix. On Beissinger's calculation, the involvement of an ethnic group in an episode of collective violence produced a 3.1 percent increase in the incidence of public demonstrations by that ethnic group in the following week.[26] Those groups that failed to mobilize at all—very small minorities within the Russian Federation and, by and large, Central Asians—were saddled with inauspicious structural conditions or had local leaders who actively blocked the tidal influences coming from other parts of the Soviet Union.

The second question, about the use or avoidance of violence, is even trickier. Overall, the collapse of the world's largest state was unexpectedly peaceful, with probably under 2,000 people killed and perhaps another 13,000 injured in interethnic violence. (The post-Soviet wars in Chechnya and elsewhere are another matter, where perhaps 200,000 people have died—but still an order of magnitude lower than in places such as Sudan and Afghanistan.) During the period of collapse, from 1987 to 1992, violence came in waves, in several senses. It started in particular regions and then moved to others. It involved large numbers of people in some periods and far fewer in others. It began with the use of less sophisticated weapons, literally sticks and stones, and then after 1991 rapidly escalated to the use of heavy artillery. Once again, however, structural factors—a previous historical experience of mass violence, demographics, institutional resources, being "Islamic"—seem to be weak predictors of the variability of violence, across both space and time. For example, groups that had the highest levels of previous violent conflict with the Soviet state within living memory, Baltic groups and ethnic Germans, engaged in virtually no violent activity. Even the Chechens, routinely tagged as perpetually resistant to Russian rule, only became involved in mass violence three years after the Soviet Union ended—and only then in response to a full-scale invasion by the Russian army.

Instead, violence seems to have emerged from three rather different sources. It could erupt as a reaction to an initial use of force by the state. It could be a strategy pursued by ethnic leaders on the back end of the mobilizational cycle, as a way of raising the stakes at a time when peaceful protests were winding down. Or it could arise, after the end of the Soviet Union, as part of the contentious politics associated with defining borders and new political institutions within the successor states. The tragic irony is that a mobilizational cycle that was relatively peaceful led on to devastating wars in some of the new political systems that it ultimately produced (see chapter 6).

In Beissinger's research, when and how any particular event occurred, in relation to others within the same mobilizational cycle, turns out to be more important than the macrolevel structural conditions that might have facilitated it. That finding is consonant with recent work on India, especially Ashutosh Varshney's important *Ethnic Conflict and Civic Life*.[27] As in the Soviet cases, social mobilization and collective violence involving India's two largest communal groups—Hindus and Muslims—has not been equally distributed geographically or temporally. Since 1947, some Indian states have experienced recurrent episodes of communal rioting with high casualties; others have remained relatively calm. Even within high-violence states, such as Uttar Pradesh and Bihar, there is a marked diversity from one city to another. In cities where the relative size of the communal populations and other structural variables are similar, some are violence-prone—that is, there has been a consistently high incidence of intercommunal rioting—while others have seemed generally immune. (A third category consists of locales where violence is rare but intense, such as Gujarat.) Varshney was able to identify this basic puzzle by creating his own original data set derived from a systematic coding of riots reported in the *Times of India* from 1950 to 1995. Just assembling the data set, as in Beissinger's work, is a hugely important task. The landscape is uncertain without it, and depending on the level of analysis—the country, the state, the city, perhaps even the neighborhood—what counts as an interesting and researchable question looks radically different.

The city seems to be the lowest level that the available data can reach, and it is also a level with a sufficient degree of complexity to ensure that some large-scale social processes are at work, something beyond, for example, violence prompted by a family feud or a stolen car in an individual village or neighborhood. But how can one explain the city-level variation in the incidence of intercommunal rioting? The answer, in brief, is that low-violence cities have strong associational ties between Hindu and Muslim communities.

It is one thing to interact on a daily basis with members of another communal group, to buy your newspaper from a Muslim, your flowers from a Hindu, and your food from a Sikh. This, in fact, is what most people mean when they talk about long histories of intercommunal concord or refer nostalgically to periods of cross-cultural exchange in diverse societies, even in those that are eventually torn apart by war. But these informal contacts are not good enough; they are ephemeral, nonbinding, and not necessarily intergenerational. Associations, on the other hand, are durable, and they have certain ancillary qualities that turn out to be crucial when exogenous shocks threaten the peace. They provide channels of communication between elite groups in the ethnic communities. They raise the stakes for those who would upset the peace. They bring together—and, indeed, even create—interest groups that do not readily emerge from everyday interactions. Associations are how the strategic decisions of elites become concretized, and they can have a major effect on the durability of communal peace.

But arguing that differences in associational life map differences in communal violence is a correlation without an explanation. As it turns out, levels of associational engagement mirror longer term patterns of communal interaction, but those patterns were not bequeathed to particular cities merely by social structure (Hindu-Muslim demographics, levels of wealth, etc.) or by an imponderable "history." Rather, they, too, were the products of political action, in this case during the period of the all-India national movement from the 1920s to the 1940s.

Elites in different cities chose different responses to the politics of mass mobilization during these decades, creating what Varshney calls a "master narrative" about the nature of intercommunal relations. In some, the master narrative became one of caste, with Hindu and Muslim elites cooperating against low-caste Hindus. In others, it became one of communal identity, with Hindu leaders reaching across caste lines to mobilize against an indigenous Muslim dominant class. In the former, the choices of elites encouraged cooperation across the Hindu-Muslim divide, a form of cooperation cemented in the creation of bicommunal associations, from trade unions to business alliances. In the latter, intercommunal differences were infused with political significance, and the salience of ethnic lines as political dividers discouraged the establishment of lasting associations. Since independence, the first road has led to relative peace, the second to deadly ethnic riots.

There is a certain practical optimism here, and its lessons are important. To reduce the chances of violence, encourage intercommunal contacts, but make sure that those contacts find expression in associations. In times of social crisis, remembering the kind member of an ethnic minority who used to repair your shoes becomes a thin foundation for intercommunal peace. School textbooks that show Germans as hardworking, Jews as frugal, and Russians as jolly—a project, incidentally, sponsored by the United Nations Development Program in a multiethnic district of Ukraine—will not do the trick. Rather, elites at all levels must be bound together in repeated, patterned, and formal interactions.

Ultimately, however, this argument is perhaps less optimistic than one might think. It is not about how to secure social peace but rather about the trade-offs involved in pursuing a particular brand of it. A concomitant of strong associational linkages across Hindu and Muslim communities has sometimes been conflict along other axes. The cities of Calicut and Lucknow, for example, emerge as models of Hindu-Muslim concord in Varshney's work. But both have experienced recurrent conflict, sometimes brutally violent, along lines of caste (low-status versus high-status Hindus) and sect (Shi'a versus Sunni Muslims).

That fact does not diminish the power of the associational argument in explaining the Hindu-Muslim relationship, but it does make one wonder whether the price of concord along one social cleavage might be violence along another. The master narratives in Calicut and Lucknow are different from those in areas where Hindu-Muslim rioting has been the norm; however, both have narratives built around other, equally divisive visions of social life. It seems a stretch to describe a dense set of associational ties between Hindus and Muslims as "civic life" when those ties do not also seem to have had knock-on effects on the city as a whole. But this may well be the crucial, sobering point: In any social setting with multiple poles of allegiance, multiple sets of grievances, and multiple exogenous shocks, peace is always a relative condition.

Mobilizational waves and intercommunal ties can lead in different directions, sometimes toward peaceful protest and rapid political change, sometimes toward violent confrontation and mass killing. Once societies have tipped into the realm of large-scale and repeated violent episodes—that is, into civil war—what dynamics govern group behavior? The most ambitious account of social violence in decades, Stathis Kalyvas's The Logic of Violence in Civil War, focuses on four puzzles at the heart of substate killing.[28] Within the context of a single civil war, what explains variation in the incidence and intensity of violence across time and space? What accounts for the seeming universality of brutality in substate conflicts, even when compared with the mechanized warfare of interstate disputes? Does a factor exogenous to warfare itself—ideology—ever drive actors and determine outcomes in substate conflicts? And why do causes and patterns of violence at micro and macro levels seem so disparate; in other words, why is it that narratives of motivation and culpability take different forms at the level of the conflict as a whole versus at the level of specific acts of violence that take place in individual towns, villages, or neighborhoods?

Each of these puzzles is one strand in a broad tapestry, and Kalyvas aims at nothing less than a systematic account of the functions of violence in the context of substate war. On Kalyvas's reading, violence is in most cases instrumental. It is a particular type of group conflict that serves identifiable ends, especially the extraction of allegiance and cooperation from noncombatants. Armies, guerrillas, and other combatant groups engage in violent behavior not only as a way of diminishing a rival's will or ability to fight but also to secure material or other resources from noncombatants. Combatants desire control over distinct populations, and they use both selective and, more rarely, indiscriminate violence to attain it.

From this basic insight, several conclusions follow. Levels of violence vary with the difficulty of controlling the geographical and human terrain of a given area. The incidence of collaboration varies with the ability of combatants to exercise authority over distinct regions, which in turn depends on the ability of combatants to provide public goods, solve collective action problems, and secure direct and indirect monitoring of noncombatants. Violence appears as a strategic response to problems of control and monitoring, with variation that can be mapped geographically. Targeted violence—against enemies, collaborators, and traitors, for example—entails not only the power to perpetrate a discrete act of violence but also the ability to gather sufficient information to be sure that the targeted person or group is likely to be guilty of the alleged transgression. Where an actor's level of control and information gathering is high, violence is unlikely to occur; if the noncombatant population can be served, monitored, and punished with some degree of ease, the disincentives for defection are high, and combatants can manipulate those disincentives to encourage loyalty. At the other end of the spectrum, where an actor's level of control and information gathering is low, indiscriminate violence is likely to be high; no party can provide the public goods that would buy off local noncombatants or gather sufficient information to use targeted violence effectively. Between these two extremes, violence exists as patterned episodes of both selective and indiscriminate attacks consonant with varying levels of coercive control over population and territory.

In each of these scenarios, preexisting ideological commitments—toward a particular party or ethnic group, for example—seem to matter little. Rather, on Kalyvas's account, violence is only one form of combatant activity in the context of civil war and one that emerges in response to the interests and aspirations of both armies and noncombatants alike. Indeed, in any conflict, actors engage in a whole variety of behaviors: building roads as well as blocking them, dispensing medical assistance while also poisoning wells, harvesting crops in addition to burning them, educating children as well as dragooning them into service as child-soldiers. The chief insight of Kalyvas's work is to see violence as only one of the actions that people caught up in large-scale conflict choose to pursue. And like paving a road or tearing down a school, large-scale killing is undertaken for reasons that are discernible, patterned, and at some level rational.

Kalyvas's contribution is not only substantive but also methodological. Beissinger and Varshney employ a combination of methods, but much of their important findings follow from event analysis: the compilation of data on a huge array of individual violent and nonviolent acts, mainly gleaned from systematic coding of indigenous newspaper reporting. Kalyvas takes things several steps further. His empirical work rests on a detailed quantitative study of violent incidents, as well as on ethnographic and archival work, in the Argolid region of the northern Peloponnesus, an area that was overwhelmingly monarchist before 1943 yet became, by turns, variably procommunist as the Greek civil war developed. In the end, inhabitants of the Argolid experienced a master narrative of violence that pitted monarchists against communists, yet they also engaged in their own "mosaic of discrete mini-wars."[29] The intensity, direction, and nature of violence varied across the region from village to village and from season to season, a finding that Kalyvas is able to demonstrate both quantitatively and via rich ethnographic data on the experience of individual villages. As the state and guerrilla groups swept into the region, they self-consciously created new incentives for active collaboration, noncommittal acquiescence, denunciation, and neighbor-on-neighbor barbarity among erstwhile noncombatant populations.

A Micropolitical Turn

In a widely cited survey of the state of the field in comparative politics, David Laitin identified a "new consensus" among comparativists.[30] Laitin noted that the most influential new work seeks to unify three methods: survey techniques and large-n data analysis, in order to identify broad patterns and develop hypotheses; microlevel anthropological and historical digging, in order to uncover evidence; and explicit, sometimes formal, theorizing, in order to link hypotheses and evidence by specifying causal mechanisms.

Something similar seems to be going on in the study of social violence. There are clear trends toward a reconsideration of the scholarly traditions on which work on social violence should draw and toward an eclectic, micropolitical approach to what constitutes cutting-edge methods. There are at least three characteristics of this emerging research program: a stress on engaging violence at analytical levels far below the nation-state, an attentiveness to how discrete episodes of violence are defined, and a skepticism about the utility of labels applied to conflicts from the outside. Each of these has important implications for methods and theory building in comparative politics and international relations in general.

Disaggregating the Case

Episodes of social violence, whether riots or atrocities committed during civil wars, may well be patterned, but they do not occur uniformly across time or space. There are lulls and peaks. Violence comes to different cities, towns, and neighborhoods at different times. It plays itself out in contrasting ways in various social contexts, even within a series of violent events that are lumped together as a single ethnic conflict or civil war. Disaggregation thus has two important advantages. It expands the number of cases, and hence the number of observations, available for large-n work, and it provides added nuance to our understanding of the diversity of violent outcomes within the dominant unit of analysis, the nation-state. Work by Elisabeth Wood on El Salvador; Steven Wilkinson on India; Jeremy Weinstein on Uganda, Mozambique, and Peru; and Abdulkader Sinno on Afghanistan—all of whom develop and test novel theories of violent behavior—moves things in these directions.[31]

Disaggregation can work in another way. Much of the literature has treated violence as merely the highest stage of mobilization. Get enough people mobilized enough—or, to use a technical expression, get them mad as hell—and you are likely to end up with someone, usually lots of people, getting killed. However, there is no reason to assume that mobilization and violence are naturally linked.[32] True, the former can sometimes lead to the latter. A strike can turn into a riot; a march can become a pogrom. Some of the same mechanisms are also no doubt at work in violent and nonviolent mobilization; killing en masse, as much as going on strike, is still a collective action problem.

Yet there are certain features of social violence that have no clear analogues in the process of mobilization. How victims are selected, why atrocities occur, and how personal revenge intersects with group goals are all themes that are critical to understanding both the variability in and the life cycles of violent episodes. All could easily become respectable research questions in their own right, even though they have too frequently been overshadowed by the macrolevel—and perhaps ultimately unanswerable—question of why violence occurs at all.

Doing research on these microlevel issues demands an extreme sensitivity to small-scale social interactions, phenomena that can be studied only through detailed ethnographic work. Consider the question of choosing victims. Groups and individuals are specifically targeted, often with surprising care, even in the midst of what seems an otherwise chaotic event.[33] But knowing precisely whom to kill, maim, or run out of town can be problematic, and perpetrators often have an array of techniques for sorting out friend from foe. Skin color may matter, but then humans have an infinite capacity for parsing gradations of skin tone; it is rarely a case literally of black and white. Linguistic ability can also be a criterion, but in environments of multiethnic interaction and multilingual repertoires, how one speaks is a slippery desideratum. Frequently, targeting seems to be based on subtler characteristics of the victim—occupation, clothing, perceived social status, the football team he supports—all of which can convey important information about religion, social status, ethnicity, or other traits. Even eyewear can matter: In Romania in 1990, rioting miners, encouraged by the government, were known to attack people wearing glasses, a sure sign that the target was an "intellectual" and therefore a supporter of the embattled prodemocracy movement there. None of this will be readily apparent, however, without carving off specifically violent acts from the broader process of group mobilization.

Interrogating the Violent Event

Violent events are often clustered spatially and temporally. Existing research practice has been to treat the cluster itself—something called "the Bosnian war" or "the Rwandan genocide"—as the only serviceable dependent variable. Cases have become coterminous with conflicts. But even at the lowest level of aggregation—the individual violent event—bounding the case can still be frustratingly difficult. Previous instances of violence may be invoked as rallying points. What outside observers see as discrete episodes may be, in the minds of participants, multiple iterations of the same dispute. Violent events, in other words, are not natural kinds. They are themselves constructed as part of the process of social violence; they are wrapped up in the constitutive power of violent collective action.

The rhetorical battle for control over defining the event can thus be as much a part of the contestation as violence itself. Anyone who has spent time in violent settings, from societies plagued by sectarian discord to an English football match, can understand how successive iterations of violence are difficult to distinguish from one another, both analytically and causally. Slicing into the complex narrative of first causes and iterated grievances can provide a cross-sectional image of a conflict at one point in time, but it can also be misleading. Any single episode of violence may be part of an intricate web of meanings connected with previous events and acting as precipitants for those to come. On the other hand, participants themselves may devise very clear ways of marking off one episode from another. That is why in societies where interfamilial feuding is common, there are also usually social rules for deciding how to terminate a violent dispute—whose blood and how much of it must be spilled for a wrong to be righted, for example.[34] The alternative would be an endless spiral of revenge, precisely the condition that complex feuding norms are meant to forestall. The point is that where any instance of collective violence begins and ends, whether it is a single riot or an entire civil war, can be determined only from within the cognitive landscape of those who are engaged in it. Marking off events as discrete by fiat of the researcher will not do the trick.

What constitutes an analytically singular event is thus both a conceptual and an empirical question, part of what Donald Horowitz and Stathis Kalyvas have both called, in slightly different senses, the "ontology" of violence.[35] But how exactly does one go about ordering the varied and often contradictory versions of who did what to whom?

One technique is simply to rely on press reports in local languages and to make sure that those reports come from many different, mainly indigenous sources. That, at least, takes one as close as possible to the action without requiring a multisource account of every killing, but it still requires building a clear protocol for coding each violent event (based on location, number of participants and their goals, and the source of the reportage itself). A second is to write an ethnography of event making, to examine systematically the various meanings attached to violent episodes and to explore the ways in which one is marked off from another. That approach is less amenable to quantitative analysis and may produce only a *Rashomon*-like series of multiple stories. But focusing on the construction of meaning can provide a valuable corrective to the idea of the violent event as a naturally occurring species.[36] A third technique is represented by what Horowitz has called a "near-miss strategy": doing enough microlevel work to know when an episode of large-scale, mass violence was truly imminent but instead turned into something smaller, a lynching, for example.[37] This is an approach much preached but rarely practiced. It is not quite enough to work at extremely high levels of aggregation, to ask why Yugoslavia's end was violent but Czechoslovakia's was not. Rather, following through on this strategy involves narrowing the research focus, both spatially and temporally, and giving greater attention to cases that really seemed, but for a few key variables, to be headed in the same awful direction. Paired comparisons of towns, villages, neighborhoods, or streets—as sociologists and anthropologists have long known and some political scientists are now rediscovering—provide much finer-grained accounts of violence than research built around larger units of analysis.

These techniques certainly dampen scholarly ambitions, but that might not be a bad thing. They cause researchers to take very seriously the bounding of both cases and events. They remind us to be honest about what we are really studying: not violence tout court, but one small, bracketed space on a scale of behaviors running from murder to total war. Knowing with some certainty why a massacre did not escalate to genocide is not nearly as attractive as saying why one country is war-torn and another peaceful. But it is probably closer to science.

Problematizing Labels

When "ethnic conflict" joined the mainstream of comparative politics and international relations research in the early 1990s, there was a tendency to look uncritically at the labels applied to violent episodes. Actors were categorized according to ascribed identities, usually ethnic but sometimes religious or linguistic. Typologies separated conflicts into analytical boxes accordingly. The easy categories of "Serb" or "Bosnian" masked a host of differences within these allegedly separate groups in the 1990s, even though journalists and policy makers alike tended to use those categories without question to describe the belligerent sides in the Yugoslav wars. The labels Sunni and Shi'a took on a similarly iconic status in Iraq the early 2000s.

There are two obvious problems with using labels without being concerned for whether they really map social groups in the world. One is what might be called the implicit teleology of ascriptive difference. It is often too easy for labels to masquerade as causes. To declare a conflict "ethnic," say, usually rests on a set of assumptions about the roots of the conflict and the unusual levels of violence said to characterize it. But emphasizing social identities can blind researchers to the mechanisms that are at work in shaping them, often in the middle of violence itself.[38] Violence raises the stakes of defection by presenting both perpetrators and victims as threatened; it makes it more difficult to move across interidentity boundaries. As one example, in the "lynching era" in the U.S. South—from the early 1880s to the early 1930s—a fifth of all lynchings were intraracial, whites killing whites and blacks killing blacks. The highest incidence of these within-group attacks occurred before the period when new racial laws had reestablished the clear social boundaries between racial groups that had been eroded by the Civil War and Reconstruction. Lynching was thus not only an abhorrent form of intergroup violence but also a method of in-group polic-ing.[39] Violence does not always make identity, of course, but it can certainly push a particular identity to the top of one's repertoire.

Another problem is that the way participants themselves label a conflict is often an essential part of the contentious event, not analytically (or even chron-ologically) prior to it. Acquiring the power to define a hegemonic discourse about a conflict is a goal self-consciously pursued by belligerents. The aim is, in part, to convince outsiders of the rightness of one's own cause and the perfidy of others, to demonstrate that the opposite side is composed only of ethnic mili-tants, fanatical hardliners, terrorists, separatists, and so on. But it is also to control the entire vocabulary that observers and participants use when they speak about the origins of the dispute, the identities of the belligerents, and what might count as a legitimate form of conflict termination. Labeling, in other words, is a political act.

Social identities morph. People switch sides. Labels change. None of this, however, is to argue for a postmodern rejection of analytical categories alto-gether. On the contrary, labels should be taken even more seriously than they normally are. What they mean, how they are used, and why some stick and oth-ers do not should be part of the raft of research questions that one asks, both of people in the middle of conflict and of the scholars who study them. In the 1990s, claims about "nationality" or "ethnicity" became a central component of the way many belligerents talked about the wars they were waging. But figuring out why and how that discourse emerged is a project very different from inves-tigating why there is more "ethnic conflict" in the world than in the past. The former problematizes the label. The latter simply embraces it.

The causative power of naming is evident even today. It would not be sur-prising to find that, a few years hence, political science data sets show a marked increase in the incidence of something called "terrorism" beginning in 2001 and rising steadily through the early 2000s. There will no doubt be significant discussion about how to explain such an upsurge: whether it came about as a reaction to unipolarity or globalization, an outgrowth of state weakness and authoritarianism, or a reflection of postmodern angst and fundamentalist nihilism. Yet just as one might now be skeptical about whether a natural cate-gory called "ethnic conflict" began to grow after the end of the cold war, one might be equally skeptical about whether a natural category called "terrorism" has now taken its place. Coding is never divorced from the particular context in which it occurs, whether the coder is in the middle of a civil war or the middle of a political science department. An appreciation for this context ought to be a more explicit part of research design.

Conclusion

The new micropolitics of social violence is explicitly theory-focused. But what is perhaps most appealing in the emerging literature is an implicit argument about what constitutes theory in the social sciences. Contemporary political science privileges a particular notion of what theory is: a set of careful propositions meant to link cause and consequence. There is debate, of course, about the epistemological status of such propositions, but those debates take place within a paradigm in which theory is conceived as a mainly positivistic statement concerned with explanation. This view is remarkably out of step with most of the other social sciences, all of which have vigorous theoretical discussions that deal with issues beyond the narrow goal of explanation. One need only have a conversation with an anthropologist or a historian to understand that the realm of theory is both broader and richer than the discipline of political science has come to understand it, involving such varied enterprises as clarifying concepts, honing analytical categories, and reflecting critically on one's own research practice.

The intriguing subtext in much of the new microfoundational work on social violence is a call for theory building as sense making: a multifaceted understanding of what constitutes theoretical work, grounded in the goal of integrating the self-conscious perspectives of participants themselves. Varshney, for example, is careful to elucidate the multiple interpretations of violent acts and to caution against broad generalizations disconnected from the particular vision of rationality in which these acts are embedded.[40] Beissinger likewise focuses on the social environment in which mobilization takes place, an environment infused with the knowledge about what other people in structurally similar situations have done or are likely to do. Most explicitly, Kalyvas has demonstrated that multiple methods—from large-n data collection to participant interviews and careful archival work—can yield a far more complex picture not only of the interests and intentions of violent actors but also of the durable social meanings with which their acts are invested. The goal of this type of work is not to reduce social behavior to simple calculations of interest (although a kind of soft rationalism is implicit) but rather to understand why a set of otherwise puzzling behaviors might, from the vantage point of those who perform them, make sense.

In practical terms, theorizing these microlevel processes entails two things, one conceptual and one empirical. First, it involves thinking hard about how to operationalize fluidity. If identities really are constructed, as most scholars seem to believe, how and why are they constructed as they are? And more important, why does that fact even matter for how one studies mobilization and violence? Demonstrating that labels, identities, and social categories change over the course of a conflict or even within the context of a single violent event is an important first step. Far too little work has been done to uncover this phenomenon in particular cases. The next task, however, is to link those changes with social behavior by treating the fact of fluidity as both dependent and independent variable: to investigate whether there are patterns of identity change within violent contexts and what accounts for them, and to examine what this says about who wins and loses in instances of large-scale killing.

Second, it implies embracing the full panoply of available empirical sources as the acceptable purview of political science and to use those sources in ways consonant with the best practices of other disciplines. If we use archives, we must use them properly: reading systematically, using accepted archival notation, and being suitably critical about the textual evidence they contain. If we use interviews, we must conduct them with appreciation for the kaleidoscopic nature of memory and sensitivity to the potential costs to our interviewees, not only in terms of their time also but the potential threats they may face to their livelihood and personal security. If we use press reports, we have to handle them with the care, skepticism, and cross-checking of the best historians. Being even more explicit about the empirical substance of our work, not just the elegance of its manipulation, is crucial.

In short, we need to consider carefully what constitutes *evidence* in research on social violence, not just the reified category of *data*, which political science has come to use for the stuff of what it studies. Data carry with them the seductive promise of their own objectivity. Evidence, as any trial lawyer knows, does not. New thinking about qualitative methodologies has rightly called for broadening and deepening discussions about what constitutes well-structured research and effective argumentation.[41] But transforming and enriching research practice, not just research design, should also be a goal. How to conduct an interview, how to use an archive, how to write systematic field notes, and how to "read" complicated social relationships must become as much a part of good method (and methodological education) as statistics, formal modeling, and process tracing. In an area as fraught with human suffering as the study of collective violence, being careful about how we engage both perpetrators and victims should be a priority. The stakes, after all, are rather high.

PART II

Eastern Europe and Eurasia

5

Post-Postcommunism

Is There Still an "Eastern Europe"?

There are two ways to speculate about the future of Russia. One is to know a great deal about the behavior of overpowerful executives and divided legislatures in environments where credible commitment is low, huge incentives for free-riding exist, institutional anarchy encourages self-help political and economic behavior, rent-seeking and patronage networks among central and peripheral entrepreneurs discourage broad cooperation, and social cleavages along ascriptive lines such as ethnicity and religion overshadow both ideology and class as a basis for political mobilization. The other is to know a lot about Russia.

The gap between these two ways of thinking about eastern Europe and the former Soviet Union was long considered a gulf between students of the region and their colleagues in other areas of political science. East European specialists worried about their estrangement from mainstream comparative research. Comparativists denounced the area studies tradition for a host of sins, including its supposed failure to predict the end of Soviet-style socialism.[1] In the 1990s, debates raged in area studies journals and the newsletters of professional associations, as regional scholars attempted to fend off assaults by colleagues calling for the elaboration of generalizable hypotheses rather than accounts that stressed cultural uniqueness or historical contingency.[2] The monumental changes in the field were evident in the renaming of scholarly journals, a phenomenon that paralleled the rechristening of streets and squares across the former communist lands: *Soviet Studies* became *Europe-Asia Studies*; *Soviet Economy* became *Post-Soviet Affairs*; *Problems of Communism* ceased to exist, before being resurrected as simply *Problems of Post-Communism*.

The major question that long preoccupied students of the communist world was how to integrate theories from mainstream political science into the study of eastern Europe. In other words, how might the theoretical or conceptual insights of comparative politics enrich the study of communism? The question was not easy to answer, since communist political systems seemed so utterly different from the west European liberal democracies that formed the basis for much of the existing comparative model building. A question that was less frequently asked, though, was how the study of eastern Europe could contribute to comparative politics in general. Although regional specialists did strive to fit their work into research programs generated by the field, it was rarer to find empirically grounded work on eastern Europe that influenced how those research programs were shaped. In fact, it is difficult to think of a single book on communism that made a major impact on the discipline of political science outside its regional subfield.

Nearly two decades after the end of the Soviet Union, the second question can now be answered. The once acrimonious debates between "area studies" and "the discipline" have largely subsided. Area studies has become more rigorous, while comparative politics has turned toward reevaluating the role of contingency, midrange theorizing, and case-based narratives. Comparativists have come to value the same scholarly attributes that area studies specialists have long prized, including sensitivity to problems of concept-stretching and cross-regional model building. Postcommunist Europe and Eurasia are fertile ground for testing theories of democratization, institutional design, interest group interaction, and identity politics that have been developed in other geographical contexts. The reinvigorated study of the region has also produced new work that promises to enrich the general study of the political economy of reform, federalism, transitional justice, and nationalism and interethnic relations. The one-lane dirt road that used to wend between area studies specialists and comparativists has, at last, become a multilane highway.[3]

This chapter focuses on one of the most significant areas of research to emerge for comparativists over the past twenty years: accounting for variable outcomes in the systemic transitions across the region. Compared with the relative homogeneity of outcomes in earlier transitions in southern Europe and Latin America—extrication from previous regimes, followed by long periods of democratic consolidation—the record in the east looks profoundly more varied: a handful of successful transitions and easy consolidations, several incomplete transitions, a few transitions followed by reversion to authoritarian politics, even some transitions that never really began at all. Why the extreme differences? And what light might the answer shed on systemic change in general?

The first section here presents an overview of the study of communism and its development before the early 1990s. Understanding the evolution of the subfield is important to appreciating the relationship between the east European cases and comparative analysis today. The second section reviews the shape of transition politics across the region after 1989 and underscores the variable pathways that countries chose in enacting (or avoiding) reform. The third section illustrates the ways in which intimate knowledge of particular cases has been coupled with serious theorizing about political problems of broad interest. The fourth section hazards a few suggestions about where "post-postcommunist studies"—if there can be such a thing—might go in the early part of this century, as the countries of eastern Europe and the former Soviet Union move toward developing new forms of politics that are touched by, but not wholly products of, their communist pasts.

From Totalitarianism to Comparative Politics

In its earliest incarnation, "communist studies" was not so much scholarly research as studious propagandizing. Sidney and Beatrice Webb's paean, *Soviet Communism: A New Civilisation?* (1935), is the best known of these early works, but the Webbs' enthusiastic endorsement of the Soviet experiment was echoed in many other memoirs and travel books from the 1920s and 1930s.[4] These early on-the-spot narratives were produced by and large by Europeans, but the Second World War made the Soviet system—and its new avatars in Poland, Romania, Yugoslavia, and elsewhere—a matter of strategic concern to the United States. The new centers of teaching and research that sprang up within American academia contributed two new features to the study of communist Europe: a focus on formal language training for nonnative speakers and the introduction of social-scientific methods into the study of the region. Whereas previously the leftist traveler or émigré historian had been the model east European specialist, after the war, a growing generation of American-born social scientists began to join the communist studies field.[5]

If the writings of the Webbs and their contemporaries were largely uncritical of Soviet socialism, early Sovietology was perhaps too tendentious in the opposite direction, characterized by denunciations of communist systems as rigid, totalitarian dictatorships led by the iron hand of the party. Interestingly, both groups tended to take communists at their word; they differed only in which words they chose to take seriously. The Webbs and others in their cohort believed the Soviet rhetoric of social justice and equality; postwar Sovietologists tended to believe the rhetoric of party discipline and the plan.[6] During the era of high Stalinism, from the war through the early 1950s, this vision of Soviet and even east European politics prevailed. However, the totalitarian model of communist politics was never really much of a model at all. It did not explain (nor, to be fair, did its adherents claim to explain) precisely how the system held together, since it was assumed that brute force was the key variable.[7]

In the 1960s and 1970s, a more complex vision of Soviet and east European politics began to emerge, a result both of changes in the region and of developments within academe. The communist bloc was hardly the monolith that some totalitarian theorists portrayed, and even the Soviet Union itself clearly witnessed intraparty struggles and elite rivalries. In response, a variety of new conceptual tools and techniques—such as increasing concern with elite-level struggles and with communist societies (rather than just the state)—made their way into writing on Soviet and east European politics.[8] As Jerry Hough wrote in 1979, in his rewritten and renamed edition of Merle Fainsod's *How Russia Is Ruled* (1953), "research and writing about western governments has centered on the policy process and the factors associated with responsiveness in political systems, and meaningful comparative political science requires that a conscious attempt be made to ask the same questions about the Soviet Union."[9] By the mid-1980s, when the rise of Mikhail Gorbachev remade the study of Soviet politics as much as Gorbachev's own perestroika would change the Soviet system, the study of Soviet-style communism had become a diverse field with competing visions of the key characteristics of the state. New writing on interest group politics, patronage networks, leadership, generational change, ideology, and political culture transformed the understanding of communist politics.[10]

In retrospect, it is clear that many of the major debates in the field, from the 1960s forward, involved at base a kind of competitive naming. Was the Soviet system "totalitarian" or just "authoritarian" under Stalin? Did it become "pluralist" under Brezhnev? Was Gorbachev a "transformative" leader or merely a "reformist" one? It is difficult to know what difference the label might really have made in actually explaining how Soviet politics worked. But in a system in which real data were difficult to obtain, being clear on the framework of analysis was a crucial step. The labels were part of an ongoing conversation among Western academics about the degree to which communist systems could be studied with the same conceptual tools used to understand other systems, such as those of advanced liberal democracies or third-world authoritarian regimes.

Given the extent of these conceptual and methodological debates, it is not only unfair but also simply wrong to assert that communist studies was wholly divorced from mainstream political science. The main criticisms of the field—that it was insular, that it reified geographical boundaries into analytical ones, that it was overly fixated on institutions, that it failed to consider serious disputes among rival interests within the party and state apparatus—are caricatures of what most people were actually writing. At nearly every turn, from the 1940s through the 1980s, students of communism were, in general, solidly in step with developments in the broader social sciences. The early totalitarian model was not a great deal more rigid than similar institutional analyses that dominated other areas of political science in the 1940s and early 1950s. Descriptive institutionalist treatments gave way to analyses that tried, as far as possible, to differentiate distinct interest groups within the Soviet and east European elite and to begin to see communist states—most of which were largely peasant economies and backward societies before the advent of communism—as evolving, modernizing polities.[11] These in turn gave way to more sophisticated accounts of Soviet politics that, by the 1980s, analyzed contests within the party leadership, generational changes among party and state elites, emerging trends in Soviet and non-Soviet societies, and center-periphery struggles between Moscow and the republics.

In a political system in which survey data were nonexistent, archival access severely restricted, elite interviews either impossible or unreliable, preference falsification prevalent, and official dissimulation the norm, that is not a bad record. Plenty of criticisms can be made of Sovietology. It was not until 1986, for example, that a major scholarly work on the politics of interethnic relations appeared.[12] But that Soviet studies concerned itself solely with interpreting the arcane rituals of party congresses and Politburo sessions is not one of them. It was, in fact, U.S. government analysts and journalists—not academic Sovietologists—who spent their time divining trends in communist politics from who stood next to whom on top of Lenin's mausoleum during May Day parades. Serious students of the Soviet Union and eastern Europe, especially those who recognized sooner than others the power of the nationalities question across the region, can be proud of their scholarly pasts.

Students of eastern Europe and Eurasia are today keenly aware of how their subfield was perceived by the wider discipline, and the transition to broad comparison has presented three particular challenges. The sudden opening of the states and societies themselves produced a flood of new empirical information. There has been, over the last twenty years, an embarrassment of riches as archives were flung open, innumerable surveys carried out by local and Western researchers, and—crucially—younger east Europeans educated in the United States and western Europe, individuals who have both the local knowledge and the formal methodological training to conduct truly pathbreaking research. These developments have revealed what may have been the chief irony of the old area studies: Despite the repeated criticisms from colleagues outside the subfield, one of the real deficiencies of communist studies was not the naiveté of its modeling but the inaccuracies in its empirical evidence. According to Peter Rutland, of the eighty-seven Ph.D. dissertations on Soviet politics completed in American universities between 1976 and 1987, the authors of only seventeen had actually spent time conducting research in the Soviet Union.[13] One cannot imagine a similar statistic today.

Furthermore, students of postcommunism, even if they were inclined to insularity, cannot afford to be separated from the wider social science world. Grant-making bodies increasingly demand cross-regional, comparative research. Even organizations that continue to fund year-long research visits to individual countries—such as the Fulbright Commission and the International Research and Exchanges Board (IREX)—have come to redefine exactly what region they cover, expanding their reach at times to include Turkey, Iran, and other neighboring states. For students of Poland, Hungary, and other locales in the northern tier, funding has almost completely disappeared, as these states have "graduated" from being of critical strategic importance to the United States and attained the stably boring status of Denmark or Spain, at least as far as congressional appropriations are concerned.

Perhaps most important, though, the collapse of communism and the disappearance of communist studies came at the same time as the ascendance of deductive theorizing, especially rational choice modeling, as one of the major (if not dominant) paradigms in American political science.[14] If not all political scientists have become rational choice theorists, they have at least been forced to become more rigorous in their research design and to think more carefully about problems of causation and hypothesis testing. One wonders, in fact, whether the shape of postcommunist studies and the sometimes acrimonious debates of the early 1990s might have been different had the Soviet system disappeared at some other point in the history of American social science. All of this has presented a unique task to students of postcommunism: to take advantage of the overwhelming wealth of new empirical information while presenting work in a way that will be meaningful to the wider discipline. The next section considers how well the subfield has fared.

The Varieties of Postcommunist Experience

In the last two decades, the raft of states that used to be known quaintly as European and Eurasian transition countries—all twenty-seven of them, from the Czech Republic to Kazakhstan (one might also include Mongolia)—have had highly variable success in the move from one-party rule and planned economies.

Some have rejected authoritarian governments, refashioned state institutions, and become fully integrated parts of Euro-Atlantic structures, including NATO and the EU. Others have rejected authoritarian regimes without managing to build authoritative governments. Still others have done little more than exchange the mantras of international socialism for those of nationalist authoritarianism.

Not surprisingly, most comparative work on the collapse of communism and its immediate aftermath has focused on the states that progressed most rapidly along the path toward free elections, responsive institutions, and good governance, places such as Poland, the Czech Republic, and Hungary. Even today, when quantitative data and local research partners are far more available than they were throughout much of the 1990s, less developed countries such as Romania, Bulgaria, and Albania still rarely figure into comparative discussions. Russia is most often treated as a country apart, more the focus of comparative-minded case studies than genuinely cross-national research; likewise for most of the remnants of socialist Yugoslavia. Central Asia and the Caucasus are barely on the comparativists' map. The reason for the exclusion of these countries, it is often said, is that they have lagged behind others in terms of political and economic reform and are thus less propitious venues for testing theories of regime change, institutional design, and the political economy of reform. But these laggards are in fact in the majority. The countries of the northern tier—roughly from Slovenia northeast toward the three Baltic countries—are the exceptions, not the norm, in postcommunist politics. More broadly, as Valerie Bunce has argued, regime collapse that ends in long periods of difficult transition and even bloodshed, as in Yugoslavia, may be the historical norm, not just the regional one.[15]

Today, the differences across the postcommunist world are even more striking than they were throughout the 1990s. According to the annual Freedom House surveys (www.freedomhouse.org), some countries (Albania, Armenia, Azerbaijan, Ukraine) have either regressed on the democratization scale since the early part of that decade or have settled into a sine-wave pattern oscillating between relative freedom and relative unfreedom. On Transparency International's Corruption Perceptions Index, a measure of corrupt business practices in ninety-nine countries, most of the old transition states still fall on the bottom half of the list (among the most corrupt), along with such countries as Colombia and Uganda. All the transition states of northern Europe (except, interestingly, Latvia) usually cluster in the top half.[16] In the human rights field, most countries are likewise part of the laggard class. The annual surveys by Human Rights Watch, the U.S. State Department, and Amnesty International catalogue a range of abuses, from periodic violence against minorities to police torture and extrajudicial killing. Oddly, the country often seen as a major outlier in the postcommunist world—the solidly authoritarian Belarus—may in many ways be closer to the norm than is often imagined. The dynamics of political change there since the late 1980s—hesitant national revival, fitful liberalization, authoritarian backlash—now seem far closer to that of several countries in eastern Europe and Eurasia than the relatively peaceful and hopeful path trod by Poland and Hungary. Indeed, even the so-called electoral revolutions of the early 2000s—in Serbia, Georgia, and Ukraine—could be analyzed either as breakthroughs for democracy or as simply new chapters in the cycle of popular revolution and authoritarian reconsolidation that other parts of the region have experienced since the end of communism. In fact, the further away we get from Georgia's Rose Revolution of 2003 and Ukraine's Orange Revolution of 2004, the more valid the second interpretation is likely to appear.

The countries of postcommunist eastern Europe and Eurasia have experienced a "return to diversity," as Joseph Rothschild's masterful history once put it—but in a rather different sense from what Rothschild perhaps anticipated.[17] There have been valiant attempts to pull similar strands from this tangled skein and to characterize "postcommunism" in general. Leslie Holmes, in the first introductory survey to be published on the phenomenon, elaborated a "fourteen point model . . . that makes it possible to distinguish post-communist countries from others with which they might initially appear to have much in common."[18] (Holmes's points, however, are slippery, ranging from "moral confusion" to "temporality" to "unfortunate timing.") In a later introductory textbook, Richard Sakwa narrowed the number to thirteen, from the "emergence of pluralistic societies" to "various facets of identity politics"—and that, he wrote, is postcommunism "narrowly defined."[19]

Sakwa's text is one of several introductory volumes on the postcommunist condition to have emerged in the last decade.[20] Books such as these have provided helpful *tours d'horizon* of the intricacies of the transition from one-party states. Yet the very complexity of the subject can sometimes make general works on postcommunism strange reads. Sakwa's text, for example, was included in the respected Open University Press series on "Concepts in the Social Sciences," along with Bernard Crick on socialism, Robert Nisbet on conservatism, and Mark Smith on something called "ecologism." The problem is that postcommunism is, of course, not just one thing (as Sakwa himself demonstrates), much less an ideology, set of behaviors, or style of politics that can be usefully compared with, say, socialism or conservatism. That label, some two decades beyond the initial transition away from communist systems, now seems bizarre as a moniker for governments, societies, and economies as vastly different as those of Poland and Tajikistan.

Comparison and Differential Outcomes

The chief challenge, then, is to explain in general terms the different forms of extrication from communism and the massive changes in the zone, not just in the rolling revolutions of 1989–1991, but in the period since. How, in other words, did similar systems become transformed in such radically different ways? Communist states were diverse entities. But there was something called the "communist system"—or as some scholars have preferred to call it, the "socialist system" or "state socialism"[21]—and the countries normally included under this rubric did share a host of comparable institutions, economic relationships, and foreign policy orientations that make it worth asking why the divergence among them has been so astronomical in the last ten years.

The temptation, especially for scholars intimately familiar with particular cases in the former communist lands, is to attribute botched transitions and stagnant economies to the idiosyncrasies of the cases themselves: leadership, public commitment, external support, political culture. But things did not necessarily turn out the way one might have predicted based on these variables. The most politically liberal and economically open European communist state—Yugoslavia—produced the bloodiest of all the transitions, spawning at least four (depending on how one counts them) full-scale wars. Some states that are relatively homogeneous in an ethnocultural sense, such as Poland, have had a far easier time than heterogeneous countries such as Romania. But other, even more homogeneous states, such as Albania and Armenia, are still among the least reformed and the most violent. No one would have expected the transitions to be exactly alike; after all, twenty-two of the postcommunist countries are also new states, facing problems of state building and nation building, as well as regime change and systemic reform. However, unlike the transitions in southern Europe and Latin America, the postcommunist states did come from similar starting points—a common ideology (with variants), state-controlled economies, single-party systems, and a sense of being part of a single, international movement—which throws into even sharper relief the differences today.

How have scholars responded to the challenges of studying such a patently diverse region? Some of the most influential work in the field has had at least three features in common. First, it has engaged with the problem of comparison itself, in particular, the degree to which the experience of southern Europe and Latin America has been useful in accounting for differences across eastern Europe and Eurasia. After years of intense debate about the shape and content of transitology as a field of study, scholars can now offer a reasonable assessment of how well transition models have adapted as they have traveled east. Work has focused in particular on the problem of institutions, not only the challenge of institutional design (which was a key subject of the older transitology literature) but also the complex interaction among postcommunist institutions and the communist substrate on which they were constructed. Second, new research has dealt with the problem of stability and state power, the extent to which the formal institutional arrangements and informal political bargains struck in the early years of the transition set in place particular incentives and habits of behavior that can either further or—more frequently—freeze genuine reform. Third, scholars have wrestled with the problem of identity, an overstudied and undertheorized topic in the postcommunist literature, especially the origins of the so-called ethnic revival across the region from the late 1980s forward. The next section addresses these features of the vast literature on postcommunist politics by examining several key works that ground discussions of the fate of eastern Europe and Eurasia in genuinely comparative work. As this section shows, there are clear ways in which the study of the postcommunist world is touching on vital debates within comparative politics more generally—and, in turn, offering a remarkable set of new cases for developing and testing general theories of political behavior.

The Record of Transitology

Transitology—the study of the extrication from authoritarian political systems and the transition toward more pluralist forms of politics—was never without its critics, even among the specialists on Latin America and southern Europe who were the field's pioneering exponents. Among east Europeanists, however, Valerie Bunce was perhaps the most important early skeptic of the wholesale migration of transitologists into the postcommunist world. In a series of spirited exchanges with Latin Americanists and other comparativists in several major journals, Bunce argued that good comparative studies were those that not only were sensitive to the surface similarities among cases but also took account of the real differences among them.[22] Postcommunist systems did come from somewhere, and the particular legacies of the past might have some bearing on the nature of politics afterward. Today, transitology and the massive "democracy assistance" and "transition aid" industries that it has spawned have come in for energetic criticism from both political scientists and policy practitioners.[23] It is thus worth revisiting some of the basic questions that Bunce and others asked in their own work in the 1990s, in particular the issue of how well transitological models have fared in their eastward migration. The short answer seems to be "not very well."

The transitions literature is highly varied, but as Bunce has argued, one can distill several general lines of argument, if not firm conclusions, from it.[24]

First, there is a stress on what she calls "proximate politics," that is, the form of extrication (pacts between old elites and the opposition, full-blown revolutions) and the design of new institutions (electoral systems, constitutions). Second, the newest wave of democratization—of which southern Europe, Latin America, and eastern Europe are all a part—is amenable to "crafting," in Giuseppe Di Palma's well-known term.[25] There is a best practice in democracy building that can usefully be applied across regions. Third, countries in transition are defined more by where they are headed, toward open societies and democratic governance, than where they have come from. Drawing comparisons based on the future trajectories of these states is more useful than attributing their problems to inherited legacies.

Transitologists might fault Bunce for being unduly cavalier with their body of literature, since throughout the 1990s, Latin Americanists have themselves come to question much of the older transitions writing from the 1980s.[26] (Bunce has herself gone into these issues in some depth.)[27] Still, she is right to ask whether the early hegemony of transitology may have blinded scholars to key variables and taken them down explanatory culs-de-sac. The eastward migration of comparative transition studies tended to ask what the experience of other regions could tell students of eastern Europe, rather than ask how theories derived from other historical experiences could be enriched in the postcommunist context. They underestimated the difficulties of crafting new regimes in multiethnic contexts and overestimated the usefulness of civil society as an explanatory variable (especially in circumstances in which vibrant, deep-rooted, nonstate associations are decidedly uncivil). They focused on how the choice of institutions shaped political outcomes, rather than on why elites chose particular institutions in the first place.[28] And they were perhaps too ready, as work by Thomas Carothers and Janine Wedel has shown, to believe that Western assistance in institution building and party development could ensure the growth of stable democracies and sustainable civic orders.[29]

In her *Subversive Institutions* (1999), Bunce engages with these issues in a series of what she terms "cascading comparisons" centered around three research questions. First, why did socialism end across the entire communist bloc? Bunce proceeds by comparing communist regimes with one another, as well as with other authoritarian bureaucratic systems. Second, what accounts for the divergent paths since the collapse of the regimes? The method here involves comparison across the transition states. Third, why did the three communist federations—Czechoslovakia, the Soviet Union, and Yugoslavia—break up in such radically different ways, the first peacefully, the second less so, and the third in fratricidal war? Here the comparison involves a detailed look at the dynamics of center-periphery relations in each of the three states.

Bunce's overall response to these questions is that starting points matter. Unlike some transitologists, who argued strongly that the obstacles to democratization "everywhere . . . are determined by a common destination, not by different points of departure,"[30] she holds that analysis of initial conditions is one crucial part of sorting out the vast variety of postcommunist outcomes. But initial conditions are not understood here as demographic factors, levels of economic development, traditions of democratic governance, or the other variables most often used to explain regime instability, reform, and collapse. Rather, Bunce focuses on the institutional structure of the communist state and the ways in which the reforms of the 1980s, working within the institutional constraints imposed by the system, provided new incentives and opportunities for both political actors and publics.

The communist system was institutionally rich but organizationally weak. The regimes constructed an elaborate network of state institutions that insinuated themselves into almost every aspect of society, from trade unions to chess clubs. In most instances, an array of multilevel party structures mirrored those of the state. The institutional density of communist systems was meant to serve as a mobilizational instrument, a surrogate for class, economic interest, religion, or other mobilizational stimuli that might be found in more open, pluralistic societies. Moreover, they were meant to work in a single direction, mobilizing economic, political, social, and even cultural resources to achieve the ends of state planning, not as channels for assessing the public mood and for enabling elites to make policy accordingly.

The "totalitarian" school of communist studies did pay attention to institutions, but what early analysts missed was that the system, although organized as a hierarchy, became increasingly feudal as time passed. Administering the various domains and levels within this institutional network depended not on central command and control (which would have been impossible as the systems aged and the societies became more diverse after the Second World War), but rather on the distribution of power and resources to institutional agents throughout the state. As time passed, the central party and state apparatus displayed an increasing tendency to try to buy off restive allies in the Soviet bloc by allowing some degree of autonomy in foreign policy, to buy off regional bureaucrats by turning a blind eye to economic overreporting, and to buy off publics by producing cheap consumer goods. More than in other authoritarian states, communist elites thus had at their disposal a vast body of instruments, both coercive and redistributive, but rather few feedback mechanisms for assessing how well or poorly those institutions were functioning.

The problems that these institutions faced by the 1980s came from both internal and external forces. The institutional density and overlap created

competing institutional interests; however, unlike the bureaucracies of pluralistic societies, there were no extrainstitutional forums in which these rivalries
could be mediated. Elites became increasingly divided, often as a result of the
passing from the scene of the first and second generations of post–Second
World War bureaucrats who had consolidated the system. Publics became more
autonomous and demanding. Efforts to reform the system from within merely
opened up channels for the expression of discontent without simultaneously
enabling the institutions to respond to demands from below. The result was a
series of multilevel defections from the institutional arrangements that had
defined the communist system for forty years or more. Opposition groups
across the communist bloc created autonomous avenues of interest articula-
tion and insisted that they be represented by the state. Regional elites in socialist federations claimed ever greater autonomy from central governments.
National leaders in the Soviet Union's outer empire asserted full independence
from Moscow. It was in this sense that the institutions were self-subversive.
Although originally designed to ensure state control over wide swaths of territory and deep into society, the institutions of Soviet-style socialism "functioned
over time to divide and weaken the powerful, homogenize and strengthen the
weak, and undercut economic performance."[31]

Bunce's story is a complicated one, but that, in fact, is part of the message
of *Subversive Institutions:* that parsimony in explaining macrolevel historical
change may necessitate unwisely cutting out precisely the variables that need
attention. (To be fair, though, most theorists would not disagree. As Adam
Przeworski and Henry Teune argued, parsimony and accuracy usually are
incompatible; which quality one stresses depends on the kind of research question being asked.)[32] The real value of her account is its concretizing exactly
what the much-discussed "communist legacies" really are. Many scholars of
eastern Europe have written, usually defensively, of the peculiarity of the region
and the reasons that models of political change imported from abroad are
unlikely to fit exactly. The reasons given usually have to do with social atomiza-
tion, weak civil society, or (the favorite obstacle to reform cited by postcommunist politicians) residual communist "mentalities." Looking more closely at the
design of the communist state, though, provides one key to understanding why
some regimes went gently while others took the state with them.

Federalism and Stability

Throughout the 1990s, there was a tendency to focus on problems of identity
and interethnic relations as the sole variables in accounting for the stability of
multiethnic and ethnofederal states, especially in the postcommunist context.

The reciprocal grievances—historical, economic, psychological—of majorities and minorities figured heavily in the literature. What is strikingly absent from many of these accounts, though, is politics: the activities of central and peripheral elites, their political interests, and the strategies of political survival that each pursues in relation to the other.[33]

One of the key questions to emerge from the postcommunist rubble is how to explain the relative stability of Russia's federal order, especially during the intense crisis period of the early 1990s. How did the Russian Federation, although faced by an array of centrifugal forces at least as powerful as those that tore apart the Soviet Union, Czechoslovakia, and Yugoslavia, manage to remain intact at the height of center-periphery tensions. One compelling answer, proposed by Daniel Treisman in his important *After the Deluge* (1999), is that a policy of "selective fiscal appeasement" allowed the administration of Boris Yeltsin to garner support from the most restive republics and regions, thereby preventing bandwagoning against the center.[34] Fiscal disbursements were targeted precisely at those regions most prone to disruptive protest actions, from strikes to voting against establishment candidates in national elections. Although more recent research has focused on other aspects of Russia's ethnofederal system—especially the power of legal, administrative, and other formal institutions—Treisman's center-periphery model has remained an influential analysis of the relationship between Moscow and its asymmetrical federal units.[35]

Why did Russia not go the way of other communist federations? Competing explanations for the shape of Russian reform, in particular the relationship between center and regions, are legion. One might point to culture and ethnicity, but any putative commitment of Russia's citizens to a unifying "Great Russian" culture did not prevent major protest behavior and the growth of protosecessionist movements. Moreover, there was no clear correlation between republics, regions, or districts with the most homogeneous or cohesive ethnic mix and their opposition to the center's policies. The fear of the center's use of force was also not a clearly powerful motivator. The October 1993 attack on the Russian parliament might have had a chilling effect on the demands of the regions, since the Yeltsin leadership showed itself willing to use brutal force against opponents. But both before and after 1993, the Russian military came to depend more and more on regional elites, as the central budget was cut, and the armed forces could not have been relied upon to implement the center's orders to clamp down on the regions. The first Chechen war (1994–1996) also illustrated the impotence of the military to deal with committed separatists.

In contrast to explanations based on culture or brute power, Treisman seeks to bring politics back into the picture. Russia's central and peripheral elites were locked into playing the same political game but for different stakes. Central elites needed to garner and maintain the loyalty of regional voters to win national elections; regional governors needed constituent support to win their own local races. Both sets of elites thus shared an interest in increased fiscal disbursements from central coffers. The former hoped that payment of wage arrears and entitlements would buy regional votes; the latter hoped that a record of making the center pay up would translate into greater support in the next regional election. "Whether or not they shared philosophical convictions, personal sympathies, or political networks, Yeltsin and his governors shared an interest in nurturing support with which to face future elections. And voters, by apparently holding incumbents at both levels responsible for declining state services, made it difficult for one to achieve his aim without also assisting the other."[36]

The argument is elegant, but there is a potential difficulty with the causal arrow. Treisman's main indicator for regional support for the Yeltsin leadership is the voting record of the regions in the April 1993 referendum on the constitution, the December 1993 parliamentary elections, the December 1995 parliamentary elections, and the 1996 presidential elections. However, it is difficult to know whether central appeasement produced desirable regional electoral outcomes because local voters responded to financial incentives, as Treisman wants to argue, or the financial incentives caused regional bosses to "deliver" the vote for Yeltsin in each of these instances. Treisman clearly recognizes this potential difficulty, and in an appendix, he analyzes the record of State Duma deputies and their votes for or against Yeltsin. "The delegates from regions where voters' approval of Yeltsin had recently increased were very significantly more likely to vote on the side supported by Yeltsin on roll-call votes in the Congress."[37] Treisman sees this outcome as evidence of democratic influence. Nevertheless, things could well have worked in the opposite direction: The record of State Duma deputies may have been the cause of regional voting behavior, not the result (a point that Treisman himself concedes in a footnote).

This issue does not affect the overall contention that appeasing the most aggressive anticenter leaders can be an effective strategy in weak federations. It does matter, though, for the contrast that we might draw with other cases. Russia seems to offer a sharp departure from other examples of imperial behavior. The Romans and Ottomans worked to bring potentially aggressive peripheral leaders into an imperial hierarchy of incentives—making bandits into bureaucrats, in Karen Barkey's suggestive formulation.[38] But Yeltsin seemed to succeed by co-opting not the regional elites but their constituencies, providing increased federal funds to pay wages and pensions in order to secure constituents' votes in national elections and, simultaneously, to hedge against regional elites' ability to mobilize those same constituents against the hands that fed.

This view depends on the idea that the regional governors are at least minimally responsive to their electorates. That, though, may be a heroic assumption. Electoral participation in many regions has been low, especially in the cities (precisely the area where the increased disbursements from the center would be expected to have the greatest effect). The early 1990s also witnessed the continued growth of regional executive authority over the power of local legislatures, the forums in which the voice of the electorate would be most readily heard. The center may have provided disbursements not so much to placate regional voters as to provide rent-seeking regional elites with sufficient funds to deliver the votes themselves—whether through legitimate channels of increased social spending or through less savory methods of electoral engineering. In the latter case, Russia's strategy of ensuring the compliance of peripheral elites looks far more like the Roman or Ottoman experience than the trappings of elections and parliaments seem to indicate.

Institutions and Identity Politics

After the Deluge includes a brief chapter comparing the Russian case with those of the Soviet Union, Czechoslovakia, and Yugoslavia. Why did the last three federal systems shatter when Russia, faced by peripheral challenges no less severe, managed to hold together? The answer, for Treisman, lies in the political decisions taken at the height of federal crises. In the Russian case, Yeltsin worked to redistribute resources to peripheral elites who, in turn, distributed resources to their own constituents, a form of cascading conciliation that produced greater public support for integration and discouraged cross-regional bandwagoning. The Soviet, Czechoslovak, and Yugoslav elites behaved differently. In the Soviet Union, the Gorbachev leadership had a decreasing ability to enforce fiscal agreements and used fiscal resources as a stick rather than a carrot by meting out punishment to the most restive areas; even if the Soviet center had been willing to buy off regional leaders through disbursements, there would still have been little ability to appeal to the publics in the regions, since there were no truly representative institutions at the center. In Czechoslovakia, the strong commitment to liberal reforms in Prague ruled out fiscal profligacy; the refusal of the Vaclav Klaus government to lessen the economic shock of reform in the less-developed Slovak half of the federation provided ample opportunities for populist mobilization there. In Yugoslavia, an institutionally weak and resource-poor federal government sought to impose fiscal austerity throughout the federation; rather than further empowering regional elites through budget payoffs, the Belgrade government sought to recentralize the federal system, ignored the demands of the most likely secessionists, and early on, demonstrated its willingness to use force against the periphery. In all these cases, the policies pursued by the center exacerbated the centrifugal forces in the federation and pushed the countries further toward dissolution.

Treisman notes that his comparative argument is meant only to be suggestive (others, such as Susan Woodward, have made the argument in greater detail).[39] But his account does provide an intriguing contrast with Bunce's institutionalist argument. Bunce highlights the major institutional differences among the four cases. In both Czechoslovakia and Yugoslavia, central institutions were unusually weak; power had been significantly decentralized as early as the 1960s to a far greater degree than in the Soviet Union or post-Soviet Russia. The crucial differences in the Yugoslav case, though, were structural. Yugoslavia was even more decentralized than the others. It had a politically weak republic (Serbia) at its center, a republic that took on the task of trying to keep the federal state together, eventually by force. That republic, moreover, came to control the one institution whose legitimacy and privileged position were predicated on the existence of a Yugoslav state: the Yugoslav National Army. For Treisman, the key issue is the strategy pursued by political actors within a given institutional context. For Bunce, it is the logic of institutional arrangements themselves—the logic of rules and established norms within which strategic games were played out.

The two accounts do share an important commonality, though: a focus on the institutions of communism and their impact on the politics of identity under postcommunism. Through the lens of the late 1980s, in which communism seemed more a brake on national development than its catalyst, it is easy to forget that the early Bolsheviks and their heirs elsewhere in Europe's east saw themselves and their mission as fundamentally modern. In more than the Soviet Union, one of the basic elements of their modernizing project was the creation of self-conscious nations. Nationalism was, in this sense, not merely an unintended by-product of the Soviet system; it was central to the Bolshevik message. Communists were not always nationalists, but they were without exception nation builders. As Ronald Suny famously noted in the case of the Soviet Union, the Bolsheviks' rhetorical commitment to the fading away of national affiliations notwithstanding, the Soviet Union was not a melting pot for old nations but an incubator for new ones.[40] The irony is palpable: A state committed to creating a supraethnic Soviet people, dominated by a party that saw classes rather than nations as the main motors of history, may well be remembered by future historians chiefly for its contribution to the growth of national consciousness across Eurasia. The same could be said for similar nation-building projects throughout eastern Europe and Eurasia, where com-munism came to be seen not as a break with a previous bourgeois national past, but rather as its apotheosis.

The lesson for students of postcommunism, and of interethnic relations more broadly, is to examine in greater detail the particular institutional incen-tives for the mobilization of ethnic issues. Growing research on interethnic conflict has reaffirmed the ways in which ethnic mobilization, far from being an atavistic resurgence of primordial identities, is often a rational response to a given set of incentives or a strategy consciously pursued by self-interested elites.[41] Philip Roeder, for example, has argued that national heterogeneity—multiple, self-conscious cultural groups living in the same state and usually tied to a particular piece of real estate—can be a serious impediment to democratiza-tion; as uncomfortable as it may be to admit, multiculturalism may be a luxury in established democracies but an obstacle in democratizing states.[42] Heterogeneity, however, is only one piece of the puzzle. The institutional arrangements inherited from previous regimes and the decisions that policy makers take in the early years of systemic reform are crucial, regardless of whether the state is culturally homogeneous or plural. Countries with more languages, more cultures, and more historical grievances obviously face a host of challenges unknown in less diverse polities, but diversity itself need not impede democracy building.

There is also a less optimistic dimension to the institutional story. If the institutions and early decisions of transitional elites create a particular trajectory from which it is difficult to deviate later on, then the politics of accommodation and appeasement may have an unwelcome outcome: rewarding ardent periph-eral elites by recognizing their control. Such a strategy may lead to a decline in center-regional tensions and even a halt to armed conflict, as it did in Russia in the early 1990s and in several post-Soviet secessionist disputes by 1994. Yet the price in some cases has been to legitimize pockets of authoritarianism in return for professed loyalty to a single central government—the strategy of old empires now pursued within new and allegedly democratizing states. It is a dark bargain, but one that has been frequently struck across postcommunist Eurasia.

Toward "Post-Postcommunist Studies"

The scholarly work produced in the two decades of postcommunism has been, at its best, empirically rich, theoretically engaged, and designed to bridge the divide between accurate accounts of real-world politics in exceptionally com-plex environments and general theorizing about the determinants of political behavior. But where are things likely to go beyond the postcommunist horizon?

Is there still an "Eastern Europe" to be studied through a distinct set of analytical lenses, or has the field—like the parties and even polities that were once its purview—slipped from political science into history?

Theory Building from Snapshots

Treating institutions in a historically aware and detailed way means viewing them "as films, not snapshots," as Bunce has it, that is, "acknowledging that institutions can appear to have one set of consequences, but in practice and over time, quite different, if not opposing ones."[43] The same might be said about the transition itself. In few areas of political research are dependent variables as skittish as in the study of postcommunism. The rapidity of change in eastern Europe and Eurasia has meant that speaking of a political scientist's favorite subject of study—"outcomes"—is inherently slippery. What seems to be an unusual outcome in need of explanation one year can deliquesce into an uninterestingly commonplace one the next, and vice versa.

Take, for example, the cases of Kyrgyzstan, Georgia, and Moldova. In the late 1990s, these three states became hopeful cases in an otherwise disappointing Eurasian array. All three experienced devastating economic crises, and two were threatened by wholesale dissolution and separatist wars. But they were normally seen as relatively successful instances of democratization. Multiple elections were held with minimal irregularities, presidents won by less than unanimous votes, and new governments were peacefully formed after shifts in parliamentary representation. However, by early 2000, none of these three looked nearly as positive as earlier enthusiastic assessments had held. Kyrgyzstan's 2000 parliamentary elections did not comply with international democratic norms, as measured by the OSCE. Research on Georgia had illustrated the degree to which the country's democratic governance was, at least in part, an illusion of Western governments and international nongovernmental organizations with a vested interest in perpetuating that image.[44] Even after the remarkable change in government in late 2003 and early 2004—the so-called Rose Revolution, which ushered out the Soviet-era administration of Eduard Shevardnadze and brought to power a younger, Western-oriented political elite—elements of the old authoritarianism remained in place. In Moldova, a power-hungry president and his supporters in a fractious parliament threatened to rewrite the constitution and introduce a strongly presidential, and potentially authoritarian, system. That, in turn, led to an ironic and world-historical event in 2001: the coming to power of the world's first elected Communist party, which formed a new Moldovan government and purged members of the previous administration.

What scholars need to explain, then, can depend on when they get around to explaining it. There is little sign that the dependent variables in this field will become any less mercurial as time passes—unless, unhappily, the "authoritarian reactions" that seemed to sweep across Eurasia by the late 1990s and early 2000s become an even more solid end-state across the region. For theorists, this means that a certain degree of humility is still in order. East European and Eurasian studies is better than ever before at elaborating the ways in which systemic change is consonant with and differs from similar phenomena in other parts of the world. However, the ability to predict which direction change is likely to go, solely from deductive theorizing rather than on the basis of intimate familiarity with the facts on the ground, is still as limited as in most other areas of political science. Even so, establishing the limits of the knowable, as Timur Kuran reminded scholars at the beginning of the east European transformations, is itself part of science.[45] Getting used to politics as cycles of change, not as transitions to or from a more or less stable end-state, will continue to be part of the post-postcommunist condition.[46]

New Area Studies

There was a time when experts on eastern Europe and Eurasia—all of it— might have existed. But today, as the individual countries move in different directions—consolidating forms of government ranging from prosperous social democracies to sultanistic or even dynastic regimes—continuing to treat all twenty-seven (or more) transition countries as a natural set has an extremely limited benefit. In fact, we have probably already reached the half-life of this particular method. Postcommunist studies, if it continues to keep within the same geographical boundaries as its predecessor, cannot last.

There are different ways of dividing up the old "transition" world, and these divisions may make more sense in the future. The utility of a particular region as an analytical tool depends not on any perennial cultural, historical, or topographical features of the region itself, but rather on the type of question that the analyst chooses to ask. Poland and most of the northern tier states can now be considered consolidated democracies; the study of policy making, electoral systems, public administration, legislative politics, transnational integration, and other subjects that occupy students of western Europe can now properly apply there as well.[47] Will we really want to think of Poland and Estonia as uniquely "postcommunist"—and, therefore, meaningfully distinct from Greece, Portugal, and other economically comparable, formerly authoritarian EU members—a few years hence?

Some research questions that are meaningful in the north make little sense farther south and east. There seems little reason to include Azerbaijan, with its rigged elections, in a study of comparative voting behavior. Students of center-periphery relations are unlikely to be enlightened by a study of Albania, where the center, frequently, has not held. Models of democratic consolidation may have little to gain from Turkmenistan, which has transited from one form of authoritarianism to another. Instead, depending on the research focus, there might be fruitful comparisons to be made with neighboring countries that come from Leninist, but not communist, traditions—a point implicit in Ken Jowitt's emphasis on the specifically Leninist dimensions of the communist experience.[48] Turkey and Iran might be brought into discussions about politics in the Balkans, the Caucasus, and Central Asia, not simply in the foreign policy arena (where their influence is clear) but also in domestic politics. Students of the Balkans and the Caucasus, for example, will be struck by the similarities between identity politics, patronage networks, and state-sponsored violence in Turkey and some of its neighbors to the north. Likewise, countries that have experienced state crises, violent territorial secessionism, and collapsing central institutions might be more usefully compared with similar cases in Africa than with other postcommunist states that have not experienced such crises. Surprisingly, only one major book has explicitly taken up this comparison in explicit ways, even though several scholars have examined the connections between political change in Eurasia and the developing world in spheres such as violence and strategies of state transformation.[49]

Comparison is crucial, but students of the former communist world should ask whether the sets they compare today might be less useful than they were two decades ago. Professional journals, regional studies associations, and graduate education programs have still not fully appreciated the impact of the last decade's changes on how they go about their tasks. In large part, research is still oriented along the same geographical lines, conducted in the same languages, and published in the same kinds of journals as during the cold war. At least in political science, those divisions surely cannot long endure. There is no need to throw out regional peculiarities altogether. Very few researchers have really taken up Adam Przeworski's admonition to "forget geography"[50]—if for no other reason than that the silent majority of comparativists still value foreign languages, enjoy getting our hands dirty in empirical research, and think both are important to understanding political life. The real challenge is to recast what counts as the geographic area (or, more likely, areas) that post-postcommunist studies will aim to cover. Today, "Eastern Europe," with two capital Es, is really no longer serviceable, except as anything more than a quick tag for all points east of the Oder River. Even "Eurasia" will be meaningful in the future only if it seriously admits Turkey, Iran, and perhaps Pakistan and Afghanistan into the mix. The *area* in the new area studies need not disappear, but it cannot be the same as it has been in the past.

The Meaning of "Method"

After the late 1980s, there developed a strong consensus among political scientists about the need to bring methods from the study of American and west European politics into the study of postcommunist Europe and Eurasia. Even scholars skeptical about the migration of transitologists eastward stressed the need to be more comparatively minded and methodologically sophisticated, which normally meant being versed in the techniques used to study the politics of Western liberal democracies. Just as a focus on where east European and Eurasian countries are headed has determined which kinds of comparisons are thought to be most valid, the same idea has tended to govern what kinds of methods are thought to be most useful for comparativists interested in postcommunism.

The broader exposure of postcommunist studies to rigorous methods has been an unequivocally positive development. But given the real character of politics in most parts of the former communist world, defining "research methodology" in overly narrow terms—as the ability to run regressions, say—can actually diminish the quality of research and graduate education rather than improve it. Today, most of the states that east Europeanists and Eurasianists study are still poor, weak, and relatively unfree. Some have central governments whose writ does not run far outside the capital city. Almost all are multinational, not just multiethnic, with distinct cultural groups now exercising considerable control over their own affairs in the absence of effective state power. Several have become the unwilling hosts of de facto independent but unrecognized states on their own territory. To explain political outcomes in these contexts, researchers need a whole host of methodological skills that are probably not captured in traditional definitions of what constitutes good methodology.

The issue is not qualitative versus quantitative research, but rather the kind of expertise that researchers need to hone to answer interesting and important questions about political behavior. In eastern Europe and Eurasia, facility in (several) foreign languages is often required, as is a sensitivity to the ways in which the results of surveys and interviews can change, depending on the language in which questions are asked. In edgily multicultural states, as much as in totalitarian ones, dissimulation and preference falsification can still be the norm. Researchers need to know where to find and how to judge archival sources, official statistics, and indigenous scholarship. They still need to root out short-run newspapers or underground publications and cart back in over-loaded suitcases invaluable work by local scholars that can be found only in streetside kiosks.

These are, of course, the same skills that characterized the communist period—learning to read between the lines and squeeze the most out of a limited and often skewed array of numbers, documents, and personal testimonies. For most of the postcommunist region, outside the small coterie of democratic and prosperous states in the northern tier, they will continue to be essential for some time to come. How anthropologists, demographers, and sociologists deal with these methodological problems in similarly underdeveloped countries and semiauthoritarian polities ought to be more widely available to students of comparative politics than a focus on the American and west European experience has so far allowed.

The Ethics of Research

The old area studies was particularly attuned to the ways in which cultural diversity and historical trajectories can make a difference in political life, an approach that is now clearly represented in the mainstream political science literature, in both its more historically grounded and more deductive strains. This was not, however, just a methodological peculiarity of interdisciplinary research. It had two ethical dimensions as well.

First, interaction with individuals, in their own languages and often around their own kitchen tables, predisposed scholars to consider how woolly things such as identity, history, and personality might condition political behavior. Explanations for why individuals behaved the way they did had to take seriously their own accounts and understandings of their actions. Second, interacting with local scholars and everyday citizens on their own turf—what is called, condescendingly, research in "the field"—encouraged scholars to package the results of their work in such a way that they would be intelligible to those whose actions the research was supposed to explain. The attention given to the ethics of scholarship, either implicitly in the way it was conducted or explicitly in the discussions that took place within area studies associations, was at times profound.[51]

Of course, no one any longer suggests that savoring a glass of fiery *rakija* in a Belgrade apartment or a bowl of fermented mare's milk on the steppe is crucial to "really understanding" east European and Eurasian politics. But the old area studies' consideration for the ethics of research design and presentation has been one of the unfortunate casualties of the field's demise. People are more than data-generators. The unspeakably brutal wars, the crushing poverty, and the human rights abuses that many men and women continue to face are the stuff of what political scientists study. They are not just propitious social-scientific testing grounds or natural experiments, as more than one writer has averred over the last ten years. Especially in the dire straits in which most east Europeans and Eurasians find themselves, it is perverse to see them as primarily test cases for broad theories of political behavior and only secondarily as purposive, suffering agents. They are equally both. Discussions of method and research practice in political science are amazingly lax when it comes to the ethics of data collection and analysis. Indeed, one of the most widely used texts in the methodology of qualitative comparative research makes no mention of this issue at all, an astonishing contrast to best practices in fields such as anthropology.[52]

So, is there still an "Eastern Europe"? Some have argued, even long after the end of communism itself, for the fundamental power of the communist experience in shaping political and social life. There may be a set of commonalities—for example, the generally low level of associational life, even when controlling for other factors such as regime type and level of economic development—that might continue to bind postcommunist states and societies together as a useful analytical unit.[53] As time goes on, however, the utility of the region qua region, irrespective of the specific analytical questions one chooses to pose about it, will diminish. The consumers of knowledge about the region—scholars, graduate students, journalists, and government officials—are already voting with their feet, gravitating toward educational programs and research projects that offer novel and creative ways of carving up the region from Poland to Mongolia and from the White Sea to the Mediterranean. Where the old area studies may survive, though, is in the particular ethical frame with which it viewed its geographical bailiwick and the people who inhabited it. In this sense, the old communist studies and its post-postcommunist progeny might find yet another way to contribute to the comparative study of politics in general: by bringing issues of responsibility, sensitivity, and morality out from the shadows and by raising questions about what makes the social sciences an inherently social activity.

6

The Benefits of Ethnic War

War is the engine of state building, but it is also good for business. Historically, the three have often amounted to the same thing. The consolidation of national states in western Europe was in part a function of the interests of royal leaders in securing sufficient revenue for war making. In turn, costly military engagements were highly profitable enterprises for the suppliers of men, ships, and weaponry. The great affairs of statecraft, says Shakespeare's Richard II as he seizes his uncle's fortune to finance a war, "do ask some charge." The distinction between freebooter and founding father, privateer and president, has often been far murkier in fact than national mythmaking normally allows.

Only recently, however, have these insights figured into discussions about contemporary ethnic conflict and civil war. Focused studies of the mechanics of warfare, particularly in cases such as Sudan, Liberia, Rwanda, and Sierra Leone, have highlighted the complex economic incentives that can push violence forward, as well as the ways in which the easy labels that analysts use to identify such conflicts—as "ethnic" or "religious," say—always cloud more than they clarify.[1] Yet how precisely does the chaos of war become transformed into networks of profit, and how in turn can these informal networks harden into the institutions of states? Post-Soviet Eurasia provides an enlightening instance of these processes in train.

In the early 1990s, a half dozen small wars raged across the region, a series of armed conflicts that we might term collectively the wars of the Soviet succession: Nagorno-Karabakh, Transnistria, South Ossetia, Abkhazia, Chechnya, Tajikistan. Each involved a range of players, including the central governments of newly sovereign states, secessionists, the armed forces of other countries, and international peacemakers. By the middle of the decade, most of the conflicts had settled into relative stability. Numerous rounds of peace negotiations were held under the aegis of the United Nations and the Organization for Security and Cooperation in Europe (OSCE). Little progress was achieved in the talks, but with the exception of the second Chechen war, which began in 1999 and ended officially in 2009, none of the post-Soviet disputes returned to the levels of organized violence experienced earlier—even with the upsurge in violence over South Ossetia in 2008.

But how can one explain the durability of these disputes, sometimes referred to as "stalled" or "frozen" conflicts, even after the cessation of violence? This chapter makes two central arguments in this regard. First, the territorial secessionists of the early 1990s have become the state builders of the early 2000s, creating de facto countries whose ability to field armed forces, control their own territory, educate their children, and maintain local economies has in some instances approximated that of the recognized states of which they are still notionally a part. The crystallization of independent statelike entities has meant that the resolution of these conflicts is not so much about patching together a torn country as about trying to reintegrate two functionally distinct administrations, militaries, and societies. (By "statelike entity," I mean a political unit that has (1) a population and (2) a government exercising sovereign control over some piece of territory—but without the imprimatur of international recognition. In Eurasia, the conceptual bar for statehood cannot be raised too high, for many of the qualities that define relatively well-functioning states in central Europe do not exist farther east, even among states that have seats at the United Nations.) The products of the wars of the Soviet succession are not frozen conflicts, but relatively successful examples of making states by making war.

Second, the disputes have evolved from armed engagements to something close to equilibrium. In many cases, both the secessionists and their erstwhile opponents in central governments have benefited from the untaxed trade and production flowing through the former war zones. Even in less unsavory ways, individuals inside and outside the conflict areas have an interest in maintaining the status quo—from poets who have built careers extolling their newfound statehood to pensioners worried about how their meager incomes might be further diminished if the country were once again integrated. It is a dark version of Pareto efficiency: The general welfare cannot be improved—by reaching a genuine peace accord allowing for real reintegration—without at the same time making key interest groups in both camps worse off. Even if a settlement is reached, it is unlikely to do more than recognize this basic logic and its attendant benefits—that is, unless one side seeks to change the status quo by opting once again for war.

This chapter examines the ways in which statelike entities have emerged and thrived in Eurasia since the earliest outbreak of violence in the late 1980s. The first section offers a brief overview of current research on civil war endings and the disjuncture between approaches drawn from the international relations literature and the work of sociologists and development economists on the functions of violence. The second section outlines the course of four Eurasian wars and identifies the de facto states that have arisen after them: the Republic of Nagorno-Karabakh (in Azerbaijan); the Dnestr Moldovan Republic, or Transnistria (in Moldova); and the republics of Abkhazia and South Ossetia (in Georgia).[2] There are other areas across eastern Europe and Eurasia that might be included on this list, such as Montenegro and Kosovo (before their independence declarations in 2006 and 2008, respectively), Chechnya in the Russian Federation (before the end of the second Chechen war), and Achara in Georgia (before its full takeover by Georgia's central government in 2004), not to mention the long-lived Turkish Republic of Northern Cyprus. But the four cases examined here are instances in which local armed forces, often with substantial assistance from outside powers, effectively defeated the armies of recognized governments in open warfare. They are also the cases in which the drive to create independent state structures has raised the most serious questions about whether any real reintegration with the central governments that the international community still recognizes as legitimate can now be reasonably expected. The third section analyzes the pillars of state building in each case, including the ways in which the interests of several major groups are satisfied by the limbo status into which these disputes have lapsed. The fourth section examines the Eurasian conflicts in light of Kosovo's successful secession from Serbia and the new republic's growing recognition by the international community. The final section describes the equilibrium that the disputes seem to have reached and suggests lessons that these cases might hold for further study of intrastate violence.

Civil War, Negotiations, and State Construction

Scholars have long recognized that civil wars tend to be protracted and that negotiated settlements are rare; even where talks have succeeded, they have produced less stable end-states than outright victory by one side.[3] Given these facts—and the apparent interest of the international community in promoting negotiations nonetheless—understanding why some belligerents come to the bargaining table while others remain on the battlefield has been of central importance.

Researchers have pointed to two broad categories of explanations. On one view, the qualities of the belligerents themselves may work against compromise. Ethnic groups may feel that a particular piece of real estate is historically theirs and that allowing it to be controlled by an alien group would be tantamount to national betrayal.[4] Committed leaders may sense that they have little choice but to push forward with the fight, lest they fall victim to even more radical comrades in their own camp.[5] If groups feel that they can get more by fighting than by negotiating—if they have not reached a "hurting stalemate," in William Zartman's well-known phrase—they are unlikely to seek peace.[6]

A second view stresses the structural environment in which decision making takes place. Using insights from neorealist theory, some writers have argued that, in the absence of institutions to ensure credible commitment, even the most well-intentioned leaders would be irrational to seek a negotiated settlement.[7] Given the host of factors that seem to work against negotiations, other observers have held that seeking peace only after one side has won or accepting the physical separation of warring ethnic groups may be the only truly stable solutions to large-scale communal violence.[8]

In all of these debates, however, the benefits of war have been largely neglected. As David Keen has observed, a major breakthrough in medicine was the realization that what might be very bad for the organism could be very good for the germ that attacked it; the same can be said for civil wars.[9] There is a political economy to warfare that produces positive externalities for its perpetrators. Seemingly perpetual violence in Sierra Leone, Myanmar, Liberia, and elsewhere has less to do with anarchy—of either the social or the institutional kind—than with the rational calculations of elites about the use of violence as a tool for extracting and redistributing resources. Diamonds in Angola, timber in Cambodia, and coca in Colombia have all become spoils of war that both fuel conflict and discourage settlement. Conflicts, in this sense, may not burn themselves out precisely because it is in the interests of their makers, on all sides, to stoke them. Although these arguments have been central to the study of conflicts in the developing world for some time, they have only recently begun to filter into the study of regional and interethnic violence in other areas.[10]

Even after one camp has secured a partial or complete victory in the military contest, the basic networks, relationships, and informal channels that arose during the course of the violence can replicate themselves in new, state-like institutions in the former conflict zones. Belligerents are often able to craft a sophisticated array of formal institutions that function as effective quasi states, from the "Somaliland republic" in Somalia to the demilitarized zone in south-central Colombia. Through these institutions, however, politics in peacetime becomes little more than an extension of war. The instruments of violence, sublimated into the institutions of unrecognized regimes, can in the long run keep existing states weak, populations poor, and full-scale war a constant possibility, even as they enrich the key players who extol the virtues of peace.

Such has been the case in the Eurasian conflicts of the 1990s. Yet there is also an intriguing twist. Erstwhile secessionists have become relatively successful state builders, but they have also sometimes done so with the collusion of central governments, external actors, and international negotiators ostensibly committed to re-creating a stable, reintegrated country.

The Wars of the Soviet Succession

The end of Soviet communism was a relatively peaceful affair. Notwithstanding the range of social grievances and disputed boundaries across the region, few of the potential rivalries actually produced open war. But in at least four instances, interethnic disputes, external interests, and elite rivalries interacted to create wars that led to serious loss of life and hundreds of thousands of refugees and internally displaced persons (IDPs). In all four cases, secessionists actually won the armed conflicts, producing recognized states of variable functionality and unrecognized ones whose ability to govern themselves is surprisingly strong.

The dispute over Nagorno-Karabakh was not the first instance of open interethnic rivalry within Mikhail Gorbachev's Soviet Union, but it was the first that directly involved the interests of two Soviet republics, Armenia and Azerbaijan. Although included within the administrative boundaries of the Azerbaijan Soviet republic since the 1920s, Nagorno-Karabakh was populated in the main by ethnic Armenians, around 80 percent by 1989. The region had enjoyed autonomous status since the very beginning of the Soviet Union, but Karabakh Armenians complained of cultural discrimination and economic underdevelopment.[11] Increasing openness under Gorbachev allowed these issues to come to the fore. In 1988, Karabakh leaders called for the region's transfer to Armenian jurisdiction. Swift reprisals followed, including an organized pogrom against Armenians in the city of Sumgait in Azerbaijan. Both sides fostered long-held grievances. Repeated attacks on ethnic Armenian communities were reminiscent of the Ottoman-era genocide, especially given the massive outflow of refugees, more than 180,000 by mid-1989.[12] From the Azerbaijani perspective, Armenians were attempting to destroy the Azerbaijani national movement by undermining the republic's territorial unity.

In 1989, the Armenian Supreme Soviet and the Karabakh local council adopted a joint resolution declaring the unification of Armenia and Karabakh. Local paramilitary groups began to form, with substantial assistance in men and matériel from Armenia. The Azerbaijanis responded by forcibly evacuating villages along the Armenian-Karabakh border and imposing a road and rail blockade on the province and eventually on Armenia as well. Hostilities escalated after the collapse of the Soviet Union. Local Armenians in the regional capital, Stepanakert, organized a referendum on independence and declared the creation of a fully separate Republic of Nagorno-Karabakh. A major offensive in 1993 created an Armenian-controlled buffer zone of "liberated" territory around Karabakh. After several unsuccessful mediation attempts throughout the 1990s, in May 1994, the Russian Federation finally managed to secure a cease-fire, which has since remained in place, although with repeated violations. As of 2009, little real progress has been made on deciding Karabakh's final status.

The dispute between Armenians and Azeris might be cast, simplistically, as a reprise of struggles between Armenians and Turks left over from the early twentieth century. But across the Black Sea, in Moldova, no one would have predicted major violence in the 1980s. Rates of intermarriage among all ethnic groups were high, there were no religious lines separating ethnic minorities from the Romanian-speaking majority, and there had been no history of widespread communal violence. Nevertheless, Moldova became embroiled in a small war in the eastern part of the country, the thin Transnistria region east of the Dnestr River on the border with Ukraine.

Transnistrians were not a distinct ethnic population; in fact, ethnic Moldovans/Romanians were the largest single group in the region. However, the importance of the zone in Soviet steel production and the military sector meant that Transnistria's inhabitants were fundamentally linked—in terms of both livelihood and social identity—to Soviet institutions such as the Communist party, strategic industries, and the military.[13] The Moldovan national movement of the late 1980s thus hit Transnistrians particularly hard. Prodemocracy groups saw perestroika as an opportunity to reassert the voice of the republic's ethnic Moldovan/Romanian majority after decades of Russian cultural domination. In 1989, the republican Supreme Soviet adopted a series of language laws that made Moldovan/Romanian the state language and mandated the use of the Latin alphabet rather than the Cyrillic.

Industrial managers and military personnel in Transnistria reacted sharply, taking control of governmental and security structures in the districts east of the Dnestr River and in the Russian-majority city of Bender on the west bank. In autumn 1990, Transnistrian leaders declared a separate republic within the

Soviet Union and later opted for full independence when Moldova itself exited the Soviet federation. War accompanied these competing declarations. In 1992, a Moldovan government offensive against Bender sparked the first major intervention by the Russian Fourteenth Army, stationed in Transnistria, on the side of the secessionists. With the superior firepower of the Russian troops, the Moldovans were driven out of the city. The uneasy balance of power after the battle produced a formal cease-fire agreement and the deployment of a tripartite Russian-Moldovan-Transnistrian peacekeeping force. Despite numerous rounds of talks, sponsored by the OSCE and regional neighbors, the final status of Transnistria has not yet been agreed.

On the surface, the relationship between Georgians and Abkhaz had little in common with that between Moldovans and Transnistrians. The Abkhaz are a distinct ethnic population, speaking a language unrelated to Georgian. During the Soviet period, the Abkhaz were given their own autonomous republic, within which they enjoyed a privileged position in the party and state hierarchy, even though they were less than a fifth of the population there. However, the pattern of events in the late 1980s paralleled those in Moldova. A revitalized Georgian national movement emerged in the waning days of Soviet power, eventually leading to a referendum on independence and Georgia's exit from the Soviet Union.

Abkhaz reacted by demanding greater local autonomy and a say in the politics of independent Georgia. Clashes erupted between the Abkhaz and the local Georgian majority. In early 1992, a new Georgian president, Eduard Shevardnadze, backtracked on the negotiations that had been ongoing with the Abkhaz leadership, and full-scale war followed. Georgian troops, marching into Abkhazia in an effort to eject the regional government, succeeded in capturing and holding the regional capital, Sukhumi. But by the end of 1993, Abkhaz militias, assisted by Russian forces and irregular combatants from north of the Caucasus Mountains, had sent Georgian troops scrambling toward the Inguri River, the geographical divider between Georgia proper and Abkhazia. An agreement in May 1994, brokered by Moscow, provided for the deployment of a peacekeeping mission under the aegis of the CIS (although in practice wholly Russian). Negotiations on Abkhazia's final status, brokered by the United Nations, have continued off and on since then. However, the tensions created by the Russia-Georgia war of August 2008 (see the epilogue to this chapter) virtually halted serious talks between Abkhaz and Georgian officials.

Unlike the Abkhaz, the Ossetians were not historically concentrated in Georgia, in the area of present South Ossetia; their cultural center was across the border in North Ossetia, now part of the Russian Federation. By 1989, however, two thirds of South Ossetia's population was ethnic Ossetian. Despite a history of strong intercultural ties between Georgians and Ossetians, the political climate of the late 1980s encouraged cascading demands for local autonomy and independence. In 1988 and 1989, the Georgian government took measures to strengthen the use of the Georgian language in public institutions and rejected calls by regional leaders to upgrade South Ossetia's status from autonomous region to autonomous republic. As in Transnistria, Ossetian leaders argued that language reforms would unfairly disadvantage them. In 1990, the South Ossetian regional administration announced the creation of a separate South Ossetian republic within the Soviet Union and organized elections for a separate South Ossetian parliament. In response, the Georgian parliament revoked South Ossetia's existing autonomous status. The Georgian state ordered troops to the region, but their entry met with fierce resistance from Ossetian irregulars, aided by supporters from North Ossetia and other parts of the Russian Federation. In July 1992, a cease-fire agreement provided for the cessation of hostilities. Final-status talks, sponsored by the OSCE, continued throughout the 1990s, but the rise of hostilities in the early 2000s—culminating in the August 2008 war, the Russian intervention, and Moscow's recognition of the independence of South Ossetia and Abkhazia—doomed hopes for a negotiated settlement. (See Table 6.1.)

The Politics of Surreptitious State Building

Today, the political elites that made these wars, both in the national capitals and in the secessionist regions, have undergone wholesale change. Presidents have been pushed out of office, via elections or death. Military commanders have retired or made lucrative careers as business leaders. Old nationalist poets have put down their pens. However, the narratives concerning the origins and evolution of the Eurasian disputes have outlived their creators. Throughout the region, elites and average citizens continue to refer to the events of the late perestroika period as explanations for why the violence erupted and why a stable settlement has been so elusive. Karabakh leaders talk of the revocation of their local autonomy and the massacre of ethnic Armenians in Sumgait. Transnistrians speak of the threat of cultural Romanianization and the unwelcome possibility of Moldovan unification with Romania. Ossetians and Abkhaz cite Georgia's oppressive cultural policies and the removal or weakening of the autonomy that both regions had during the Soviet years.

These putative root causes, however, are slippery explanations for the absence of a final settlement. Cease-fires, by and large, have held, at least up to

TABLE 6.1. Eurasia's Recognized and de Facto States

	Capital	Independence and Recognition	Population	Ethnic Composition	Territory	Armed Forces
Azerbaijan	Baku	Declared Oct. 18, 1991. Joined UN Mar. 9, 1992	8,480,000	Azerbaijanis 90% Dagestani ethnic groups 3% Russians 3% Armenians 2%	86,600 km^2	66,740
Republic of Nagorno-Karabakh (also known as *Azat Artsakh* in Armenian)	Stepanakert	Declared Sept. 2, 1991	Est. 150,000	Armenians 95% Kurds, Greeks, Assyrians 5%	4,400 km^2	15,000–20,000 (incl. 8,000 from Armenia)
Georgia	Tbilisi	Declared Apr. 9, 1991. Joined UN July 31, 1992.	4,430,000	Georgians 70% Armenians 8% Russians 6% Azeris 6% Ossetians 3% Abkhaz 2%	69,700 km^2	21,150
Republic of Abkhazia (also known as *Apsny* in Abkhaz)	Sukhumi	Declared Aug. 25, 1990. Recognized by Russia and Nicaragua as of Sept. 2008.	Est. 150,000	Mainly Abkhaz, but compact Armenian population in north and Georgians (Mingrelians) in south.	7,867 km^2	1,500

(continued)

TABLE 6.I. (continued)

	Capital	Independence and Recognition	Population	Ethnic Composition	Territory	Armed Forces
Republic of South Ossetia (also known as *Iryston* in Ossetian)	Tskhinvali	Declared Sept. 20, 1990. Recognized by North Ossetia (itself not a sovereign state) in 1993. Recognized by Russia and Nicaragua as of Sept. 2008.	Est. 70,000	Mainly Ossetians, but some Russians and Georgians.	2,732 km^2, minus a few villages still under central government control.	Unknown
Moldova	Chisinau	Declared Aug. 27, 1991. Joined UN Mar. 2, 1992.	3,830,000	Moldovans 65% Ukrainians 14% Russians 13% Gagauz 4%	33,700 km^2	6,750
Dnestr Moldovan Republic (also known as *Pridnestrov'e* in Russian and *Transnistria* in Romanian)	Tiraspol	Declared Sept. 2, 1990.	Est. 670,000	Moldovans 33% Russians 29% Ukrainians 29%	4,163 km^2	7,500

Notes: Figures for the unrecognized states are, at best, imperfect estimates, but they are as close as one can come, given the available evidence. Most unrecognized states declared sovereignty first within the context of the Soviet Union and then declared full independence; the first date is the one usually celebrated as the national holiday. Territory and population figures for recognized states also include the unrecognized republics. Military figures, as of 2008, do not include reserves, which can quintuple the number of men under arms.

Sources: *The Military Balance, 2000–2001* (London: International Institute for Strategic Studies, 2000); *The Military Balance, 2008* (London: International Institute for Strategic Studies, 2008); K. G. Dzugaev, ed., *Iuzhnaia Osetiia: 10 let respublike* (Vladikavkaz: Iryston, 2000); *Sakartvelo/Georgia* (Tbilisi: Military Cartographic Factory, 1997); *Atlas of the Dniester Moldavian Republic* (Tiraspol: Dnestr State Cooperative University, 1997); www.worldbank.org; author's interviews.

August 2008. Negotiations have continued under the aegis of the UN and the OSCE, with the support of the United States and the Russian Federation. Governments have, to varying degrees, changed their constitutions, citizenship laws, educational statutes, and local administrative structures to guarantee civil rights and some degree of local autonomy for ethnic minorities. These steps allowed all three recognized states—Azerbaijan, Moldova, and Georgia—to join the Council of Europe, the human-rights body that has become something of a waiting room for eventual applicants to the EU.

The real brake on a final settlement has been the fact that, beneath the rhetoric of unresolved grievances and international negotiations, political elites have gone about the process of building functional states. These unrecognized entities, moreover, are buttressed by independent militaries: 15,000 to 20,000 men in Karabakh, 7,500 in Transnistria, 1,500 or more in Abkhazia, and an uncertain number in South Ossetia, all with substantial supplies of armor and equipment.[14] Interest groups outside the conflict zones—that is, inside the rec-ognized states proper—have learned to live with the effective division of their countries and have even found ways to profit from a chronically weak state. The economic benefits of state weakness, the support of key external actors, the legitimization of statehood through cultural and educational policies, the com-plicity of central governments, and in some instances, the unwitting assistance of international negotiators are some of the mechanisms of this surreptitious state building.

The Political Economy of Weak States

By any measure, Azerbaijan, Georgia, and Moldova are exceptionally weak states. Per capita national income in 2006 was under $2,000 in all three countries. In the first two, public revenues (including foreign grants) account for 20 percent or less of GDP, a figure too low to support some of the most basic state functions.[15] Significant portions of each country's territory, popula-tion, and wealth-producing potential—the secessionist regions—remain wholly outside central government control. Karabakh and the occupied buffer areas are around 20 percent of Azerbaijan's territory; Abkhazia and South Ossetia together are 17 percent of Georgia's; Transnistria is 12 percent of Moldova's. Even outside the secessionist republics, there are many parts of the country where the central government's power is virtually nil, areas where banditry is common, local notables run their own affairs, and the institutions of the central state are conspicuous by their absence. The lives of average Azerbaijanis, Georgians, and Moldovans rarely intersect with the state, and where they do, it is often in the form of a policeman demanding payment for an imagined traffic offense. Indeed, massive emigration abroad and domestic immigration to the national capitals have made all three countries appear, in demographic terms, something close to city-states, with the cities of Baku, Tbilisi, and Chisinau sitting like islands in countries virtually bereft of people and economic activity.

State weakness is of obvious benefit to the unrecognized regimes.[16] Business can be carried on with neighboring states without paying production taxes or tariffs. Luxury goods, especially cigarettes and alcohol, can be brought in for resale or export. The republics differ, though, in terms of their relative economic success. The lowest on the development scale is probably Karabakh. Situated in a mountainous area where most roads are barely passable, and with little indigenous industry and a collapsed agricultural system, Karabakh is a largely poverty-stricken region. Its total population, estimated at 150,000, survives mainly on the basis of subsistence farming or resale of goods imported from Iran and Armenia. Important urban centers, such as the city of Shushi, have yet to rebuild apartment buildings and offices gutted during the war. Although demining of fields and villages has progressed since the cease-fire, with the assistance of international relief agencies, agricultural production has remained stunted by the fear of unexploded ordnance. Nevertheless, local authorities have been able to construct something resembling a state, with its own foreign ministry (which charges visitors a nominal fee for visas), armed forces, police, and court system. Even in Karabakh's dire straits, citizens have been able to find economic potential. The export of wood to Armenia and farther afield has become a booming enterprise, but it has also caused serious worries about deforestation and the long-term effects on Karabakh's eroding agricultural land, a situation that also obtains in Abkhazia.

Abkhazia and South Ossetia are only marginally better off than Karabakh. During the Soviet period, both were reasonably important regions. Abkhazia supported a booming tourist trade along its Black Sea coast, as well as a substantial hazelnut industry. In South Ossetia, lead and zinc mines and factories producing enamel fittings, wood products, and beer and fruit juices were important parts of the Georgian economy. Now, however, few of these enterprises function, since the outflow of refugees and IDPs more than halved the populations of both regions, which stand at perhaps 150,000 in Abkhazia and up to 70,000 in South Ossetia.

Local inhabitants have turned to other pursuits. In Abkhazia, tangerines and hazelnuts remain an important source of revenue, particularly since there are no taxes to pay to the central Georgian government; local gang activity, in fact, tends to be seasonal, centered around attempts by bandits to steal hazelnut shipments in the late summer and early autumn. Trade in scrap metal, both from dysfunctional industries and from power lines, is also important. South Ossetia has little in the way of functioning industry or export-oriented agriculture, but the region's geographical position has been its chief asset. Until its shutdown by the Georgian government in 2004, South Ossetian highway police maintained a customs checkpoint just outside the entrance to the regional capital, Tskhinvali, to monitor the vigorous trade along the highway to Vladikavkaz, the capital of the Russian republic of North Ossetia. The police, however, were more facilitators of this commerce than its invigilators. A massive market in petrol and wheat flour flourished along the roadside, with hundreds of trucks laden with goods from the Russian Federation.[17] Controlling this trade (which has reproduced itself in other locales since 2004), the road link to Vladikavkaz, and especially the passage through the mountain tunnel linking North and South Ossetia has provided a major source of revenue for the South Ossetian administration. In 2000, OSCE officials estimate that some $60–70 million in goods passed through the tunnel each year, compared with an official South Ossetian budget of roughly $1 million.[18] In both Abkhazia and South Ossetia, drugs, especially heroin, have also reportedly joined the list of transit goods.[19]

Of all four unrecognized republics, Transnistria's economic position is probably the best. During the Soviet period, Transnistria was the mainstay of Moldovan industry; while areas west of the Dnestr River were largely agricultural, most heavy machine industries and power-generating plants were located to the east. Many still operate on the basis of barter trade, but some have managed to secure contracts with firms abroad. The Rîbniţa mill, in northern Transnistria, was one of the Soviet Union's most important producers of high-quality rolled steel, especially for munitions. Originally built in 1984 using German technology, the plant remains one of the best in the former Soviet Union, and firms from western Europe continue to sign contracts with the plant—so many, in fact, that by the late 1990s, the firm was already employing a bevy of translators to process foreign orders.[20] It is indicative of Transnistria's international links that the "Dnestr Moldovan Republic ruble," introduced as the region's official currency in 1994, was printed in Germany. In addition to steel, small arms—an important local industry during the Soviet period—are also manufactured, and Transnistria's president, Igor Smirnov, once hailed their export as a sign of his republic's importance on the world stage and its links with other embattled peoples in Kosovo, Chechnya, Abkhazia, and elsewhere.[21] Given the dire state of Moldova's own economy, Transnistria looks rather better in some areas. Throughout the 1990s, average household income was higher, and in every major field except consumer goods, the secessionist region was a net "exporter" to the rest of

Moldova, delivering more construction materials, chemicals, ferrous metals, and electrical energy than it receives.[22]

Russia, Diaspora Politics, and Inter-"State" Cooperation

From the earliest days, these conflicts were never simple confrontations between an embattled ethnic minority and a nationalizing central government. The relationships involved were even more complex than Rogers Brubaker's "triadic nexus"—ethnic minority, central government, external homeland—would suggest.[23] Indeed, many interested players have been crucial in assisting the secessionist republics not only in winning the wars but also in consolidating statehood afterward.

By far the most significant has been the Russian Federation. The Russian official history of the post-Soviet wars argues for Moscow's pacifying role in each of the conflicts.[24] It is clear, though, that Russian assistance was a crucial component in the early stages of state building. Whether prompted by the whim of brigade commanders or by a policy directive from Moscow, Soviet armed forces, later to become Russian Federation troops, were the main supplier of weaponry (and often soldiers) to secessionist groups. Throughout 1991 and 1992, the Moldovans issued numerous notes to the Soviet and Russian governments protesting the involvement of the Fourteenth Army on the side of the Transnistrians.[25] In December 1991, the army's commander left his post to become head of the Dnestr Guards, the newly created army of the Dnestr Moldovan republic; he was followed by his former chief of staff, who became the republic's defense minister.[26] Azerbaijan was able to secure the complete withdrawal of Russian troops from its territory by mid-1993, but the forces that remained in Armenia—the Russian Seventh Army—are known to have aided both Armenian government troops and Karabakh irregulars during the war. Russian newspapers published the names of soldiers who participated in the fighting, and in 1992, the Russian defense ministry promoted the commanders of both the Fourteenth and Seventh armies for their leadership in the Transnistrian and Karabakh campaigns.[27] Leakage of weapons and soldiers from the Russian 345th Airborne Regiment, based in Abkhazia, as well as the influx of freelance fighters from Russia's north Caucasus, contributed to the Abkhaz defeat of Georgian forces.[28]

Russian foreign and security policy since the wars has been complex in each of these cases, but it has centered around three main elements, all of which have turned out to be crucial resources for the unrecognized republics. First, Russian economic support has been essential. The Russian gas monopoly Gazprom, while pressuring Azerbaijan, Moldova, and Georgia to pay their massive energy debts, has continued to supply subsidized gas to the secession-ist areas. Russian officials have even staffed positions within key economic institutions. Until late 1996, the head of the Transnistrian central bank was reportedly a member of the Russian intelligence service; even after that, bank officials continued to receive training in Moscow and St. Petersburg.[29]

Second, negotiations with Moldova and Georgia regarding the withdrawal of Russian troops have been linked with the resolution of the secessionist dis-putes. In 1999, both Moldova and Georgia managed to secure Russian agree-ment to an eventual full-scale withdrawal, but in both cases, the devil has been in the details. The Moldovan government, under both Russian and OSCE pres-sure, signed an agreement in 1994 mandating that the withdrawal of the Fourteenth Army be "synchronized" with the final status of Transnistria. That agreement has effectively blocked real progress in withdrawal negotiations, since it is unclear whether withdrawal should precede resolution or vice versa. Russian troop strength is much lower now than in the past—by 2008, about 1,200 men organized as an "operational group" rather than an "army"—but the military presence continues to be a boon to the Transnistrians, providing civilian and military employment for local citizens and a sense of security for the unrecognized regime.[30]

In Georgia, the Russian military began downsizing in 2000. However, much of the matériel was moved to Armenia, with which Russia has a long-term basing agreement; that, in turn, raised Azerbaijani fears that some of the equipment would eventually find its way into both Armenian and Karabakh hands. The Russian military base in Abkhazia serves much the same function as the troop presence in Transnistria, providing employment and security for an effectively separate regime. The Russian and Georgian governments suc-cessfully concluded negotiations regarding the transformation of the base into a convalescence station for Russian peacekeepers, but that change of label did not substantially alter the strong role that the facility plays in Abkhaz political and economic life.[31] In both Moldova and Georgia, even the salaries of Russian soldiers and peacekeepers, paid in rubles, have ensured that Transnistria, Abkhazia, and South Ossetia remain economically tied to Russia rather than to their recognized central governments, because local goods and services are purchased using rubles rather than national currencies.[32] For these reasons, both the Transnistrians and the Abkhaz have insisted that the bases remain in place or, if they are closed, that the Russian military equipment be transferred to Transnistrian and Abkhaz control.[33]

Third, Russian citizenship and visa policy has encouraged the secession-ist regions to see themselves as effectively independent states. Azerbaijan, Moldova, and Georgia have all been wary of allowing dual citizenship for fear that inhabitants of the unrecognized republics would secure foreign citizenship and therefore become further disconnected from the center.[34] Plenty have taken Russian citizenship nevertheless. According to the Transnistrian administration, by 2000 as many as 65,000 people (about 10 percent of the population) had taken Russian citizenship; less than a decade later, it was widely believed that the vast majority of Transnistrians were actually Russian passport holders.[35] Abkhaz and South Ossetians have done likewise, especially since much of their livelihood depends on their ability to travel easily to the Russian Federation.[36] The citizenship option is another reason that contract work in Russian Federation forces in Abkhazia and Transnistria has been an attractive option for many locals, since it often leads to a passport and citizenship. Even for those who are not citizens, changes in Russian visa policy have also widened the gap between the secessionist zones and the central governments. Under a previous visa regime, citizens of former Soviet republics could travel visa-free to Russia. But as part of a move to tighten border security in the wake of the Chechen wars, Russia announced that it would pull out of the agreement and begin requiring visas for citizens of particular post-Soviet states. From late 2000, regular Russian visas were required of citizens of Georgia—but not inhabitants of South Ossetia and Abkhazia. Since then, Russia has increasingly behaved as if the two districts were informal parts of the Russian Federation itself, such as by opening polling stations there during Russian national elections without the consent of Georgian authorities.

While overwhelmingly significant, Russia is not the only external dimension to state building. Diaspora politics has also played a role. Armenia and the Armenian diaspora have been the sine qua non of Karabakh's existence. For all practical purposes, Karabakh is now more an autonomous district of Armenia than a part of Azerbaijan. The Armenian *dram*, not the Azerbaijani *manat*, is legal tender. Substantial numbers of Karabakh inhabitants enjoy Armenian citizenship and travel abroad with Armenian passports; some have even risen to political office in Armenia—including Robert Kocharian, who has the distinction of having been president of both Karabakh and Armenia. The highway connecting the Armenian city of Goris to Stepanakert, the so-called Lachin corridor carved out during the war, may now be the finest road in the entire south Caucasus. Built to European standards, it was financed in part by Armenians abroad, which accounts for the bizarre sign outside Stepanakert, in Spanish, acknowledging contributions from Argentina in its construction. Military convoys regularly journey back and forth along the highway, taking fuel to Karabakh and returning with timber to Armenia, and there is nothing more than a small police checkpoint at the putative international frontier. Foreign investment from abroad, usually from Armenian communities, has picked up. Already in

2000, Swiss-Armenian businesspeople invested some $900,000 in a watch-manufacturing facility; others have spent $2 million to renovate Stepanakert's central Hotel Karabakh; still other investors have pledged some $17 million to build tourist facilities near Karabakh's striking medieval monasteries.[37]

The four unrecognized states also act in the international arena as if they were independent entities and, to a great degree, cooperate with one another. They have officially recognized one another's existence. The four presidents exchange visits during each republic's national day celebrations. Official delegations sign trade agreements, and firms execute import and export deals. Security services share information on possible threats. For example, in autumn 2000, a delegation of leaders of Moldovan nongovernmental organizations arrived in Georgia for a brief tour. The Moldovans asked, via the local OSCE office, if they could arrange a trip to South Ossetia as part of their program. After approaching the South Ossetian leadership, the OSCE came back with a categorically negative response. As it turned out, the deputy speaker of the Transnistrian parliament had been in South Ossetia only weeks earlier, to attend the celebrations surrounding the tenth anniversary of South Ossetian independence, and he had strongly advised the Ossetian interior and foreign ministries against approving the Moldovan visit.[38] Networks such as these were formalized in November 2000, when the four republics' foreign ministers held an official conference in the Transnistrian capital, Tiraspol, and pledged to coordinate their bargaining positions in talks with the three central governments. In 2006, they formed a new international body, dubbed the Community for Democracy and Human Rights, to coordinate their policy positions and represent a counterweight to the GUAM Organization for Democracy and Economic Development, a forum founded in 2001 to link Georgia, Ukraine, Azerbaijan, and Moldova.

Making Denizens into Citizens

From early in all four conflicts, local authorities moved to take over educational and cultural institutions within the conflict zones. Polytechnics were upgraded to universities. New "academies of science" were established. New national festivals were inaugurated. History curricula were redesigned to highlight the citizens of the secessionist regions as the indigenous inhabitants of their territory and to strengthen the connection between earlier forms of statehood and the current, unrecognized states. For example, the new ministry of information of the South Ossetian republic began to reproduce works of nineteenth-century travelers who described the customs of the Ossetians, in order "to bring to the masses the most interesting pages in the history of Ossetia and the Ossetians."[39] The Ossetians located the origins of their modern statehood in ancient Iryston, the lands of settlement of the Iranian-speaking Alans; they were thus considered, as a new Ossetian encyclopedia argued, the true "autochthonous population" in their republic.[40]

Local intellectuals also worked, as far as possible, to discover cultural or historical heroes around which semiofficial cults could be built. In Transnistria, Alexander Suvorov, the eighteenth-century field marshal who conquered Transnistria for the Russian Empire, became a symbol of the Dnestr Moldovan Republic, his visage appearing on the newly minted Transnistrian ruble. In South Ossetia, the statue of Kosta Khetagurov, a nineteenth-century poet, became one of the focal points of the annual republic day in September. Previous instances of statehood, no matter how tenuous, were marshaled to serve the cause. Armenians in Karabakh pointed to their own briefly independent republic, which existed before Karabakh's absorption into Soviet Azerbaijan in the 1920s. Abkhaz writers lauded their 1925 constitution, which established an autonomous regime. Transnistrians identified the Moldovan Autonomous Soviet Socialist Republic, which existed inside Soviet Ukraine between the two world wars, as the basis of their modern statehood.

The armed conflicts themselves also became sanctified as a struggle against external aggression. Children who were not even born when the conflicts began are now, in 2009, young adults, schooled in the view that the republics they inhabit not only represent ancient nations but also have been forged in the crucible of war and sacrifice. A Transnistrian textbook characterized the decisive battle of Bender in 1992 in unmistakably patriotic terms:

> The traitorous, barbaric, and unprovoked invasion of Bender had a
> single goal: to frighten and bring to their knees the inhabitants of the
> Dnestr republic. . . . However, the people's bravery, steadfastness, and
> love of liberty saved the Dnestr republic. The defense of Bender
> against the overwhelming forces of the enemy closed a heroic page in
> the history of our young republic. The best sons and daughters of the
> people sacrificed their lives for peace and liberty in our land.[41]

As strange as they may sound, such arguments are little different from the equally tendentious views often used to justify the existence of Azerbaijan, Moldova, Georgia, and other new Eurasian states.

As in these instances, there were rational reasons for the narrative strategies that intellectuals and academics pursued. In Karabakh, the opportunity for greater connections with educational and research institutions in Armenia was at the center of the early movement for transferring the region to Armenian jurisdiction. Many Karabakh writers and educators eventually moved to Russia or Armenia, but others found themselves catapulted into new jobs as professors and administrators of the new Artsakh State University in Stepanakert. In Moldova, the effective purge of Soviet-era scholars in the late 1980s created a class of disgruntled researchers and writers who looked on the Transnistrian cause as their own. Although not native to the region, some moved to Transnistria, where they could continue to thrive by writing the same Soviet-style versions of history and socialist internationalism that had made their careers— and become the shapers of Transnistrian national identity in the process.[42] In South Ossetia, professors at the local polytechnic found that increasing ties with institutions in Vladikavkaz, Moscow, and St. Petersburg was more appealing than continued existence as a backwater in an increasingly "Georgianized" educational system. While the new ideologies of nationalism and statehood usually did violence to historical fact, most grew as much from the professional backgrounds and interests of their makers as from a romantic commitment to nationalist ideals.

The Complicity of Central Governments

Central authorities frequently point to the modalities of state building just outlined, complaining that the secessionists and their external supporters are indeed constructing states that have come to depend less and less on the recognized governments. But that is only part of the story. In Georgia and Moldova, central policy elites have also played a role in prolonging the disputes. The benefits of state weakness accrue not only to the secessionists but also to the institutions and individuals who are ostensibly responsible for remedying it. Both countries are arguably among the most corrupt in the former Soviet Union, indeed, the most corrupt in the world.[43] The links between corrupt central governments and the secessionist regions have further imperiled already weak state structures while enriching those who claim to be looking after the states' interests.

In South Ossetia, the illegal trade with Russia benefits all sides. The South Ossetian government receives money from resale and haphazardly applied "transit taxes," while Georgian authorities, especially the interior ministry, are able to take a cut by exacting fines from truck drivers on the outskirts of Tbilisi. The expansion of international humanitarian aid to the region has also provided another cover under which goods can be traded; organizations are set up in Tbilisi to receive assistance destined for South Ossetia, and the goods are then sold in local markets.[44] It is partly for these reasons that relations between Tskhinvali and Tbilisi were—at least until the rise to power of a new presidential administration in Georgia in 2004—generally cordial, notwithstanding the lack of a final settlement. The South Ossetian president, in fact, openly supported Eduard Shevardnadze in his campaign for Georgian president in early 2000.[45]

In Abkhazia, similar formulas apply. Police officials in Zugdidi and Tsalenjikha, the two districts on the Georgian side of the border with Abkhazia, carry out periodic crackdowns on illegal transborder commerce, but local observers are convinced that these efforts are designed less to enforce the law than to root out small-time smugglers who might disrupt the police monopoly on transborder trade.[46] None of this is lost on local Georgians, who express deep skepticism about their own state institutions: In 2000, some two thirds reported having no faith in parliament or the president, and some 80 percent had no faith in tax and customs officials.[47] Although those figures diminished over succeeding years with the ouster of the Shevardnadze administration, connections between secessionists and corrupt local institutions remained in place.

These connections are even easier to document in Transnistria. In accords signed in 1996 and 1997, the Moldovan government, encouraged by the OSCE, agreed to establish joint customs posts with the Transnistrian administration, providing official customs stamps and export licenses to the secessionists. Transnistria was also given the right to import and export goods, directly or via other parts of Moldova, without paying duties at the point where the goods entered Moldovan-controlled territory. The agreement was intended as a measure to build confidence between the two sides, but in practice, it represented little more than a conduit for illegal commerce under the cover of law. The scale of this trade is easily traceable, since customs duties are duly registered with the Moldovan central government, even if the money never makes it into state coffers. For example, in 1998 Moldova imported around $125 million in goods subject to import taxes. At the same time, another $500 million was registered with Moldovan customs officials as entering the country for transit on to Transnistria.[48]

The figures are as instructive as they are incredible: A piece of territory that holds around 17 percent of Moldova's total population imported four times as much merchandise as the country as a whole, including around 6,000 times as many cigarettes—all with the full knowledge of the central tax inspector's office. Although some of the imports no doubt do reach Transnistria, the majority found their way onto the Moldovan market. The country's senior presidential advisor on Transnistria, Oazu Nantoi, resigned in protest when he discovered these figures, and later he put together a series of broadcasts on public television that brought this illegal trade to light. But in late 2000, the director of Moldovan National Television ordered the broadcasts stopped, reportedly on the order of senior government officials.[49] Throughout these conflict zones, the weak state is not a condition that has somehow simply happened. Continued weakness is in the interests of those in power, whether in the secessionist regions or in central governments.[50]

Even in less unpalatable ways, there have been powerful disincentives for central governments to change the status quo. Even politicians who may be committed, in good faith, to resolving the dispute must deal with radical domestic forces pushing in the opposite direction. In Georgia, the Apkhazeti faction in parliament, the remnants of the former Georgian administration in Abkhazia that fled to Tbilisi during the war, proved to be a brake on genuine compromise. The Apkhazeti, who enjoyed set-aside seats in parliament before 2004, functioned as a regional government-in-exile; although they did not control enough parliamentary votes to challenge the strong government majority, they were vocal opponents of any move that might seem to compromise their own interests in returning to power in Abkhazia.[51] For example, they blocked legislation to provide resettlement and integration of the 250,000 people displaced during the Abkhaz war, people who spent much of the 1990s living in "temporary" accommodations in run-down hotels and resorts. Resettling the IDPs in Georgia proper, the faction leaders feared, would reduce their own political and economic power since they controlled state budgetary disbursements to the IDPs and the provision of social services. The Apkhazeti group, in turn, proved a useful foil for the most independence-minded Abkhaz. The failure of negotiation could always be blamed on the militaristic language of the Apkhazeti and on their supporters on the ground, the ethnic Georgian guerrilla movements that harass Abkhaz troops. The Abkhaz, the Apkhazeti, and the Georgian government—although radically distinct groups—had a common interest in blocking real change. Similar situations have existed in Moldova (where pro-Romanian intellectuals have opposed concessions on Transnistria) and Armenia (where militants assassinated the prime minister in 1999 when he seemed to be moving toward a compromise with Azerbaijan).

International Intervention as a Resource

In each of these conflicts, international involvement has been frequent, if not frequently successful. In Azerbaijan, the OSCE-sponsored Minsk Group has provided good offices and a mechanism for negotiations since 1992. In Moldova, an OSCE mission that has been active since 1993 has sponsored numerous rounds of negotiations. In Georgia, a United Nations observer mission was deployed in 1993 to provide a basis for negotiations on Abkhazia's future and to monitor the peacekeeping operation conducted by the CIS forces in the Georgian-Abkhaz security zone. In South Ossetia, Russian peacekeepers have been in place since the end of the war, and negotiations on South Ossetia's final status have continued apace, involving Russia, North Ossetia, and the OSCE as mediators.

Despite this active engagement, little of significance has been achieved, even despite political change in each of the recognized states. In Moldova, the quasi nationalists of the early 1990s have been replaced by the world's first elected Communist government. In Azerbaijan, political transition involved the handover of power from the president to his son, who has focused on building Azerbaijan's oil and gas wealth. In Georgia, a bloodless coup led to the ouster of Shevardnadze and the ascent of the young Mikhail Saakashvili as the new president. Still, there are three broad reasons for the lack of real progress. First, in all cases, the incumbent governments have argued from positions of weakness. They were the military losers in the conflicts and therefore have little to offer the secessionist regimes. That basic dynamic is compounded by the parlous state of their own economies—at least outside the national capitals—which makes reintegration of little interest either to secessionist elites or to their constituent populations. In all four disputes, the secessionists have insisted that full recognition of their independence should come first, after which they might be willing to negotiate some form of loose confederation with the incumbent governments. Central governments, on the other hand, want precisely the opposite: an acceptance of state unity first, followed by discussions about devolution of power.

Second, because of the beneficial economies of conflict, no key elites on either side have a major incentive to implement the agreements that have been signed. The belligerents have been favorably disposed to negotiate, even if scheduled sessions are routinely canceled or postponed, but rarely have the talks produced more than an agreement to maintain dialogue—an outcome that both sides seem to see as acceptable. And so long as the sides maintain "dialogue," they receive the political support and financial assistance of the international community. The major players have been willing to talk to each other precisely because the stakes are so low; few people on either side believe that what happens at the bargaining table will ever be implemented on the ground.

Third, at times the policies of international negotiators have actually strengthened the statehood of the secessionist regions. International intervention can itself be a useful resource for the builders of unrecognized states. Even accepting the secessionist delegation as a negotiating partner confers some degree of legitimacy on that side's demands, but in more important and subtle ways, otherwise neutral facilitators have bolstered the secessionists' hands. In Karabakh, the difficulty of crossing the trenches between Karabakh and

Azerbaijani forces—not to mention the excellent road link from Armenia—has meant that humanitarian and development programs, including those sponsored by the United States government, are managed from Armenia, not from Azerbaijan.[52] In Transnistria, the local OSCE delegation strongly encouraged the Moldovan government to sign the agreements that provided customs stamps to the Transnistrians, thereby facilitating illegal commerce through the region. Later, the OSCE pressured the Moldovans to sign another accord that committed both sides to existence within a "common state," a form of language that the Transnistrians now interpret as Moldovan acquiescence to no more than a loose confederation.[53] In Abkhazia, humanitarian relief agencies have become a pillar of the local economy, injecting as much as $5 million into the economy each year through rents, services, and payment of local staff.[54] Even the most dedicated peacemakers thus find themselves in a no-win position: pushing an agreement with secessionists who have no incentive to negotiate in good faith, central leaders who benefit from the status quo, and an impatient international community looking for any symbol of progress, regardless of whether it actually contributes to resolution.

Outside organizations and interested states frequently refer to the ongoing negotiations over Eurasia's de facto countries as conflict resolution. But as time has wound on, that term has come to seem decreasingly applicable to the rounds of fruitless talks, canceled meetings, and rhetorical resolutions. Indeed, the interests of the outside parties—the United States, Russia, and the EU—are inextricable components of the negotiating process. None of these parties is a genuinely disinterested observer, willing to accept whatever solution the parties to the conflict might propose. As was the case with international negotiations over Bosnia and Kosovo, outside powers have a distinct interest in the shape of a final settlement and are willing to block proposed solutions that fail to protect those interests. In the case of Moldova, the Chisinau government and Transnistria were at the point of signing a peace accord in 2003. That accord, penned in large part by the Russian government and known as the Kozak Memorandum after Dmitrii Kozak, the first deputy chief of President Vladimir Putin's presidential staff, would have made Moldova into an asymmetric federation while ensuring long-term basing rights for Russian troops in the region. Although both Chisinau and Tiraspol were prepared to sign the agreement, these provisions were opposed by the United States and other outside parties, which pressured Moldova to withdraw its support for the Kozak Memorandum. By the middle of 2004, the Kozak plan was a dead letter. As in the other conflict zones, "conflict resolution" in Moldova became as much of a misnomer as "frozen conflict." Neither one accurately captures the complexities of interest that swirl around Eurasia's unrecognized countries.

The Kosovo Precedent

The declaration of an independent Republic of Kosovo on February 17, 2008, represented a major change in the direction of territorial issues in the postcommunist world. (I use the spelling already common in English, rather than the Albanian *Kosova*, with no political significance intended.) The armed interventions by Western states in the 1990s—in Somalia, Bosnia, even the first Gulf War—were by and large intended to restore the status quo ante in the wake of an illegitimate invasion or to preserve an existing territorial arrangement. When world powers recognized secessionist entities, they tended to do so in a limited set of circumstances: if these new countries were built within the confines of defunct federations, and only then if the borders of the newly independent states followed the internal boundary of one of the major constituent parts of those federations. For these reasons among others, Montenegro and Kazakhstan became fully fledged countries. Abkhazia and Transnistria did not.

Kosovo marked a shift in these dynamics. In structural terms, the NATO-led attack on Yugoslavia/Serbia in 1999, followed by the UN-sanctioned peacekeeping mission, represented Western governments' siding with the secessionist aims of a minority population, principally ethnic Albanians, within a larger state. That minority population, furthermore, did not reside in a territory that enjoyed formal status as one of the major administrative constituents of a former federal state.

Of course, the details are important. Since the mid-1970s, Kosovo had held a prominent position in the machinery of the Yugoslav federation; in practice if not in name, it was treated very much like republics such as Croatia and Macedonia. Moreover, the administration of U.S. President Bill Clinton, in leading the NATO alliance toward war, in no sense claimed to be assisting the Kosovo Liberation Army (KLA) in its effort to create an independent Kosovo. At the time, there were laudable and honorable reasons for pressuring Slobodan Milošević to end the horrific attacks on ethnic Albanian civilians that had come to characterize his administration's response to the rise of the KLA. But even at the time of the NATO air strikes, it was difficult to distinguish an intervention to prevent genocide from one intended to support the long-term political aims of a guerrilla army. An independent Kosovo was fated from the moment the first U.S. fighter-bombers took off from the NATO air base in Aviano, Italy.

A really existing Kosovo, now seeking membership as a nation-state in the world's major international organizations, is today a fact of life. Serbia's political system has yet to adjust fully to this reality, but the reaction—as of 2009—has been exactly of the sort that most informed Balkan watchers would have predicted. Whereas journalists routinely underscored Kosovo's status as the "spiritual homeland" of the Serbs, hordes of young men did not rush from Belgrade to drive out the infidel Muslim. Although Russia was frequently labeled the "historical ally" of Serbia (something that would have been news to Serbs in 1804, 1877, and 1948), the Kremlin's support for Belgrade was more vocal than real.

Kosovo is the first instance in the postcommunist world of a newly independent state that (1) achieved de facto independence in large measure because of the intervention of external powers, (2) has boundaries reflecting something other than the internal borders of a highest level administrative component of a preexisting federation, and (3) has achieved widespread de jure recognition. When commentators in Washington, Brussels, and Moscow ponder the "Kosovo precedent," it is this combination of factors that comes immediately to mind.[55] Indeed, even Kosovo's own declaration of independence explicitly addresses it. The preamble "observes" that "Kosovo is a special case arising from Yugoslavia's non-consensual breakup and is not a precedent for any other situation."[56] That statement surely makes the declaration a historic rarity: a document in which the basis for independence is claimed to be unique and circumstantial. It contains no reference to the universal principle of the self-determination of peoples, nor does it make claims to sovereignty based on history or identity—both of which have been braided into the preambles of most other declarations of independence over the last two decades.

Yet the impact of Kosovo's independence and growing recognition will have reverberations that are only beginning to be felt. For all its unique qualities, Kosovo nevertheless shares a certain set of common features with the four Eurasian secessionist disputes. All of them ended with the battlefield victory of the secessionist side. All produced a significant flow of refugees and internally displaced persons, in addition to substantial casualties. All involved some form of direct external military intervention. All produced cease-fire agreements that languished for years without final peace settlements. And all have resulted in de facto states that have acquired some of the basic accoutrements of statehood. Some of the Eurasian cases have elements of democracy, such as contested local elections; others are solidly authoritarian fiefdoms. None has gone nearly as far as Kosovo in adopting, at least in theory, European norms with respect to human rights, return of refugees, multiethnic tolerance, and the rule of law. But from the grassroots perspective of individual citizens resident in these liminal zones, Kosovo has simply done what all of Eurasia's unrecognized states achieved half a generation ago: declaring independence and winning it with blood and sacrifice on the battlefield. The real precedent, from this perspective, is not Kosovo's declaration of independence but rather its swift recognition by the same Western governments that routinely condemn Eurasia's other unrecognized regimes as separatists or, worse, terrorists.

That view, one might argue, misses several key points. Following on from more than a decade of underground state building during the Yugoslav and Serbian periods, in the nine years after the Kosovo war, leaders in Prishtina were engaged in building structures of governance that seemed to mirror those of other European democracies, all under the aegis of the EU, the UN, and NATO. The Kosovar government took pains to incorporate state-of-the-art legislation on human and minority rights, and its state symbols stress the multicultural past of its inhabitants. Its geographical position alone will make it, down the road, a reasonable candidate for eventual membership in the EU. None of the other unrecognized states can claim all these qualities. Yet in denying that any sort of Kosovo precedent exists, the Kosovars themselves—and the Europeans and Americans who had a strong hand in drafting the actual declaration of independence—have ignored the ways in which that precedent has already been defined. And it is here that an interesting parallel between policy and scholarship has emerged.

One of the pressing questions for political scientists over the last decade has been why conflict erupted in some parts of eastern Europe and Eurasia but not in others. What made large-scale ethnic disputes turn into full-scale wars in a few places but only simmer in others, despite the fact that grievances, guns, and simple greed created plenty of environments that seemed ripe for violence? Several answers have been proposed, from the administrative structure of the Soviet state to patterns of elite manipulation to long-standing structures enabling or inhibiting social mobilization (see chapter 4).

This research question and its cognate programs have produced important and sophisticated work.[57] In some ways, however, posing the question in this way misspecifies the basic issue at stake. The immediate reason for violence in the four Eurasian cases surveyed in this chapter (as well as in Chechnya) may be far simpler than scholars have often allowed. At base, these places became sites of war simply because the recognized countries of which they were a part decided to use military force to quash secession. Imagine the counterfactual. Had Mikhail Gorbachev sought to prevent the secession of Georgia with the response that Eduard Shevardnadze used in Abkhazia, we would now be busily analyzing the causes of the bloody (but thankfully nonexistent) Russo-Georgian war of 1990–1991—and presumably offering historical, structural, and identity-based factors to explain it. Asking why nation-states use force to prevent secession in some instances but not in others is a rather different project from seeking to understand the origins of things we now label "ethnic conflicts."

All this leads us back to the question of precedent. Worries about the knock-on effects of Kosovo, by scholars as well as by policy makers, have perhaps blinded observers to another precedent. The real lesson that elites in the post-communist world are likely to take from the recent Balkan experience may not be Kosovo but rather Krajina. In August 1995, the Croatian army swept into the Serbian Republic of the Krajina, the small enclave that had been maintained by local Serbs along the Croatian-Bosnian border. The international community's action was, at best, flaccid. The United States, by some accounts, provided intelligence to Croatian military units in planning the operation and, at the very least, gave a green light to the operation.[58] The results for Serbs were disastrous; hundreds of thousands were forced to flee a region that they had inhabited for centuries. The results for Croatia and, to a degree, Bosnia were profoundly positive, at least in the short term. The disappearance of the Krajina republic restored Zagreb's control over all Croatia's territory, paved the way for state consolidation, and eliminated a back-door threat to the embattled Bosnian government.

The "Krajina precedent" may ultimately prove to be a more powerful model than the Kosovo one, as it did in August 2008. Five years into the war in Iraq, Georgia was the third-largest troop contributor (a point that probably said more about the nature of the international coalition there than about the military readiness of Georgian forces). Azerbaijan, flush with new gas and oil wealth, has poured money into equipping and modernizing its armed forces. The day may come when political elites in Tbilisi and Baku reckon that a swift, successful war to retake Abkhazia, South Ossetia, and Nagorno-Karabakh would receive the same green light from the United States that enabled the Krajina offensive. (The Moldovans, burdened by structural poverty and having little pull in Washington, seem less inclined to this way of thinking.) That would surely be a miscalculation. Georgian and Azerbaijani forces would probably win the first days of such a war—and then lose miserably once Russia, Armenia, and the entire north Caucasus were fully mobilized on the other side. But war has frequently been the result of the inadequate analysis of incomplete information.

Today, it is easy to forget that the difference between an independence movement and a separatist movement depends entirely on the normative perspective of the beholder. In the 1990s, the United States and Europe treated some secessionists as the former and dismissed others as the latter. The reasons for this distinction were arguably sensible and even praiseworthy. After all, inconsistency is the foundation of great power politics. But on the ground across eastern Europe and Eurasia, the differences between one group's fight for freedom and another group's illegal separatism have sometimes seemed ridiculously fine-grained. To plenty of political elites and average citizens, the sorting out of borders and sovereignties in that vast region is not yet finished. Kosovo has convinced them that, in some circumstances, the West probably agrees.

Conclusion: Peace as a Public Good

Eurasia's de facto countries are informational black holes. Traveling there is difficult and sometimes dangerous. Elections have been held but never under the eyes of disinterested international observers. Economic and demographic data are not included in statistics compiled by national and international agencies. Locally published books and newspapers barely circulate within the secessionist regions themselves, much less to national capitals or abroad.

For all that, they may seem instances of what Freud called the narcissism of small differences. In most instances, the leaders of these republics and their counterparts in central governments speak a common language—Russian—during negotiating sessions. Many had similar professional backgrounds during the Soviet period. The territory that separates them is in some cases minuscule: Tiraspol is fifty kilometers from the Moldovan capital, Chisinau; Tskhinvali is under two hours' drive from the Georgian capital, Tbilisi. Yet the problems they have spawned are immense. They are the central political problem for the recognized states whose territory they inhabit, and they have become conduits for trafficking in drugs, arms, and even people across Eurasia into Europe and beyond. Especially after the independence of Kosovo, they have become bones of contention among Russia, the United States, and the EU.

Since the end of the wars, secessionist elites have moved on with the process of building states, and even central elites and average citizens have learned to accommodate themselves to that process. But the cessation of the armed conflict has perversely made a final political settlement even more difficult to achieve. Peace has now become something like a public good, an outcome from which all groups might potentially benefit but which entails some sacrifice from all interested parties. Just as the political economy of war can perpetuate violence, so, too, the institutions of Eurasia's unrecognized states have ensured that the benefits born of conflict continue to accrue to belligerents on both sides, the erstwhile losers as well as the winners.

To a certain degree, the energetic institution building in the secessionist regions is a legacy of the Soviet system. Three of the conflict zones had some of the basic institutions of statehood already (through their status as "autonomous" areas), and even in Transnistria, local party organs and city councils provided the germ for what would later become a parliament, presidency, and security structure. The Soviet era provided a convenient template for how national issues ought to be channeled, a template that placed a premium on having and controlling statelike institutions drawn along national lines. It is indicative of the power of the Soviet model that among the first official acts of secessionist elites in the late 1980s and early 1990s was to set up a parliament and to adopt legislation on a national flag, anthem, and seal—long before they were able to secure the territory they claimed as theirs. The supply of stateness in the Soviet system was there even before the demand.

Still, once the accoutrements of statehood have been put into place, they are extremely difficult to deconstruct. Why be mayor of a small city if you can be president of a country? Why be a lieutenant in someone else's army if you can be a general in your own? Of course, those calculations might be different if Azerbaijan, Moldova, and Georgia were strong, wealthy, or even marginally functional states, in which individuals in the secessionist regions could see some advantage to reintegration. So far, however, life inside a recognized state beyond the capital cities is little different from life in one of the unrecognized ones. Traveling in the far reaches of Georgia or the backwoods of Abkhazia, for example, one is hard-pressed to tell if one is in a real country or an imaginary one.

There is an obvious solution to this conundrum. Central governments could simply recognize the power of the secessionist regions and opt for the maximum devolution of authority to them, in exchange for commitment to the existence of a single state. That has been the recommendation repeatedly put forward by the Russian Federation and generally supported by other external mediators: the idea of a final peace settlement based around the concept of a "common state" (*obshchee gosudarstvo*). As the Russian defense ministry's official history of these conflicts argues, the only possible course now is "the preservation of the existing de facto independent status of Abkhazia, Nagorno-Karabakh, and South Ossetia as juridically legitimate entities, as something like associated parts of internationally recognized states."[59] But even though this course might provide some diplomatic cover—a document that would allow the international community to claim that the conflicts had been solved—it would do little to alter the basic structure of power. In fact, it would simply legitimize the continued division of these states into areas controlled by central governments and areas where their writ does not run. That may have been a workable solution in empires, where rebellious peripheral elites were granted tax-farming powers in exchange for loyalty to the center. It is not, however, a viable option for new, fragile, and allegedly democratizing states.

These issues call into question the academic lenses through which researchers have addressed the problems of intrastate war. Given the Western policy interest in the Balkans and the Caucasus in the 1990s, the study of conflict in these regions became of serious interest to security studies and, by extension, to international relations as a whole. Research has normally focused on the dimensions of conflict research derived largely from confrontations between states, such as the security dilemma. But seeing ethnoterritorial confrontations as mainly a security problem can blind researchers to the deep political and economic incentives that sustain disputes and fossilize networks of war into institutions of de facto states. The lesson of Eurasia's unrecognized countries is that these mechanisms are precisely where one should look to explain the conflicts' intractability. In civil wars, as in politics, asking cui bono can be illuminating.

Epilogue

The editing of this chapter was completed shortly before Russia intervened in Georgia, in August 2008, to repel a Georgian attack on South Ossetia. After five days of fighting, a ceasefire brokered by the EU brought open hostilities to a halt. In the weeks that followed, Russia beefed up its military presence in both South Ossetia and Abkhazia and, on August 26, formally recognized the two republics as independent.

The Russian intervention and recognition changed the dynamics of Eurasia's unrecognized states, but it was a change that was, in many ways, predictable. Kosovo had set a clear precedent, despite repeated denials by Western governments, for how territorial issues were to be treated across the postcommunist world. Russia's own go-it-alone approach to foreign policy, along with the blind eye that Western governments had turned to the problem of Eurasia's secessionist struggles over the last fifteen years, produced the "five-day war" of summer 2008. Although Western governments and news agencies were quick to see a revived Russian imperialism as the chief cause, this chapter elucidates the rather more complicated prehistory of the August crisis.

7

Diasporas and International Politics

When and why does ethnicity matter in the making of foreign policy? When do states act to protect the interests of coethnic populations living abroad? Although the perils of ethnic conflict have been an important theme in international security over the last two decades, scholars and analysts have only begun to understand the relationship between dispersed ethnic groups, the states in which they live (host states), and the actions of governments that might make some historical or cultural claim to represent them (kin states). Are transborder diasporas—ethnic communities divided by state frontiers—necessarily a source of insecurity, or can nation-states use "their" diasporas as tools of nation and state building without threatening the interests of their neighbors? As many scholars have argued, transborder ethnic ties can or may increase the insecurity of states.[1] But under what conditions do these latent ties become actualized? Why, in particular, have the "beached diasporas" created by the implosion of the Soviet Union—especially ethnic Russians—been less important in regional security than many observers originally predicted?[2]

Like nations, diasporas are constructed by political and cultural elites. But this fact does not explain why some efforts to use ethnicity as a tool of international politics succeed where others fail. Defining the relationship between national states and the nations they claim to represent is often one of the major preoccupations of politicians and cultural entrepreneurs, especially in post-communist Europe and Eurasia. However, even if political elites look nostalgically across a state's frontiers, stressing the duty to protect the interests of their

I thank Neil J. Melvin for permission to publish this revised version of our originally co-authored article.

coethnics in another host state, there is no reason to believe that such an identity will automatically find expression in foreign policy.

This chapter presents a comparative analysis of three transborder ethnic groups in post-Soviet Eurasia: Russians, Ukrainians, and Kazakhs.[3] The case of ethnic Russians in the non-Russian republics has received considerable attention, but rarely has the Russian question been placed within the broader context of territorially dispersed ethnic groups and their relation to existing and newly independent states.[4] Each of the cases addressed here provides insights into the interaction between states and ethnic populations whose identities and potential loyalties are divided between their countries of residence and states that define themselves as the historic homeland of a distinct ethnocultural nation. They also reveal the constraints on the ability of homelands to mobilize diaspora issues in the international arena: domestic struggles in the kin state over the importance of relations with the diaspora, cultural solidarity (or lack thereof) and sense of attachment to the homeland among the dispersed ethnic group, competing foreign policy priorities within the kin state, and the economic resources that the kin state can wield to reach out to its diaspora.

This chapter contains four parts. The first section discusses the concept of diaspora politics and its particular relevance to the Soviet successor states. The next section details the cases of Russians, Ukrainians, and Kazakhs, three very different manifestations of transborder ethnic issues in the former Soviet space. The third section explicitly compares the three cases and highlights the reasons for the relative ineffectiveness of diaspora politics as a tool of foreign policy in the 1990s. The final section draws conclusions about transborder ethnic groups and international relations in general. Although the rhetoric of nationalism is usually unpalatable to liberal Western observers, there are specific brakes on the ability of diaspora issues to become the object of overt foreign policy moves by kin states.

Homelands and Host States in Eurasia

Research situated along what James Rosenau has termed the "domestic-foreign frontier" proliferated in the 1990s and early 2000s.[5] One of the newest subfields on this frontier is the relationship between ethnicity and international affairs, in particular the origins, spread, and termination of communally based conflict and its impact on international security. Even in nonconflict situations, though, there are clear international components to ethnic ties. In many regions of the world, the traditional ethnic homelands of particular ethnic groups have attempted to cultivate a sense of community with coethnic populations living in foreign host states.[6] Kin states can reach out to their ethnic diasporas in low-key ways, such as by sponsoring cultural exchanges or lobbying for increased opportunities for bilingual education among coethnic immigrants in the host state. In other instances, the policies of both kin states and host states can be less benign. In eastern Europe, the problems surrounding ethnic Hungarians in Romania, Slovakia, and Serbia; ethnic Albanians in Serbia and Macedonia; and ethnic Serbs and Croats in Bosnia are well-known examples of connections between transborder ethnic groups and foreign policy.

Two major developments in the 1980s and 1990s reduced the obstacles to states' taking a more serious interest in the fate of their ethnic diasporas. First, the treatment of ethnic minorities became a decidedly transnational—or more accurately, a transstate—issue. States are today more willing to subordinate their domestic politics to the scrutiny of foreign countries and multilateral institutions such as the Council of Europe and the OSCE. The special interest of kin states in the cultural affairs and general well-being of their diasporas is now generally recognized and enshrined in a host of bilateral and multilateral agreements in Europe. In 2008, for example, the OSCE's High Commissioner on National Minorities issued a set of recommendations specifically designed to regulate—and even facilitate—a kin state's interest in the status of coethnic minorities abroad.[7] In eastern Europe, interstate treaties on good neighborly relations regularly include a provision acknowledging the signatories' interests in their cultural diasporas in neighboring states. In the important 1996 accord normalizing interstate relations between Hungary and Romania, by far the longest section—Article 15—concerned the reciprocal duties of Budapest and Bucharest toward their ethnic Romanian and Hungarian minorities.

Second, the proliferation of new, national states in Europe has called into question the relationship between the political boundaries of states and the amorphous and ascriptive cultural boundaries of nations. From Croatia to Kazakhstan, newly independent states have been engaged in tortuous processes of defending statehood and defining nationhood, staking out unique claims to ethnic proprietorship over lands that are home to manifestly heterogeneous populations. In all these countries, there is some tension between an inclusive vision of the state, in which citizenship and nationality are considered to be coterminous, and a more exclusive conception of the state as "*of* and *for* a particular ethnocultural 'core nation' whose language, culture, demographic position, economic welfare, and political hegemony must be protected and promoted by the state."[8] Domestic debates over such issues as citizenship laws, voting rights, state symbols, language policy, and immigration no longer take place in a vacuum. They are increasingly shaped by patterns of action and reaction involving the state, national minorities within the state, external homelands claiming a special interest in the fate of cocultural minorities abroad, and international norms and institutions.

What is most intriguing in these processes is the semantic malleability of the label "diaspora"—its appropriation by and application to a variety of vastly different ethnocultural groups, many of which may bear little resemblance to archetypal dispersed peoples such as Jews or Armenians.[9] The role of states in defining a particular group as a diaspora is crucial. Both newly independent and established states can reach out to coethnic populations through electoral rules, constitutional provisions, regulations on the repatriation of assets, citizenship laws, and other legal structures to facilitate the participation of coethnics in the affairs of the putative kin state. Both states and nonstate actors in the ethnic homeland may shore up ties with coethnics abroad by encouraging investment from coethnic business elites, using the ethnic population as a source of influence in the state in which it resides, or forming links with criminal syndicates associated with distinct ethnic communities. The homeland's attempt to define a community as a diaspora and to create a privileged relationship with it is a tricky enterprise, for it depends on the state's ability to distinguish the privileges of membership in a transstate cultural community from the rights and duties of membership in a legal community defined by citizenship.

There are a variety of institutional innovations that can signal a state's engaging in diaspora politics. Within a kin state, citizenship laws may be changed to allow for dual citizenship or dual nationality. (The former normally allows an individual to vote in national elections, hold a passport, and enjoy all the rights and duties associated with full membership in the political community. The latter, as in the case of Mexico's relationship with Mexican Americans, is a status that normally allows the individual to hold a passport and travel freely to the homeland but limits the ability to vote or otherwise participate in domestic politics.) Legal guarantees of the right of return to the homeland may be put in place, even if the returnees were born into long-established communities abroad, as in the case of ethnic German migration from the defunct Soviet Union to a reunified Germany. Firms within the kin state may be given economic incentives to cooperate with coethnic entrepreneurs. The kin state may establish cultural centers, consulates or quasi-governmental support institutions in foreign territories with sizable coethnic populations. The kin state may advocate the rights of coethnics in international forums or may intercede directly with the host state to ensure that the cultural and political rights of the coethnic minority are respected.

States that arrogate to themselves a *droit de regard* toward coethnic communities abroad are normally seen as potential destabilizers of regional orders. As Stephen Van Evera hypothesized, war is more likely in circumstances in which states view diasporas and the territory they inhabit as targets of foreign policy making.[10] In situations in which elites on one side of a border are linked by culture or religion to communities across the frontier, Kalevi Holsti has maintained that "reasons of affinity and sentiment rather than . . . power or more hard-headed cost-benefit analyses" are likely to determine a state's decision to engage in aggression.[11] These worries are based on two common misperceptions about the nature of ethnic diasporas. First, they exaggerate the connection between the rhetoric of identity politics and the actual foreign policies of particular states. The determinants of a state's attempt to reach out to coethnic populations across international frontiers—to interfere in the domestic affairs of a foreign state because of a sense of duty toward ethnic confreres— are usually rather pedestrian. The fiery language of nation builders and would-be nation expanders notwithstanding, the constraints on a state's ability to make a coethnic community a target of foreign policy are very strong indeed. Although it is often assumed that transborder populations are ethnic conflicts waiting to happen, in most instances the exigencies of old-fashioned politics (wrangling among domestic interest groups, resource scarcity, and competing policy priorities, for example) matter more than stentorian calls for the defense of ethnic kin or the imponderable workings of identity.

Second, the basic categories of analysis employed in the study of dispersed ethnic groups—"homelands" and "diasporas"—are not given and static. Labeling states as national homelands and dispersed ethnic groups as their diasporas does not automatically make them so, nor does their taking on these labels necessarily lead to foreign policy moves that reflect them. In Europe, there are myriad ethnic groups that extend across international frontiers, and there is no shortage of states that define themselves constitutionally as the homeland of a distinct ethnic population. But the instances of states' acting accordingly—at a minimum, cultivating strong ties with their diasporas and, at a maximum, intervening militarily to protect them—are very rare. Turkey's invasion of Cyprus in 1974 is the only unambiguous case of such behavior in Europe since the Second World War. Russia's intervention in Georgia in 2008, although similar to the Cypriot example, involved Moscow's attempt to protect groups that enjoyed Russian citizenship, not an ethnic Russian population. Serbia's intervention in Croatia and Bosnia in the early 1990s was based on ethnoterritorial claims within the context of a collapsing federation.

Diaspora politics plays a special role in the context of the fifteen successor states to the Soviet Union. Soviet communism created an array of incentives for the mobilization of diaspora interests. The Soviet Union, although supposedly based on the withering away of ethnic allegiances, privileged ethnicity as a source of individual identity and a focus of group solidarity. The Bolsheviks and their successors ultimately had only marginal success in building socialism, but their skills as builders of nations proved quite remarkable indeed. The Soviet Union was divided, at various times, into a territorial and administrative hierarchy of union republics, autonomous republics, regions (*oblasts*), areas (*okrugs*), territories (*krais*), districts (*raions*), and councils (*soviets*), many defined according to linguistic, ethnic, or ethnoreligious criteria. Within the republics, other institutional structures, from local parliaments and councils of ministers to folk ensembles and "national" restaurants, reinforced the image of the fifteen union republics as the homelands of distinct historical nations. Individuals (through ethnic designations on internal passports), as well as entire populations (through the administrative structure of the state), were defined in terms of their ethnic provenance—a form of identity that was itself in many cases consciously constructed by Soviet ethnographers, linguists, and historians in the early years after the Bolshevik revolution.[12]

As political elites in the republics breathed life into their "national" institutions in the late Gorbachev period (ca. 1988–1991), the problem of diasporas quickly arose. If the newly sovereign states were the national homelands of their respective nationalities, what was to become of individuals who, because of changes in political borders, suddenly found themselves beyond the frontiers of "their" national states? For the seven decades of Soviet power, forcible resettlement, internal labor migration, haphazardly drawn borders, and what is now called ethnic cleansing ensured that there was little correspondence between the ethnically defined administrative divisions of the Soviet federation and the demographic boundaries of the ethnic groups that these divisions supposedly represented. In 1989, a quarter of all Soviet citizens (more than 73 million people) lived outside the borders of the administrative regions defined as the homeland of their respective ethnic groups. At the end of 1991, the Soviet Union gave way not only to an array of newly independent states but also to a mass of newly stranded diasporas, populations that were suddenly separated from countries now defined as their proper national homelands.

Many Eurasian states have come to use the general label "diaspora" in speaking of several distinct groups: immigrants who came to western Europe or North America in the last century, political exiles who fled abroad during the communist period, and communities that were separated from the homeland in 1991 by changes in interstate boundaries. Virtually all east European and Eurasian states have official agencies (affiliated with the executive, the legislature, or separate institutions in each branch) charged with dealing with all these diaspora groups, from sponsoring cultural exchanges to implementing a right-of-return policy for coethnics from abroad. However, the forms that diaspora politics have taken in Eurasia and the outcome of official diaspora policies have been various and multifaceted. Politics, not identity, has been the major determinant of when and how successfully foreign policy has reflected existing ethnic linkages.

Diaspora Politics in Eurasia

Since 1991, the variety of diaspora policies in the Soviet successor states has been immense. Some states have actively encouraged the return of diasporas to the homeland. Others have feared that reaching out to coethnic populations might produce a massive and unwelcome influx of immigrants. Some states have created high-level government institutions to maintain links with coethnic communities. Others have made work with the diaspora a low policy priority. The following sections present a brief synopsis of diaspora issues in three cases—Russians, Ukrainians, and Kazakhs—and analyze the reasons for the various policies adopted by kin states in each instance.

Russians: Incipient Diaspora

The sudden collapse of the Soviet system had a profound effect on the Russian populations of the region, a group supposedly numbering 25 million outside the Russian Federation.[13] Russianness as an identity category had developed over the past four centuries or more in conjunction with the expansion of the Russian and Soviet empires. In both the tsarist and communist periods, Russian identity was inextricably linked to the Russian state; the expansion of both empires across Eurasia ensured that Russians and the Russian-speaking descendants of imperial settlers dominated important positions in the economy, society, and political institutions of the territories subordinated to the imperial metropole.

The disintegration of the Soviet state and its replacement with a set of (at least nominal) nation-states struck directly at the leading position of Russian communities. The rise of powerful ethnonational independence movements on the periphery undermined Russian political, economic, and linguistic dominance. Russians went from being the privileged bearers of modernity in a backward periphery to often unwelcome colons caught in the center of movements of national resistance and national renaissance.[14] At the same time, the growth of an anti-Soviet political movement inside the Russian federal republic, a movement that initially saw the Russian nation as largely coterminous with the Russian Soviet republic, broke the historic bond between the Russified settlers in the non-Russian republics and the political power center in Moscow.

The gradual emergence of a Russian diaspora after 1991, both as an object of Russian foreign policy and as a tool of domestic political struggles inside Russia itself, served two major purposes. First, diaspora politics provided a means for the political elite within the Russian Federation to regroup following the disorientation of the perestroika years. In an environment with very few markers to indicate future policy directions, the discovery—or, more accurately, the invention—of a self-consciously Russian ethnic community beyond Russia's newly internationalized borders became the basis for developing a consensus about Russia's new identity.[15] Russia came to be defined as an ethnic homeland, a state with responsibilities toward a cultural community that extended beyond its frontiers. The idea was not that Russia was somehow the continuation of the Soviet Union (although the administration of Boris Yeltsin argued that, in relations with the West, it should be considered such), but rather a new state with particular interests and duties vis-à-vis a territorially dislocated nation.

In 1992 and 1993, a consensus arose among Russian policy makers that the Russian state was organically linked to the settler communities and bore responsibility for their well-being, a consensus that was first crystallized in Yeltsin's decree "On the Protection of the Rights and Interests of Russian Citizens outside the Russian Federation" in November 1992. The Russian state's perceived abandonment of coethnics outside Russia had earlier been a weapon that nationalist and neocommunist forces could use against the Yeltsin leadership, but by late 1992, the government itself had taken a clear stand on Russia's position as de facto kin state for a de facto Russian diaspora. The Russian government agreed to grant citizenship to anyone born in Russia or any former Soviet citizen who did not take citizenship of another state, and to permit unrestricted immigration of Russians and Russian-speakers from the former Soviet territories—a provision that also allowed inhabitants of Eurasia's unrecognized states to apply for citizen status.[16] A Federal Migration Service was established to assist with relocation and to regulate the inflow of new immigrants.

The success of Vladimir Zhirinovsky and the extremist Liberal Democratic Party in the parliamentary elections of December 1993—a group that had made relations with Russians and Russian-speaking settlers a campaign slogan—prompted the Russian government to adopt an even more active policy toward coethnics abroad.[17] In autumn 1994, hearings on the subject were held within the Duma's Committee on Commonwealth of Independent States (CIS) Affairs and Compatriots Abroad, the primary state institution for dealing with the diaspora. Soon, Moscow elaborated a comprehensive policy of political and, in some cases, financial support for Russian communities.[18] Driven by an assertive nationalist opposition, the Russian government came to define the Russian Federation as the locus of Russian national identity, including for those coethnics left outside the borders of the state in 1991. By 1994, the protection of Russians abroad had become one of the few issues, along with opposition to NATO expansion, on which political elites could agree.

Second, diaspora politics legitimated an active Russian engagement with the internal and external affairs of the new states of Eurasia. At a time when many of the non-Russian successor states and the international community were harshly critical of Russia's potential neoimperial designs, the Russian government was able to couch its interests in the near abroad in broadly humanitarian terms. Concern for the cultural, linguistic, educational, and political rights of the Russian diaspora became an important component of Russian official discourse. Denunciations of human rights violations against Russians, particularly in the Baltic republics, became a standard feature of debates in the Russian Duma and public addresses by Yeltsin and foreign ministry officials.[19] In April 1998, for example, the Russian government announced that it would cut oil exports via Latvia by 15 percent, ostensibly because of Latvia's perceived violations of the rights of ethnic Russians.[20]

However, Russian diaspora politics was not without its difficulties. Identifying an obvious and clearly bounded Russian community outside the Russian Federation that could legitimately be called a diaspora was problematic. The history of gradual Russian imperial expansion since the sixteenth century had produced a multiethnic, multiconfessional, and multilingual population whose sense of Russianness and attachment to the newly independent Russian Federation were mutable and contingent.[21] The boundaries between Russians and other ethnic groups, in both the Slavic and non-Slavic republics, were often indistinct.[22] The notion of a Russian diaspora therefore emerged from a hybrid of ethnic, linguistic, historical, political, and crypto-spiritual definitions. In numerous official policy documents, the diaspora was variously described as "ethnic Russians" (*russkie*), "citizens of Russia" (*grazhdany Rossiiskoi Federatsii*), "inhabitants of Russia" or "cultural Russians" (*rossiiane*), "Russian-speakers" (*russkoiazychne*), "compatriots" (*sootechestvenniki*), and even the oxymoronic "ethnic inhabitants of Russia" (*etnicheskie rossiiane*).[23]

Some observers predicted that millions of Russians would flow from the successor states to Russia or western Europe, fleeing discrimination and seeking jobs.[24] However, the movement of Russians has been a highly complex phenomenon. Migration of Russians (variously defined) to the Russian Federation has been significant—on the order of 5.5 million since 1989—but the motivations of the migrants probably have as much to do with the perception of an improved standard of living in the federation as with any desire to return to the cultural homeland.[25] The movement of Russians to the federation began in the 1970s as internal labor migration. Migration accelerated considerably after 1991, but the peak seems to have been reached in 1994, largely in response to the relative economic prosperity of Russia at the time. Net Russian migration from the CIS states to the Russian Federation doubled between 1991 and 1992 and again between 1992 and 1994, peaking at 612,400 persons in 1994. But the net migration figure was only half that number by 1996 and continued to decline for the rest of the decade. Significant outflows occurred mainly from Kazakhstan and Central Asia and from states in which armed conflict prompted both Russians (and many others) to seek safety in other republics. Tajikistan and Armenia lost about half their Russian populations in the 1990s, with Azerbaijan and Georgia losing nearly as much. The fact that more than 30 percent of all Russian migrants came from Kazakhstan (a country generally more sensitive to Russian cultural rights than other republics and where Russians actually outnumbered ethnic Kazakhs at the time of independence) illustrates the degree to which the causes of migration have more to do with economic incentives than with a sense of attachment to Russia as homeland.

The presence of Russian-speakers outside Russia permitted Moscow to claim a legitimate right to speak on behalf of the diaspora. But the cultural hybridity of these populations provided little basis for concrete policy programs. Throughout the 1990s and early 2000s, the meaning of Russianness, both at home and abroad, remained as ill-defined as before. Russia's policy pronouncements concerning its diaspora, while provoking strong reactions from nervous post-Soviet governments, produced little in the way of practical assistance to communities abroad. Indeed, the diaspora issue surfaced only when it reinforced other economic or security interests of the Russian state. There was no instance of the Russian government's acting on behalf of its diaspora when broader state interests were not served, a fact that militant nationalists in Moscow and Russian community leaders in the post-Soviet republics often decried. The threat of a major intervention by Russia solely to defend the diaspora proved far less significant than Western policy makers had feared. When Russia did eventually intervene militarily in its neighborhood—during the five-day war in Georgia in August 2008—one of Moscow's goals was not to protect ethnic Russians but rather to shield ethnic Ossetians (many of whom were also Russian citizens) against Georgia. The legal relationship of a state to its own citizens abroad seemed to win out over the responsibilities of a nation-state toward its conationals.

Ukrainians: Bounding the Nation

During the Soviet years, Ukrainian communities in the West, especially in Canada and the United States, constituted a powerful lobby promoting

Ukrainian national ideals and calling for an independent Ukrainian state.[26] These groups maintained a sense of intergenerational solidarity through community centers, local Ukrainian Catholic churches, and summer camps for youngsters. The collapse of the Soviet system allowed the western diaspora to influence developments within Ukraine directly and openly, either as diaspora returnees or as advocates for Ukrainian interests in Western capitals. The Soros Foundation established a council of advisors to the Ukrainian president that consisted mainly of diaspora Ukrainians, while Bohdan Krawchenko, a prominent Canadian-Ukrainian scholar, established Ukraine's first genuine public policy institute.

By mid-1992, however, the Ukrainian government's enthusiasm for the western diaspora had already worn thin. The diaspora represented a challenge to the interests of local politicians and entrenched economic elites, with President Leonid Kravchuk threatening to expel diaspora returnees who were critical of the government.[27] At the same time, the emergence of an independent Ukraine also meant that Kyiv was in a position, for the first time, to address the question of its "eastern diaspora"—the 6.8 million persons in the former Soviet republics outside Ukraine (mainly in Russia) who claimed Ukrainian ethnicity in the 1989 Soviet census, as well as the estimated 180,000 Ukrainians in Poland, the 66,000 in Romania, and the 40,000 (including Ruthenians, sometimes considered a separate ethnic group) in Slovakia.[28]

In this new environment, some Ukrainian political actors, especially those associated with national-democratic and nationalist parties, sought to reach out to Ukrainian communities in the states of the former Soviet Union and eastern Europe and to engage them in the process of state and nation building after the Soviet collapse. Even during a period when the Ukrainian parliament was dominated by the political left—the groups least enthusiastic about the nation-building program—the constitutional duties of the Ukrainian president were redefined in 1992 to include "securing the national-cultural, spiritual and linguistic needs" of Ukrainians abroad. Although the wording was softened in the 1996 constitution, the state was still given the task of "providing for" ethnic Ukrainians living beyond its borders.[29] Interstate treaties signed with Russia and Romania in 1997 explicitly recognized the interest of Ukraine in coethnic communities in those states. A state-sponsored Ukrainian World Coordinating Council was established in January 1993 to oversee these tasks, and Ukrainian national-democratic groups such as Prosvita and People's Rukh have used the council to pressure the government to speak out for Ukrainian cultural rights abroad.

Even more than in the Russian case, however, official state engagement with the eastern diaspora has been limited by the problem of sorting out the complex forms of interaction, assimilation, and engagement that have developed over the centuries between Ukrainians and Russians, Belarusians, Romanians, and Slovaks along the borderlands of eastern Europe. Who counts as a Ukrainian has never been a straightforward issue. The ambivalence that many ostensible Ukrainians feel toward their newly established homeland often conflicts with the state's interest in shoring up independence and carving out of history a distinct and continuous national identity.[30] Furthermore, the factors shaping diaspora politics have frequently been contradictory. On the one hand, Ukraine's own weakly developed sense of nationhood has prompted some Ukrainian politicians to forge ties to the eastern diaspora to reinforce their nationalist credentials in the homeland. On the other hand, the multiethnic and multilingual character of Ukraine, with around a quarter of the population composed of Russian and Russian-speaking communities, who continue to form important segments of the political and economic elite, has provided a check on the state's ability to build links to a diaspora defined in monoethnic terms. In other words, are ethnic Russians, Poles, or Crimean Tatars who originally hail from the territory of Ukraine to be considered part of the Ukrainian diaspora, or should the government cultivate ties only with those groups that define themselves as culturally Ukrainian?[31]

The Ukrainian government has been concerned that an active diaspora policy might establish a precedent for interference from states with coethnics inside Ukraine, such as Russia and Romania. Building bridges to coethnic Ukrainians could encourage Moscow and Bucharest to do the same with Russian and Romanian communities in Ukraine. Both groups also inhabit territories that Russian and Romanian nationalists do not recognize as a part of Ukraine—Crimea in the south, northern Bukovina and southern Bessarabia in the west, or for the most ardent Russian nationalists, the whole of Ukrainian territory—thus providing a potential link between concern for coethnics and territorial revisionism. For these reasons, successive Ukrainian governments have opposed the idea of dual citizenship, claiming that all inhabitants of Ukraine regardless of ethnicity should feel comfortable with citizenship in the multicultural state. The needs of civic nation building at home have thus undermined attempts to create a clear diaspora policy targeting all Ukrainians abroad. Calls for cultural renewal and the signing of cultural and educational agreements with neighboring host states, rather than an active effort to build a cohesive national community stretching beyond the republic's borders, have been the primary ways in which Ukraine has sought to engage its eastern diaspora.

The relatively low level of return of Ukrainians from abroad is illustrative of the complicated relationship between identity and affinity for the homeland. Ukrainians began moving to the Ukrainian republic in the late 1980s during the upsurge in the local national movement, reaching a peak already in 1990, when 150,800 moved there from other Soviet republics.[32] As in the case of Russians, conflicts in the CIS states prompted further migration throughout the 1990s, with the total figure reaching around 1.4 million by the end of the decade. There was, however, a major counterflow of ethnic Ukrainians—especially skilled workers, engineers, and scientists—to the Russian Federation. In the first post-Soviet decade, Ukraine actually experienced a net population loss, including among ethnic Ukrainians, down to under 50 million by the new millennium. In 1996, 17,029 more ethnic Ukrainians left the country than arrived from other CIS states; self-identified Ukrainians formed the second largest group of out-migrants, behind ethnic Russians. In the same year, nearly as many Russians as Ukrainians moved to Ukraine, while the country has remained the second-lowest (behind Belarus) source of Russian emigrants in Eurasia—an indication of the degree to which ethnic Russians, both locals and new immigrants, continue to feel relatively comfortable inside Ukraine. The relationship between the Ukrainian nation and its new state are thus far more complex than an assumed link between ethnic affinity and foreign policy would lead one to believe.

Kazakhs: The Perils of Repatriation

The experience of Kazakhstan since the late 1980s points to yet another form of diaspora politics. Independence for Kazakhstan in 1991 took place in the context of relatively low nationalist mobilization. Other republics had long traditions of resistance to Russian and Soviet domination, but Kazakhstan became independent largely as an unanticipated consequence of independence movements in other parts of the Soviet Union. However, diaspora relations soon emerged as an important element of the new political regime. Kazakhstan was the only post-Soviet republic that approached independence with a titular nation that was a minority in its own republic; ethnic Kazkahs were only 39.7 percent of the total population in 1989. This demographic deficit, along with a shaky historical justification for an independent Kazakh state, provided an incentive for Kazakhstani elites to look beyond the new state borders and forge ties with a dispersed Kazakh nation.

Proto-Kazakh communities (defined mainly by language) had emigrated from Central Asia long before the establishment of a modern Kazakh national identity during the Soviet period. As a result there was little affinity within these communities for post-Soviet Kazakhstan as a national homeland. Nevertheless, following independence the Kazakhstani government moved quickly to forge links with these newly discovered diaspora groups—numbering as many as a million in China, 700,000 in Russia, and another million in

Uzbekistan, Mongolia, Kyrgyzstan, Turkey, and Iran—and to encourage their return to the newly independent Kazakh kin state.[33] Beginning in 1992, the Kazakhstani government established a series of preferential immigration quotas for ethnic Kazakhs, or "persons of indigenous nationality" (*litsa korennoi natsional'nosti*) as they were termed, and set up an elaborate network to help the repatriates: appropriating funds to assist returnees, providing housing and unemployment support, allowing dual citizenship (even though this was prohibited for natives of Kazakhstan), and for nomadic Kazakhs from Mongolia, even providing transportation of livestock.[34] Between 1991 and 1996, some 154,941 persons identified as ethnic Kazakhs moved to the republic, with roughly 55 percent (84,828) coming from Russia, Uzbekistan, and other CIS states; 40 percent from Mongolia (62,126); and the remainder from Iran (4,617), China (640), and Afghanistan (418). In 1992, the government began setting annual targets for Kazakh return: 10,000 families in 1993, 7,000 in 1994, 5,000 in 1995, and 4,000 in 1996 and 1997.[35]

Encouraging diaspora return was a way of bolstering the legitimacy of Kazakhstani independence by appealing to a national community abroad and cultivating a sense of attachment to the newly independent homeland. But the principal rationale for this policy was the need to alter the country's demographic balance in favor of ethnic Kazakhs. The early years of independence saw wide-ranging debates about whether Kazakhstan was to be defined primarily as a national homeland for Kazakhs or as a multiethnic state, but for the Kazakhstani leadership, shifting the demographic balance toward Kazakhs was essential for national survival.[36] In the 1993 constitution, Kazakhstan was defined as the national homeland for ethnic Kazakhs (even though other laws pointed to a more inclusive, civic conception of nationhood), and cultural groups such as *Qazaq Tili* (the Kazakh Language Association) worked to promote a rebirth of Kazakh language and culture. Increasing the ethnic Kazakh component of the population and finding support for the government's policy of increasing ethnic Kazakh representation in state institutions, however, depended on immigration of Kazakhs from abroad.

The practical problems of integrating the new arrivals proved more serious than many had anticipated. Repatriates were encouraged to settle in areas with small Kazakh populations, but problems with the provision of social services, employment, and housing led many repatriated families to become disillusioned with the Kazakhstani government. Quotas for repatriation were never fully filled in the 1990s, usually hovering around two thirds of the target number for repatriates, and those who did arrive found Kazakhstan less welcoming than they had imagined. Perhaps one in twenty repatriated Kazakhs have left Kazakhstan since 1995.[37]

In foreign policy terms, the repatriation policy placed Kazakhstan in a difficult bind. On the one hand, encouraging diaspora return seemed the only way of redressing the demographic disadvantages of the titular nationality, and the populations with the clearest sense of a specifically Kazakh identity (as opposed to a generic Turkic or Central Asian identity) were those living in adjacent states. On the other hand, establishing links with coethnic communities in neighboring states (such as Russia and Uzbekistan) might encourage those governments to take a more active interest in their own coethnic populations inside Kazakhstan—populations that were likely to suffer as a result of the government's emphasis on the "nativization" of the local economic and political institutions. The Kazakhstani government thus focused a great deal of its propaganda on encouraging the emigration of Kazakhs from Turkey and Mongolia, even though the sense of connection among these groups was the weakest. Members of these groups have also been the least willing to remain in Kazakhstan after a brief experience of life there. The former found life attractive in economically more prosperous Turkey; the latter were reluctant to trade open pastures in Mongolia for inadequate housing and niggardly support in Kazakhstan. Thus the very policy that might best have redressed the internal demographic problem—focusing on return from Russia and other CIS states—came up against the exigencies of foreign policy. In the end, most returnees did in fact hail from the former Soviet republics, but the government's publicity campaigns continually portrayed the archetypal repatriate as a long-lost brother returning from Turkey or Mongolia.

In the late 1990s and early 2000s, other demographic and political dynamics within Kazakhstan began to alter the relative power balance between Kazakhs and Slavs in favor of the former. Emigration of Slavs and other Europeans to Russia and other states and a high relative birthrate among ethnic Kazakhs reversed the demographic trend of the 1980s. Already by 1995, Kazakhs formed at least 46 percent of the population, a figure that tipped into an absolute majority over the next decade.[38] Debates among political elites about the nature of the state—as an ethnic homeland or a multicultural republic—were reflected in a retreat from the ethnic exclusivism of the early 1990s; the new 1995 constitution dropped the definition of Kazakhstan as the homeland of ethnic Kazakhs, and the provision of dual citizenship for diaspora returnees was undone.[39] In the second post-Soviet decade, the return of ethnic Kazakhs continued to serve an important symbolic function, justifying Kazakhstani independence as a potential kin state for the world's Kazakh diaspora. But the state-led effort to reach out to coethnic communities lost much of its earlier salience. Diaspora return was no longer an important focus of Kazakhstani foreign policy.[40]

How Politics Trumps Identity

While some governments have concentrated on establishing cultural and political ties (Russia and Ukraine), others have encouraged the return of the diaspora to the homeland, even if the historical bond between diaspora and kin state is tenuous (Kazakhstan). The extension of blanket citizenship to returnees and diasporas has become the centerpiece of diaspora politics in some cases (Russia), while other states have avoided dual-citizenship provisions (Ukraine). In some instances, the diaspora issue has been closely linked with the pursuit of kin state interests within host states (Russia), while in others a clear distinction between the kin state's international relations and its obligation to the diaspora has been established (Ukraine).

Despite the diversity of outcomes, the evidence presented here points to common patterns in diaspora relations and a common set of factors that seem to have produced the lattice of relationships among kin states, host states, and diasporas in Eurasia. Diaspora identities, like all forms of social allegiance, are made, and states have an important role in their making. But to say that "diaspora" is an identity negotiated among a variety of actors does not explain why efforts to instrumentalize such an identity become prominent in some states but not in others. Nation-states may label a variety of different groups to be diasporas—whether produced by forced migration or by alterations in state borders—but the ability of kin states to make the label meaningful and to craft foreign policy accordingly is determined by a set of concrete political factors. Most of these factors, moreover, are far more straightforward than explanations that focus on the vagaries of identity politics.

Domestic Politics and the Diaspora Question

Domestic politics within the kin state has a profound effect on the development of diaspora politics. The kin state's discovery, or invention, of its own diaspora draws on nationalism by helping postindependence elites with the task of constructing a legitimate locus of political power: the national homeland and its duties toward the historical nation of which it is a representative. The presence of sizable and powerful ethnic minorities within the kin state, however, serves as an important constraint on the ability of political elites to use diaspora issues as a major domestic political resource. The multiethnic nature of the Ukrainian state, for example, has weakened the ability of Ukraine to define itself as a political instantiation of a single ethnically defined nation.

Moreover, like all domestic political issues, relations with the diaspora are rarely a subject of universal agreement among political actors. Diaspora policy on the part of kin states emerges as a result of domestic wrangling among actors with divergent visions of the homeland and its ties to territorially displaced coethnic communities. Kin states with the most far-reaching diaspora policies have been those that have been able to develop a domestic political consensus on the need for stronger ties with the diaspora and to mobilize domestic resources for such a project. Most often, such a consensus has arisen not in response to a strongly felt sense of national identity and obligation toward the diaspora within the kin state, but in response to specific domestic interests.

In Russia, nationalist and neocommunist politicians found the status of Russian communities in Eurasia to be an emotive issue on which to attack the record of the Yeltsin leadership. As other questions took center stage after 1992, such as the pace of economic reform and relations among Russia's constituent units, the domestic utility of the diaspora question quickly receded—only to be reborn as a concern with Russian citizens (not just ethnic Russians) abroad under the administration of Vladimir Putin. Likewise, in Kazakhstan, encouraging diaspora return was a direct response to the disadvantageous demographic position of ethnic Kazakhs within their own republic. By the late 1990s, as the demographic balance began to look more favorable after the out-migration of Russians, Kazakhstani policy toward the diaspora became a secondary concern. In both instances, the domestic uses of the diaspora were ultimately one of the key variables in determining the strength and shape of the state's diaspora policy.

Communal Solidarity

The institutional strength and resources within diaspora communities—the power of political organizations, the level of economic resources, and the degree of communal solidarity—shape diaspora politics. Diasporas with well-developed internal organizations, extensive financial resources, and a strong intergenerational sense of ethnonational identity (usually older diasporas in the West) have been most effective in challenging the leading role of indigenous elites within the homeland and in becoming powerful independent actors both within the kin state and in the international arena. The comparative weakness of ethnic identity and communal solidarity among Russian, Ukrainian, and Kazakh diasporas within the former Soviet republics has reduced the kin state's ability to build bridges to them. That states have not, by and large, intervened on behalf of their diasporas in the former Soviet Union should not come as a surprise. After all, in the cases addressed here, it is extremely difficult to know who exactly those diasporas are supposed to be. In the only case of direct intervention—Russia's August 2008 war with Georgia—the state relied on legal, not ethnic, definitions of its embattled "diaspora."

Relations between diaspora populations and other ethnic communities within the host state (including the titular nationality) can also have an impact on both the kin state's willingness to engage with the diaspora and the receptiveness of the diaspora to overtures from the kin state. For example, the indistinct cultural and linguistic boundaries between Ukrainians and Russians, Belarusians, and other groups in the western borderlands of the former Soviet Union have made any efforts by Ukraine to treat these communities as its legitimate diaspora extremely difficult. The overlapping and situational identities within this region have also helped to prevent conflict around diaspora questions. Even if Kyiv were in a position to launch an aggressive diaspora policy among its eastern diaspora, there are few clearly identifiable groups that the Ukrainian state could target and even fewer that would express enthusiasm for Ukraine as an ethnic homeland.

In other cases, such as Russians in Central Asia, where interaction between titular and minority groups has historically been rather limited, it has been far easier for kin states to shore up ties with their diasporas (hence the greater degree of Russian out-migration from Central Asia than from the western borderlands in the 1990s). In addition, where the diaspora has been clearly targeted by the host state as the object of discriminatory policies, calls within the kin state for protecting the interests of the diaspora are likely to meet with more support. Observers in the West have been concerned that policies in the former Soviet republics aimed at increasing the power of indigenous elites might prompt the Russian Federation to intercede on behalf of its embattled minority. But the picture that emerges from the cases here is more complicated. The solidarity of the diaspora, its relations with neighboring ethnic communities, and the degree to which clear cultural lines separate it from other, closely related ethnic groups within the host state are vital in influencing the kin state's willingness to make the diaspora a foreign policy priority.

Competing Foreign Policy Goals

The priorities of and constraints on foreign policy making in the kin state also influence relations among homelands, coethnics abroad, and host governments. The emphasis of Ukraine and Kazakhstan upon contact with the external diaspora in the West rather than the internal diaspora in other post-Soviet states has been driven by the consideration that engagement with the latter would involve setting an unwelcome precedent—a precedent that the Russian Federation might use to argue for closer engagement with sizable Russian communities in Ukraine and Kazakhstan. In contrast, Russia's desire to embrace a diaspora has been used to bolster the Russian Federation as a great power and to underscore Russia's special foreign policy role throughout the former Soviet Union.

The degree to which kin states focus on diaspora issues is thus determined in part by the broader foreign policy agendas to which political elites are committed and the particular constraints that those elites face in crafting policies toward host states. Most of the states in eastern Europe and Eurasia are, to some degree, self-defined "diasporic states." That is, political elites and majority populations see the state as constituted by a particular cultural nation whose demographic boundaries stretch beyond the territorial boundaries of the country. At the same time, however, translating this notion into actual foreign policy always competes with other local priorities and the constraints of the international environment in which political elites must operate.

Economic Resources

Finally, the availability of economic resources has affected all actors in the diaspora politics of the post-Soviet world. The virtual economic collapse of some states in the 1990s and the continuing economic difficulties in them all have frustrated the ability of the kin states to engage with potential diasporas. The costs of developing contacts with the diaspora, as well as the limited economic gains that such contacts are likely to bring, have meant that relations between kin state and diaspora are often more a matter of rhetoric and moral support than concrete policies buttressing the cultural or economic development of coethnic communities. Why take on further obligations to the nation abroad, the logic goes, if the state cannot even provide for the nation at home? In fact, the kin states of the former Soviet Union have been most willing to engage with their diasporas in instances in which the homeland has been the beneficiary and the diaspora the benefactor, rather than the other way around. For the time being, the duty of wealthier diasporas—such as long-established communities in western Europe and North America—to help their newly independent homelands will be more prominent than the duty of the homeland to help its newborn diaspora in the east.

Conclusion

Ethnic groups that spread across international borders are not simply ethnic conflicts in waiting. States that scholars or policy makers label "homelands" and ethnic groups label "diasporas" need not see themselves in these roles. Even if they do, there is no necessary connection between these identities and the foreign policies that elites choose to pursue. Transborder ethnic groups may indeed represent one potential source of conflict, but admitting as much says nothing about how diaspora issues really matter. There are a host of obstacles—from competing policy priorities in the kin state to the vagaries of identity and cultural solidarity among the diaspora community—that inhibit kin states from building active and successful policies to reach out to coethnic populations abroad.

States that take an interest in the fate of coethnics abroad are not necessarily future aggressors. States attempt to reach out to coethnic communities for a variety of reasons, many of which have more to do with domestic politics in the kin state than with foreign policy. In some instances, host states may actually welcome the kin state's interest, touting the diaspora as an important cultural link or even economic resource binding the kin state and host state together. The host state may encourage dual citizenship or facilitate the right of return. It may encourage local ethnic groups to establish joint ventures and other economic links with coethnic businesspeople in the ethnic homeland. In each of these instances, the focus for both states is on exploiting the uses of diversity— using ethnic heterogeneity to open up foreign policy options that might not exist in relatively more homogeneous polities. In Eurasia, kin and host states have shown a remarkable ability to cooperate on issues of transborder ethnic groups, incorporating mutual recognition of the special interest of kin states in coethnics abroad into interstate treaties and other documents.

Although diaspora politics and irredentism are usually treated as two sides of the same coin, they have more often turned out to be opposite rather than complementary claims. Imbuing a coethnic population with a diaspora identity and creating institutions to look after the community's well-being can be a way of defusing outstanding territorial issues between states. Irredentism is a charge often made against states that express an interest in coethnic communities located on the other side of international boundaries. The state's interest in the cultural or political rights of its coethnics is denounced as a mask for historical or legal claims to territory and an effort to redeem lands lost through war or treaty. Diaspora claims, however, are different. Instead of calling the population to return to the fold, a state may label a coethnic group as a diaspora to ensure that the population remains abroad; a diaspora identity implies that the group's existence outside the borders of the homeland is both a normal and permanent feature of its members' sense of self and community. Political leaders are often eager to dissociate the question of their interest in the affairs of coethnic communities abroad from the prickly issue of interstate borders. One way of separating these issues is by expressing interest in the status of ethnic communities—the right to use national languages, the ability to travel to the homeland, the establishment of state-supported communal institutions, and so on—rather than forwarding overt claims to territory. Diaspora politics is in this sense more an antidote to irredentism than a catalyst for territorial conflict (see chapter 8).

Moreover, an ethnic conception of the nation need not imply either discrimination at home or costly adventures to acquire unredeemed members of the nation abroad. Most states in the former Soviet Union do indeed see themselves as the political instantiations of distinct historical nations, even though they are at the same time home to a multiethnic population. No amount of preaching from liberal Western—usually American—democracy builders will change this fact. What is crucial is to determine under what circumstances homeland identities actually matter in foreign policy making and under what conditions dispersed ethnic groups look to the homeland for protection. The obstacles to both are usually very high indeed.

Ethnic definitions of the state and the linkage between state identity and dispersed ethnic populations can have an impact on interstate relations, but observers should be sensitive to circumstances in which a heightened sense of connection between kin states and diasporas is a result rather than a cause of conflict. If the diaspora is seriously threatened, kin states may feel pressured to protect the interests of coethnics abroad. A stronger sense of attachment between homelands and diasporas may then come about as a result of conflict within the host state. Ethnic ties may be a source of the spread of conflict across international borders, but it need not be a source of tension between states on its own. In this sense, it is not politics in the kin state that matters so much as politics in the host state. Even then, there is no guarantee that ethnic linkages alone will be enough to persuade a kin state to mortgage political stability and expend economic resources by plunging into war. The experience in eastern Europe and Eurasia in the last two decades has been that the default for most kin states is to ignore the interests of coethnics, not to mobilize in support of them.

Still, one other dimension of post-Soviet diaspora politics is only now becoming apparent. Besides the coethnic populations left behind by alterations in the Soviet Union's internal administrative boundaries, there is another, even younger diaspora that may become significant in the future. All of the former Soviet states are now producing new diasporas, sending coethnic individuals and families abroad not because of trade, famine, and war—the traditional generators of global diasporas such as the Irish, Greeks, and Jews—but because of independence and openness. These new diasporas, traveling abroad as students, guest workers, and permanent émigrés, fully embrace the independence of their homelands. After all, it was independence that allowed them to leave. In the future, the states of Eurasia will find it more profitable to reach out to these new post-Soviet diasporas than to the poorer and less ethnically conscious communities in the successor states. These emerging global diasporas, spawned by the breakup of the Soviet Union, are likely to prove a far more significant foreign policy target for the newly independent states than the coethnic populations still residing in Eurasia. Los Angeles and London may well become the new loci of Eurasia's diaspora politics.

8

Migration, Institutions, and Ethnicity

States and empires are both wary of movement. Modern states seek stable borders, safeguarded by competent guards checking on the comings and goings of their inhabitants. They want some way of keeping undesirables out and of benefiting from the productive capacities of those who live there permanently or temporarily. They may also desire that their denizens become genuine citizens, feeling that they have a stake in the state, rather than simply being governed by it. Visas and passports accomplish the first thing, tax collectors the second, and elections the third.

Empires, especially those that stretch over vast portions of contiguous territory, are similar in some respects, but the difficulty of fixing the bounds of their dominion is compounded by the very vastness of the imperial landscape and the loose political allegiances on which imperial power normally depends. Rival powers might threaten to pull away outlying territories or convince particular groups to shift their allegiance. Populations along the frontier might play off the center against another patron, using their position on the periphery as a lever against the imperial capital.

Historically, states have worried about keeping people out; empires have more often worried about keeping them in. However, the distinction between the two kinds of problems can fade away in instances when empires are in the process of transforming themselves into modern states—when the structures of state power remain weak, lines of authority uncertain, and the territorial boundaries of the new political entity disputed. Over the last two decades, that has been the case across eastern Europe and Eurasia, the former inner and outer empires of the Soviet Union. The demographic changes of the 1990s—the movement of people out of conflict regions, the return of ethnic groups to newly created national homelands, the out-migration to neighboring states and even farther afield—may well have changed the population structure of the region in as profound a way as the tragedy of Soviet collectivization in the 1930s, the Second World War, and the forced deportations of the 1940s and 1950s.[1] The real effects of these changes are poorly understood, however. The social and political outcomes of demographic change usually appear only gradually, and with the exception of a few areas (such as job competition among migrants and locals, for example, or conflict between refugees and host populations), they are rarely of immediate concern to politicians. Still, the postcommunist world provides a magnificent setting in which to study the impact of population movements on social structures and political behavior, particularly interethnic relations and ethnic politics.

The first section of this chapter briefly surveys the literature on migration, an interdisciplinary field that has grown considerably in the last decade but so far has found only limited representation in mainstream comparative politics. It also gives an account of the current state of international migration in postcommunist Europe and Eurasia based on the available data, which are admittedly imperfect. The second section illustrates how a study of postcommunist migration can speak to one of the core concerns of comparative politics: the functions of formal and informal institutions and their effects on political and social behavior. There are, of course, many ethnic dimensions to international migration. People might move abroad because they feel discriminated against in their home countries. They might become refugees from ethnic conflict. They might use networks of coethnics to facilitate migration. However, getting to the heart of how ethnicity matters—and doesn't—in international migration is difficult. This section presents two case studies as a way of addressing this issue. One concerns the policies of postcommunist states toward coethnic populations abroad; the second addresses the international migration of sex workers. The cases deal with two different aspects of migration: the attempt by states to develop a legal regime for dealing with coethnics abroad and an undesirable form of irregular migration, the trafficking of women. They also focus on different types of institutions, the formal ones created by states to regularize relations with potential migrant groups and the informal ones that arise among migrant populations themselves. The third section follows on from the case studies by arguing for the reducibility of ethnicity, that is, the interrogation of the very term itself and the elucidation of the precise political processes that the label often masks. Exploring these processes in more detail can help bring international migration more squarely within the comparative politics subfield and, by extension, sort out the relationships among ethnicity, migration, and postcommunism.

International Migration, Comparative Politics,
and Postcommunism

Over the past half century, much of the social-scientific literature on migration has been dominated by debates about the economic or social causes of movement. Initially, theorists focused on the microeconomic rationality of potential migrants (such as the desire for higher wages) or the structural push-pull factors in sending and receiving countries (excess labor supply on the one hand and labor demand on the other). In the last few decades, the field has moved toward more nuanced interpretations: structural explanations that highlight the peculiar conditions of postindustrial economies, world systems theories, and the rise of global cities, among others.[2] The focus throughout, however, has been on understanding the basic cause of international migration as a phenomenon: why individuals and households choose to move across international frontiers.

That way of defining the basic subject of research has tended to treat the state only obliquely—as an intervening variable acting on underlying structural causes—or simply to ignore it altogether. In the rare instances in which state policies, institutions, and actors have come into the picture, the emphasis has normally been on explaining the development of immigration policy in receiving states. But that literature, in turn, has had to do mainly with the arcana of bureaucratic politics and international treaties, the negotiation of reciprocal agreements between states, and their execution through some of the lowest levels of a state's foreign policy bureaucracy. (It is not for nothing that the entry-level position in foreign embassies has long been the visa officer.) There was good reason for all this. Immigration issues are only intermittently matters of high politics. When they are, they frequently reduce to debates about whether immigration is good or bad, how many people should be let in, and how to keep tabs on them once they have arrived, debates that are usually more important as matters of symbolic politics and political rhetoric than they are of actual policy making.

This research program began to change in the late 1980s and 1990s, largely in response to real-world changes in international migration. As in the past, high labor supply in the developing world coincided with high demand in the developed West (both because of, among other things, differential birth rates). But this natural push-pull scenario was now accompanied by the receiving countries' desire to confine immigrants to the labor market and discourage their long-term settlement.[3] Wealthier countries sought to reap the productive benefits of labor immigration without shouldering the burdens of social integration.

In the same period, both intrastate and interstate migration increased in virtually every region of the world. New international arrangements, such as the North American Free Trade Agreement and the deepening commitment of EU states to coordinated immigration policies, placed migration questions at the forefront of state policy. As the 1990s progressed, the tightening of immigration and asylum laws in the global North was accompanied by an upsurge in illegal migration from the South, which in turn gave rise to anti-immigrant politicians and parties in Europe and North America. New armed conflicts in Europe and Eurasia, along with ongoing ones in sub-Saharan Africa and South and Southeast Asia, created new tides of refugees, while a growing norm of humanitarian intervention meant that external states were more likely to intervene to assist them. Most spectacularly, in the aftermath of September 11, 2001, the lowly visa officer, both in the U.S. Foreign Service and in many other countries' diplomatic corps, was raised from bureaucratic obscurity and made the first line of defense against the influx of potential "terrorists."

By and large, however, the political science field has not kept up with such changes in the importance of migration as a political issue. The study of international migration is a relative newcomer to political science. Its natural home has long been in departments of sociology, anthropology, and demography. Where political science has drifted into migration issues, it has usually been in only two areas: the study of immigration as a security threat—one of the "soft security" concerns increasingly analyzed in the security studies subfield—or the study of the determinants of immigration policy in receiving states: why some states, for example, adopt more liberal policies than others and how these policies intersect with conceptions of citizenship.[4]

But there are clearly several areas in which the core interests of political scientists, particularly comparative politics specialists, intersect with the concerns of other social scientists who have long studied migration. Migration cuts to the heart of how politicians and citizens define the polity: who can and cannot be a member and how such questions are decided. It is a good rough measure of state capacity—the degree to which the state is capable of regulating movement in and out of its borders—and the policy area on which much else that the state does depends. It can play a role in electoral politics, by changing the structure of voting populations and by becoming a rhetorical resource for politicians. It can change the nature of debate in a variety of public policy arenas, from tax policy and the provision of social services to state-supported education and the status of minority languages.

Migration is also perhaps the preeminent example of the link between domestic politics and international relations, and it is in this area that the potential for large-scale population movements in the postcommunist world attracted attention in the early 1990s. Young people, especially in the former Soviet Union, seemed to evince a strong willingness to move abroad. Conflicts from Moldova to Azerbaijan to Tajikistan pushed people from their homes. The economic attractiveness of western Europe and North America also seemed to be an irresistible magnet. In the first half of the decade, several scholars and policy analysts predicted a vast wave of migrants, both legal and illegal, from the former communist world, a wave that would put an immediate strain on social systems in the target states and bleed off the productive potential of the postcommunist countries.[5]

Most of these fears turned out to be unfounded. By and large, observers overestimated the willingness of east Europeans to move permanently and underestimated the power of restrictive immigration policies in western Europe as a discouragement to migration. After an initial upsurge, permanent emigration from the postcommunist world, especially from central Europe to the EU, decreased as the decade continued.[6] However, in certain areas, population movements have been significant, and they have begun to have an impact on domestic politics and international relations in eastern Europe and Eurasia. International immigration has been of three major types, although these categories are, to some degree, overlapping.

Long-Term International Migration

The flow of permanent migrants out of postcommunist Europe and Eurasia rose rapidly in the late 1980s, peaked at all-time highs in most countries in the early 1990s, and then fell off as the decade progressed. In part, this pattern was the result of the exhaustion of pent-up demand for migration; however, it also reflected the gradual tightening of immigration laws in receiving countries. Considerable numbers of migrants were able to take advantage of their special status as members of "unredeemed" ethnic minorities, such as Jews and ethnic Germans (the so-called *Aussiedler*), who benefited from special laws facilitating immigration to Israel and Germany. Even for these privileged groups, however, permanent immigration declined throughout the decade. (See Table 8.1.)

Yet this general trend masked two other important developments. One was an increase in the flow of asylum seekers to western Europe and North America in the late 1990s. As channels of regular migration narrowed, potential migrants found asylum laws an attractive, although uncertain, route to a new life in advanced democracies. The traditional first ports of call for migrants— Germany, Austria, Italy—had already tightened their asylum policies in the early part of the decade, and the flow of newcomers was redirected toward countries with more liberal regimes farther to the west, such as Britain and

TABLE 8.I. Migration Flows between Eastern Europe/Eurasia and the West, 1980–1998 (Documented migration only)

	Emigration from Eastern Europe and Eurasia to the Developed West	Immigration to Eastern Europe and Eurasia from the Developed West
1980–1984	1,167,000	511,000
1985–1989	2,708,000	746,000
1990–1994	6,074,000	1,811,000
1995–1998	3,255,000	1,442,000

Source: Population Division, Department of Economic and Social Affairs, United Nations Secretariat, *International Migration from Countries with Economies in Transition: 1980–1999* (New York: United Nations, 2002), I.

Canada. Evidence for the fact that migrants use asylum applications strategically—a back-up route abroad if other forms of legal migration are closed off—comes from the simple fact that the level of political repression or the presence of armed conflict in the sending country has never been a clear predictor of the likely source of asylum applicants. Throughout the 1990s, the largest number of applicants in western Europe came, predictably, from the former Yugoslavia, but the second largest source was Romania, which experienced no significant social violence. Slovak asylum applications skyrocketed *after* the political demise of the authoritarian president, Vladimir Meciar. Moldovan applications increased *after* the end of the war in the secessionist Transnistria region. A large-scale survey project by the World Bank demonstrated in 2007 that economic motivations and migrants' expectations about improvement in the quality of life were the primary drivers of long-term, short-term, and circular migration within and from the postcommunist world.[7]

Second, short-term labor migration accelerated in the 1990s. The mechanism seems to be the classic push-pull in sending and receiving states: surplus labor supply in the poorer postcommunist countries and labor shortages (at particular wage levels) in the richer postcommunist countries and in western Europe. This form of movement can be either extremely short term (a weekend) or rather longer (a year or more); it may also, of course, be legal or illegal. Small-scale traders take advantage of multiple-entry visas and set up shop in border regions between wealthier and poorer countries, establishing sprawling weekend markets that are now almost universally known in western and eastern Europe alike as "Russian bazaars." Longer term immigrants may gain work permits for legal employment. In the better-off postcommunist states, most of the legal labor migrants are from other parts of the postcommunist world. In the late 1990s, more than 40 percent of work permits in the Czech Republic were granted to citizens of Ukraine, and nearly 50 percent of those in Hungary went to citizens of Romania.[8]

Refugees and Forced Migrants

The wars of the communist succession—in the former Yugoslavia and across the former Soviet Union—produced a wave of refugees and IDPs. The conflicts increased the number of asylum seekers in western Europe and put pressure on overburdened governments that bordered the conflict zones. The cessation of violence in most of the conflicts by the mid-1990s led to a decrease in international migration from these zones, but in some instances IDPs were still in dire straits. In Azerbaijan, some 570,000 IDPs remained without permanent resettlement after the end of fighting in the Nagorno-Karabakh conflict in 1994. In Georgia, more than 250,000 IDPs were in a similar predicament because of the continuing standoff over the status of the secessionist regions of Abkhazia and South Ossetia. Some half a million or more refugees fled the two wars in Chechnya. By the early 2000s, these problems had become the concern not so much of international relief agencies, which had largely wound down their operations in the postcommunist world, but rather of immigration bodies in particular states. The savviest potential migrants were learning that IDP status could be parlayed into a reasonable case for asylum in the EU or North America.

Transit Migration and Postcommunist States as Destinations

An unexpected dimension of international migration in the region has been the rise of former communist states as transit countries for migrants from farther afield. Over time, some of these original transit migrants have even come to see the postcommunist countries as permanent destinations. Especially in the postcommunist north—Poland, Hungary, the Czech Republic, and the Baltic states—the relatively better economic conditions have made these countries attractive destinations for migrants from the postcommunist south, the Middle East, and East and Southeast Asia. Likewise, in Romania and the Balkans, the relatively lax border controls made these countries attractive staging grounds for eventual illegal migration to the EU, both before and after the countries' accession to the union in 2007.

Throughout the region, loose visa and asylum laws encouraged immigration in the first half of the decade; however, as some countries began to alter their immigration policies in advance of their accession to the EU, legal immigration began to fall off. In 2000, the Czech Republic instituted a visa regime covering migrants from most of the countries of the former Soviet Union. Estonia, Poland, Bulgaria, and Hungary soon adopted similarly restrictive policies.[9] Those new restrictions were cemented with the enlargement of the EU to include eight former communist states in 2004 and a further two in 2007. Unlike the early years of the postcommunist transition, there is now a clear migration barrier that cuts through the former communist world itself. However, migration within the postcommunist region, both legal and illegal, has already had a profound effect on local demographics. Although many of the states of the region have naturally declining populations because of emigration and falling birth rates, immigration has in some instances helped stem the tide of population loss or substantially reduce a natural population explosion. Russia's population, for example, had a natural decline of 5.9 percent from 1989 to 2004, yet because of the influx of migrants from other parts of the former Soviet Union, Russia's net population decrease fell to 1.9 percent. Dramatically, Tajikistan's natural increase of 45.1 percent over the same period was reduced to 30 percent because of substantial emigration.[10]

Diasporas and the Regionalism of Sex Work

Studying migration across eastern Europe and Eurasia is not easy. Weak states find it difficult to collect data. Strong states have an incentive to falsify data. Individuals have an incentive to misrepresent their preferences about migration and generally to stay below the radar of state institutions, including census bureaus and border guards. In any setting, finding out why people move is difficult. Surveys by the International Organization for Migration (IOM) found that more than a quarter of irregular migrants transiting through Bosnia into the EU were doing so because of political repression. Yet it is difficult to know to what extent this response may have been conditioned by simple farsightedness. Declaring political repression to a nosy IOM official might be the first step toward filing an asylum claim within an EU state.

More than in other areas of political life, migrants seek to avoid the state altogether. It is not surprising, therefore, that people who study them have likewise tended to leave the state out of their analyses. The following case studies present two examples of how states matter in international migration and how institutions—formal government institutions as well as the informal ones that underlie all social order—intersect with ethnicity, sometimes in unexpected ways.

Kin States, Migration, and Diaspora Laws

Almost every country in postcommunist Europe and Eurasia is defined, at least in part, as a national state, the political instantiation of a distinct, culturally defined nation's struggle for liberation. Yet all the states that are so defined also have a portion of the nation located outside the national homeland, communities that were left out of the territorial changes that produced the countries' current boundaries.

Over the last decade, most of these imperfect nation-states have developed specific laws that define their relationship with the unredeemed portions of the national community, laws that might be termed "diaspora laws."[11] In broad terms, the coethnic group is described as part of the greater national community, with certain rights and privileges to be expected from the kin state, while the kin state itself is cast as the guarantor or protector of the cultural, spiritual, and administrative (and sometimes political) rights of the kin group abroad. An individual's nationality, as distinct from his citizenship, is thus considered to be a sufficient reason for a kin state's interest in his well-being.

The laws differ, however, in the kin state's level of engagement with the coethnic minority. The Romanian law (1998) established a special center under the education ministry to sponsor cultural and educational activities among Romanians abroad. The Russian law (1999) guarantees Russian "compatriots" (which includes potentially any former citizen of the Soviet Union) the state's support "in exercising their civil, political, social, economic and cultural rights, and in preserving their distinctive identity." Bulgaria's law (2001) grants ethnic Bulgarians abroad the "right of protection of the Bulgarian state," with no clear indication of what form such protection would actually take. These laws are not a uniquely postcommunist phenomenon, of course. Several other European states, including Germany, Italy, Austria, and Greece, have long had laws that either guarantee coethnics privileged immigration rights and access to social services in the kin state or seek to promote the cultural and economic development of coethnics abroad.[12] The separation of citizenship from ethnicity is not even a particularly European phenomenon. In the 1990s, one of the greatest innovations in Mexico's relationship with Mexican Americans was the state's effort to separate its relations with "co-nationals," people with an affective connection to Mexico and Mexican culture, from "co-citizens," people with Mexican citizenship and, crucially, voting rights (see chapter 7).

That such legal regimes exist is not surprising. There is often considerable domestic pressure to reach out to coethnic populations abroad, and especially in instances in which the coethnics are the subject of discriminatory policies in their host states, the kin state is the natural spokesperson for the rights of the embattled minority. The real questions about such laws are not why they come about, but rather what their actual effects are: Do they promote or hinder immigration—or have no effect at all? Do they promote disloyalty to the host state or, instead, a unique form of multilocal or transstate politics? Do such laws promote the kind of cultural "unmixing," in Rogers Brubaker's phrase, that has characterized the postcommunist world over the last decade or more? An answer to these questions may lie in the newest and most technically detailed diaspora law in the region, Hungary's Act on Hungarians Living in Neighboring Countries, the so-called Status Law.

The Status Law applies to ethnic Hungarian communities in six states around Hungary, but given the size of the minorities in Slovakia and Romania (9.7 percent of Slovakia's population, 6.7 percent of Romania's), these are the host states most directly affected. The special relationship between Hungary and coethnic minorities was mentioned in Hungary's bilateral treaties with its neighbors throughout the 1990s, but the Status Law, adopted by the Hungarian parliament in June 2001, aimed to codify that relationship: to set out what precisely the legal and administrative ties between the state and the minority would be and what status members of the minority were to have if they entered Hungary. Except for Germany's long-standing law on the return of ethnic Germans, Hungary's is so far the most serious attempt in the region to specify what the practical relationship between a kin state and an ethnic minority should be.

The reaction of the Slovak and Romanian governments to the new law was swift. Both complained that the law represented an attempt to interfere in the domestic politics of a foreign state. They also argued that it unfairly privileged some of their citizens over others solely on the basis of ethnic affiliation. That was a particular concern to Romania, which at the time was still on the European Union's list of countries whose citizens required visas to enter the Schengen area, the last of the twelve EU accession countries still under a visa requirement. (That policy was lifted in January 2002, five years before Romania entered the EU.) Both states appealed to international organizations such as the OSCE High Commissioner on National Minorities and the Council of Europe to issue statements condemning the new law as a violation of international norms on citizenship and territorial integrity. In October 2001, at Romania's request, the Council of Europe's Venice Commission produced an analysis of the law. The text of the report was interpreted differently by the various sides in this dispute. The Romanians and Slovaks said the text condemned the law; the Hungarians said it supported it. But over the course of 2002, active diplomacy by Hungary and the recasting of several provisions in the law helped ease tensions, although plenty of problems remain. An amended version of the law was finally adopted in June 2003.[13]

It is easy to see the Status Law, and indeed most of the other laws on coethnic populations abroad, as a simple attempt to reach out to a distinct group based on criteria of identity other than citizenship. At worst, they can even seem like violations of concepts of territorial integrity, as the Romanians and Slovaks argued, or perhaps a novel form of "virtual nationalism."[14] But the fascinating thing about the Status Law is its implicit linkage of ethnicity and migration.

First, it is a mischaracterization of the Status Law to see it primarily as an effort to craft a role for the kin state in the life of its diaspora. That function, in fact, is usually covered by reciprocal clauses in interstate treaties of friendship and good-neighborliness (e.g., Article 11 of the 1996 Romanian-Hungarian treaty). Rather, it concerns the relationship between a kin state—or, more properly, simply the state—and noncitizens who enter the state through legal channels. The Status Law governs access to social services, work permits, and other aspects of short- and long-term migration for coethnic citizens of neighboring states once they reach Hungary. It does not, however, specifically ease permanent immigration or allow easy access to citizenship, as do classic laws on return, such as those in Germany or Israel. Indeed, the Hungarian law has to do with the minority's status inside Hungary, not with Hungary's status among the coethnic community abroad.

Second, as a result, Hungary's law is primarily about the relationship between a kin state and individuals, not about minority populations as collectivities. That distinction is important. The Status Law has nothing to say about communal governance in the host state or about group rights. It is silent on the question of cultural institutions abroad, such as responsibility for the maintenance of churches, schools, or clubs (something, again, usually covered in bilateral agreements).[15] It has nothing to say about the use of the minority's language in social interaction or in relations with government institutions. Although often criticized as promoting group rights, the Status Law is quintessentially individual in its language and application.

Diaspora laws such as Hungary's are relatively new. Most were passed only in the very late 1990s or early 2000s, although they build on a much longer tradition of similar legal regimes in western Europe. So far, however, there is little evidence that they have encouraged migration from kin states to host states; that movement occurred mainly in the early 1990s, long before the diaspora laws were on the books. There is a reason for this: If Hungary's Status Law is representative of a general trend, diaspora laws are, in fact, the antithesis of diaspora politics as described in chapter 7—the effort by a kin state to leverage its coethnic minority abroad to influence domestic politics in or international relations with the host state. They are not simply the product of a kin state's desire to protect members of the nation abroad. Rather, they respond to a need to regularize a relationship with the group deemed most likely to migrate from poorer areas to a relatively more privileged kin state. Ethnic identity, in this instance, matters less as an impetus for policy making than as a convenient predictor of the most migration-prone group abroad.

Seeing diaspora laws such as Hungary's as simply an outgrowth of a government's desire for a privileged relationship with its coethnic community abroad rather misses the point. The special relationship emerges from a desire by states to control migration, not from their desire to encourage it (or, much less, from their desire to change territorial borders). The leveraging of diasporas turns out to be more about keeping people out than about trying to return them to the homeland—especially if, as in Hungary's case, the diaspora inhabits a piece of territory (Transylvania) that many Hungarians continue to see as rightfully belonging to their nation, not to its present owner, Romania. Hungary thus had a dual incentive for structuring its relations with the nation abroad in this way: to discourage immigration and the attendant strains on Hungary's domestic resources and to encourage ethnic Hungarians to remain firmly planted on lands that were fundamental to Hungarian national narratives. It is not surprising, then, that one of the most energetic proponents of diaspora laws, Hungary, was also one of those states in central Europe first in line to join the EU—countries that were of necessity most concerned about the influx of potential migrants once the border of the EU, and of the common migration regime known as the Schengen area, shifted to the east.[16]

Brigid Fowler has argued that diaspora laws are an example of the rise of "fuzzy citizenship" in Europe, in which multilocal identities and multiple definitions of the polity can exist at the same time and for the same individual.[17] One wonders, however, if Hungary's law and others like it are rather more prosaic: an attempt to regularize the movement of potential migrant populations from neighboring states and to take advantage of their labor capacity, yet to limit their full integration into the societies in which they have moved. That has been the pattern followed by most advanced postindustrial states since the Second World War, and it seems to be repeating itself in the postcommunist world. For all the rhetoric surrounding a kin state's duty to defend the interests of its ethnic minority abroad, the most advanced of the diaspora laws—Hungary's—looks little different in real intent from the immigration policies pursued by other economically successful states.

Today, postcommunist diaspora laws are a mixed bag. Some are mainly declarative. Others combine policy toward coethnic populations with policy toward expatriate citizens. Still others deal mainly with the general support of the kin state for the cultural development of the diaspora inside the host state. But Hungary's law may well be a portent of things to come across the region. Kin states that find themselves the most attractive destinations for future migration—either because they are or are likely to become members of the EU or because they are simply better off economically than most of their neigh-bors—may well follow Hungary's course: attempting to combine a special rela-tionship with an ethnically defined diaspora with the desire to limit that diaspora's ability to participate fully in the polity.[18] Having your nationalism while also protecting your borders against unwanted migrants may turn out to be one of the practical advantages of postmodern conceptions of identity and community.

Sex Workers and Social Networks

As both a topic of research and as a policy problem, there are few subjects in the international migration field whose importance is more evident than the issue of trafficking in women.[19] Beginning in the late 1990s, there was an upsurge in interest in this phenomenon, and a variety of states, multilateral institutions, and nongovernmental organizations began to develop policies and programs to address the problem. In 2000, the United States created a designated office to oversee policy on combating human trafficking, especially forced prostitution and the international commerce in sex workers. The office, housed within the Department of State, is now required by law to issue an annual "trafficking in persons report" and to survey the steps taken by the United States and other countries against trafficking, much like the annual reporting and certification processes in the "war on drugs" and the "global war on terrorism."[20]

Several countries and international organizations have adopted specific legislation on trafficking. The European Commission has developed a variety of programs to encourage judicial cooperation and has allocated funds for vic-tim assistance. Various EU member states, most notably Ireland, now have a clear legal framework for prosecuting traffickers on their soil. Multilateral and nongovernmental organizations have also been extremely active in this field. The UN High Commissioner for Refugees has set up working groups on the problem. In 2008, the Council of Europe's Convention against Trafficking entered into force, mandating that member governments provide comprehen-sive assistance and protection to trafficking victims. Human Rights Watch and other monitoring organizations have issued numerous reports. Specialized nongovernmental organizations such as the Coalition against Trafficking in Women and the Global Survival Network have provided forums that bring together a variety of organizations interested in women's rights, trafficking, sexualized violence, and related themes. Even a made-for-television miniseries entitled "Human Trafficking" aired on U.S. networks in 2005, with frightened sex workers and courageous law enforcement officers played by Mira Sorvino and Donald Sutherland.

It is not difficult to see why the issue of female trafficking has garnered particular attention. Women, and often young girls, are moved across international frontiers and placed in positions that are at best indentured servitude and at worst outright slavery. They are made to work in clubs and restaurants and are sometimes engaged in the pornography industry, all in addition to being expected to service paying clients and their (usually male) bosses. They are often prevented from making contact with their homes or families. Their passports or other identity documents are seized, making them wholly reliant on their traffickers in an otherwise alien environment.

The problem is not restricted to any particular region. The reach of the coercive sex industry is genuinely global, with both short-distance migrations from poor villages to burgeoning cities in the developing world and long-distance journeys directly to Europe and North America. As one example, in 2001, police uncovered a trafficking scheme operated by a research assistant at the University of Texas at El Paso, which brought women from Uzbekistan to work as nude dancers in the United States.[21] Like the drug trade, the precise dimensions of the business are difficult to gauge, and there are few reliable data on the scale of industry. Unlike drug trafficking, however, estimates of the scale of the problem come from assisted returns, not from arrests, which makes gathering reliable information even more difficult. Traffickers and prostitutes are notoriously tough to apprehend, especially given the fact that prostitution is in some measure legal in many countries and that few countries have adequate legislation for prosecuting traffickers. The disparity between estimates and the real world of prosecution is evident in a revealing figure. The IOM estimates that some 700,000 women or more are trafficked globally each year, of which a sizable number—perhaps several hundred thousand—go to or through eastern Europe. (The U.S. Department of State reckons the global number to be 800,000, of which roughly 80 percent are women.[22]) But in one large-scale raid by several east European law enforcement bodies in September 2002, only 237 women and 293 suspected traffickers were arrested across the entire region.[23]

Beyond assessing the scope of the problem, another difficulty has been determining exactly why and how women enter the global sex industry in the first place. Given that there are many ways to move beyond borders—legal migration, nonsexual illegal migration, guest worker status—how is it that such large numbers of women become involved in trafficking? Is sexual trafficking purely a human rights concern, or does it intersect with the classic migration issue of human smuggling, the illicit but (in theory) noncoercive and nonexploitative movement of people across borders?[24] Of course, in some instances, outright abduction is the simple answer. Yet this form of trafficking seems relatively rare compared with the much larger number of women who enter the system to some extent voluntarily—women who are themselves complicit in the illegal movement across frontiers, if not in the sexualized businesses in which they eventually become engaged. There is an important distinction, of course, between the ideal types of migrant exporting schemes and slave importing operations. Women may initially believe they are getting involved in the former—that is, a system for moving them abroad in contravention of immigration restrictions—but end up falling into the latter. As David Kyle and John Dale observe, "As with many cons, it is the victim's own complicity in a relatively minor crime (illegal border crossing) that leads to the final snare of the confidence scheme."[25]

In the postcommunist world, another problem has been understanding the significant disparities in the sources of trafficked women. An overwhelming number of women who make their way directly into the EU or into first-stage migration countries such as Bosnia or Albania come from a surprisingly small number of countries farther east, particularly Moldova, Ukraine, and Romania (now an EU member). In 2000, of the 652 trafficked women whom the IOM assisted in voluntarily returning to their countries of origin from southeastern Europe (including Greece), 48 percent were from Moldova, 26 percent from Romania, and 12 percent from Ukraine.[26] Some parts of eastern Europe and Eurasia are barely on the trafficking map. The south Caucasus states and Central Asia, for example, are a comparatively insignificant source of trafficked women (although there does seem to be an increasing flow of women from these areas to the Persian Gulf and Turkey). In addition, some countries that are extremely important as routes or as first-stage target destinations before entry into the EU—particularly Turkey and Bosnia—seem to be less important as sources of women. Why do some countries become routes but not sources, and why do other countries never seem to become much of either?

There are two obvious answers to these questions, in particular, about why women become involved and about the different levels of participation in trafficking in different states. First, it is often argued, women from the most economically depressed regions are the most willing to move abroad to earn money by whatever means, and second, women become victims of trafficking because they are tricked into doing so. Both answers have become part of how the trafficking problem is generally conceptualized. As Michael Specter of the *New York Times* reported in 1998, "selling naive and desperate young women into sexual bondage has become one of the fastest-growing criminal enterprises in the robust global economy."[27] (There is also a third explanation, of course. At a conference in Odessa some years ago, when I raised the question of why women from Ukraine are more frequently trafficked than, say, Georgians, the Ukrainian presidential advisor on women's issues—a woman, incidentally—responded: "It is because Ukrainian women are more beautiful." The subjective preferences of traffickers cannot be discounted, but this is almost certainly not of primary significance.)

None of these answers is adequate. In the first place, there is no clear correlation between economic deprivation and participation in trafficking. Women who end up in western Europe or farther afield are, by and large, from the worst-off states in the former Soviet Union, measured according to general macroeconomic indicators. But within this group, the depth of misery is no predictor of involvement in the transstate sex worker industry. Moldova and Georgia, for example, are similar on several macroeconomic indicators, but the latter is far less important as a source country for trafficked women than the former. Moreover, women who become involved in the sex industry are by and large from cities, especially national capitals, where the effects of economic crises are generally more muted than in the countryside.[28] If economic factors were the primary source of differentiation in the industry, one would expect rural migrants to be most vulnerable.[29]

Second, arguments about economic misery and trickery as the primary motivations and means of sex-worker trafficking leave out what seems to be one of the most important players in the trafficking game: states. One of the major criticisms that human rights organizations have leveled at the annual U.S. Department of State's report on international trafficking has been the department's refusal to address corruption and state complicity in trafficking in many parts of the world.[30] Rather, the global trafficking industry is attributed to the nebulous specter of organized crime or, particularly in eastern Europe, to an ill-defined "Russian mafia."[31]

However, trafficked women do not usually sneak surreptitiously across international borders. They and their handlers are allowed to do so by state authorities. Sex workers in receiving states do not ply their trade clandestinely. They often work in licensed clubs as hostesses, waitresses, and dancers, clubs that local police know also function as illegal brothels. The lines of state complicity are in many cases very long, indeed. State-licensed travel agents book tickets on state-supported airlines. State-licensed taxi drivers shuttle women to and from state-controlled airports. Receiving countries issue state-sanctioned visas. State police turn a blind eye to, or actively benefit from, the sex industry itself.

The obvious arguments about the sources of international trafficking are problematic for a third reason: They overemphasize forced prostitution as the essence of international trafficking. The standard narrative about sex-worker migrants runs as follows. Young women answer an advertisement in a local newspaper that promises work abroad in the hospitality industry—as waitresses, hostesses, or other professions—in glamorous and cosmopolitan settings in western Europe, North America, or elsewhere. Their passage abroad is arranged by the "businessmen" who sponsored the advertisements. Once at their destination, the job turns out to require working as, at best, an exotic dancer. At worst, the women are eventually forced into prostitution, usually on the pretext of paying back their handlers for the passage costs from their home countries. If they refuse, the women are beaten or raped, or their families threatened with harm.

This is the narrative that has largely defined the American and, to a great degree, international responses to the trafficking issue. It has also become the major way in which the status and needs of women in postcommunist societies get framed by outsiders, regardless of the many other dimensions of gender politics.[32] Congressional hearings on the matter have featured testimony by women who confirm that they were misled from the moment they first read of the possibility of work (or advantageous marriage) abroad in their local newspaper. However, this narrative does not fit perfectly with the reality of trafficking as a general phenomenon. A sizable proportion of trafficked women are fully aware that they will be involved in some wing of the sex industry when they go abroad, perhaps even as prostitutes. The clarity begins with the newspaper advertisement itself. In Russian-speaking areas, an advertisement for women *bez kompleksov*—with "no complexes"—is a clear signal that the employment involves some form of sex work. In many countries, there is a social stigma attached to sexual labor, but that stigma can also be somewhat flexible. In a survey of more than a thousand women in Ukraine, the IOM found that all age groups agreed that "a job in the sex industry" was an unacceptable form of employment abroad. However, when asked if being a dancer or stripper was acceptable, all the women in the fifteen–seventeen age bracket answered yes.[33]

From a legal perspective, the real problem with international trafficking is not the sex. In most countries, sex work in one form or another, from pornography to prostitution, is a legal activity. Rather, the central issue is illegal servitude. Women typically are stripped of their passports and other identity papers, they are made to work without pay, and they are prevented from leaving their "employer" or returning home. It is because the reality of transstate trafficking comes up against the narrative of forced prostitution that human rights organizations sometimes even underemphasize women's own complicity. If one is trying to sell a U.S. senator on the importance of combating trafficking, it is clear which narrative is a better strategy: one that features an innocent woman taken from her home and forced to work as a sex slave overseas, or one that features a woman who is complicit in her own illegal migration but perhaps finds herself in over her head once she arrives abroad.

Arguments about economic deprivation and narratives of trickery fail to consider the context in which trafficking occurs: the set of formal and informal institutions, some drawn along ethnic lines, that facilitate movement and, in part, account for differentiation in routes, rates, and ramifications of the phenomenon across the postcommunist world. This context, particularly the intersection with ethnicity, is explored in more detail in the sections that follow.

WEAK STATES AND THE GEOGRAPHY OF MOVEMENT. The passage of many first-stage migrants—that is, from one part of eastern Europe to another, before onward movement into Turkey or the EU—often takes place through legal channels. Women simply board airplanes with tickets, passports, and visas in hand. In many instances, however, migration itself is illegal, effected clandestinely across a poorly guarded international frontier. The relative weakness of the border regime in any particular country is a reasonable indicator of the strength of human trafficking through it, and it is not surprising that countries that have experienced secessionist violence or have unrecognized secessionist regimes on their own territory are either sources of trafficked women or important transit zones: Moldova (host to the unrecognized Dnestr Moldovan Republic), Georgia (with the unrecognized republics of South Ossetia and Abkhazia), Bosnia (with its largely self-governing but nonsovereign Republika Srpska), Serbia (before the independence of Kosovo in 2008), and Macedonia (with the western region around Tetovo largely under local Albanian control). (See chapter 6.) Of course, each of these states has an obvious incentive to overemphasize state weakness as a facilitating condition for trafficking, largely because it absolves state institutions from any active role in the trafficking industry. However, even if state institutions made a good-faith effort to combat the phenomenon, the very weakness of the institutions—including the basic inability of many states to control the territory they claim as their own—would hinder their efforts.

Geography is also important. For example, rivers account for some 40 percent of the border between Bosnia and its neighbors, Croatia and Serbia; of the more than four hundred potential crossing points, only fifty-two are registered and regularly monitored.[34] The border between Georgia and Turkey is easily transgressed, by either land or sea. The border between Russia and Georgia, including via the two secessionist areas (Abkhazia and South Ossetia), is barely controlled at all. The distance between Albania and Italy across the Strait of Otranto can be crossed in very short order, especially in high-speed boats used by traffickers and smugglers. Over the last two decades, the assistance of the IOM and the EU has been crucial in helping postcommunist countries improve and professionalize border crossings. However, for countries that still have preternaturally weak state structures, even the most incompetent traffickers are able to move people across the postcommunist world and even into the EU with relative ease.

VISA AND ASYLUM REGIMES. The visa and asylum regimes of postcommunist states and EU members are a critical dimension of the trafficking phenomenon. In most instances, postcommunist countries (and Turkey) have relatively liberal visa regimes, especially those that are not yet on the list of EU accession states. That means that first-stage migration from the former Soviet Union to eastern Europe through legal channels is relatively easy. The jump from eastern Europe to the EU can then be accomplished illegally through one of many trafficking networks in the Balkans or elsewhere, many of which use the routes just outlined.

An estimated 400,000 to 500,000 migrants are smuggled into the EU each year, of which perhaps 50,000 arrive via southeastern Europe, principally through Bosnia and Albania.[35] Of these, a sizable number are trafficked women, many of whom enter first-stage migration countries legally. The numbers of transit migrants can be staggering. In 2000, just more than 30,500 persons registered as tourists at Sarajevo International Airport from Iran, Turkey, India, Bangladesh, and China; only about 6,000 were recorded as having left.[36] Obviously, not all or even most of these people are trafficked women, but they are certainly among their number. The point is that traffickers can use even legal channels of transit migration or nonexploitative smuggling networks for the first-stage move from Eurasia to eastern Europe.

STATES AND ETHNIC NETWORKS. In transit countries in particular, there is an entire informal economy of human trafficking that has little or nothing to do with the sex industry. The taxi driver who transports migrants from an airport to a land crossing, the travel agent who books a flight or arranges fictional hotel accommodation, and the farmer who may allow a migrant to stay in his house are all part of the informal economy of human trafficking.[37] There is also, however, often an ethnic dimension to these networks, and it is here that we might look for clues to the differential rates of participation in female trafficking and the routes that traffickers use. Conclusive data on this phenomenon are still lacking, but what evidence exists suggests an intriguing set of hypotheses about ethnicity, social networks, and exploitative migration.

Traffickers move people because doing so is profitable. Profit derives from three major sources: first, fees levied on the trafficked women before they leave their home countries, ostensibly for setting up a job in the target country and providing transportation or other overhead expenses initially borne by the trafficker; second, revenue produced by the labor of the women themselves, as dancers in nightclubs or as prostitutes; and third, the sale of women to other traffickers. Of these, the first and third are largely supplementary to the second. Women are rarely able to provide much of an up-front fee, which is one of the reasons that traffickers are able to hold over them the cost of their transport to the target country and insist that they pay it back through labor. Likewise, the "price" of women in trafficker-to-trafficker transactions seems to be remarkably low: In Albania in 2000, the market price was supposedly a thousand dollars, and women would be sold only in instances in which they became too "difficult to handle," that is, by repeatedly attempting to escape, refusing to work, or publicly disgracing their (male) bosses.[38]

Given the importance of women's labor as the primary source of profit, traffickers desire stable routes for moving women from east to west, that is, a stable network of relationships that will ensure that tickets can be purchased, visas granted or forged, ground transportation made available, and the necessary state institutions circumvented or co-opted along the way. In many instances, these networks can be built on top of preexisting ethnic or regional connections. Such networks are sometimes given the catchall label "mafias," but they are usually very different from the extensive system of "private protection" provided by the classic Sicilian mafia model.[39] Rather, they are simply informal groups of friends and family, often from the same ethnic group and the same town or village, who are then able to extend their primary relationships across international borders. These networks can also be self-reproducing. Significant numbers of recruiters—up to 70 percent in Ukraine, by one estimate—are women who return to their own towns or neighborhoods to engage in the recruitment of even further waves of women from the same ethnic group or region.[40]

These networks, which extend all the way down to the city or neighborhood level of a woman's country of origin, provide the essential sanctioning mechanism that allows the trafficking system to work. When a trafficker says that a woman's family will suffer if she tries to escape or goes to the police, it is usually not an idle threat. A cell phone call can be sufficient to command an associate in the home city or village to carry it out. Indeed, without this mechanism, there would be little disincentive for women to attempt to escape from traffickers in the host country or, what is even easier, confess to police when a brothel or nightclub is raided and the women taken into custody. Police and human rights groups, however, report that women are almost universally unwilling to testify against the men who have kept them in effective bondage. (It is for that reason that the Council of Europe's convention on human trafficking now includes explicit provisions for creating safety nets for women who choose to aid the state in trafficker prosecutions.) The very real ability of traffickers to sanction women—and their families back in the sending country—who do not comply with the system depends on the network itself. The sanction can also be a positive one. In Armenia, traffickers' agents occasionally bring money to a woman's family and tell them that their daughter sent it from abroad. That scheme creates good will in local communities and helps ensure a future supply of women prepared to use the traffickers' services if they decide to go abroad.[41]

In attempting to account for the variability of women who are trafficked and the regions they come from, researchers have traditionally looked mainly at classic push-pull factors: the depth of misery in the sending country or the desire for sex workers in the host country. But the relative strength of the social networks that facilitate movement has gone largely unexplored. It may well be in the broader structure of organized crime—which forms of illegal commerce are the most profitable and what kind of networks facilitate which kinds of crime—that an explanation lies. In other words, it is not the fact that Ukrainian women are more desperate or social institutions in Ukraine more lax (or, indeed, that Ukrainian women are more beautiful, as my Odessa interlocutor argued) that accounts for the differential levels of participation in international trafficking. Rather, broad, interstate networks of traffickers have found the business of moving people to be particularly lucrative. Moreover, those networks are in large part built on top of older linkages of ethnic group and regional provenance. Given other circumstances, members of the same network might be engaged in smuggling hazelnuts and copper wiring (as in Abkhazia) or Mercedes cars and heroin (as in South Ossetia). The trick is to discover why, in some cases, the profitable commodity turns out, tragically, to be women.

Theorizing Ethnicity and Movement

The unifying theme of the two case studies in this chapter is the degree to which institutions—both the formal ones of states and the informal ones of social networks—might trump ethnic identity as an explanation for particular migration policies and types of migration. As the first case study showed, what seems to be an ethnic phenomenon—the effort by states to reach out to coethnic, diaspora populations abroad—may in fact be another version of a state's attempt to limit new immigrants to particular labor markets. The second case study illustrated the ways in which ethnicity might matter less as an explanation for why and how immigrants move abroad—why, for example, members of particular ethnic groups seem more involved in the female trafficking—than as a convenient label for the ability to sanction at a distance. In both cases, ethnicity is both less and more than it might appear. It is less in the sense that it rarely functions as an inscrutable form of identity, working itself out in the lives and behaviors of individuals, like the mysterious *Geist* of German Idealist philosophers. It is more in the sense that it masks a variety of social networks of trust and mechanisms of sanction, all of which need to be investigated on their own terms.

Especially in instances in which ethnic allegiances are strongly felt, it is tempting to reify ethnicity as a catchall cause for complex social phenomena, from the relationship between kin states and diasporas to the differential rates of participation in sexual trafficking. However, without an understanding of the particular constraints on ethnicity, or the particular social institutions through which identity is channeled, one risks attributing far too much power to individual identity as a cause of such varied outcomes as ethnic conflict, ethnic separatism, migration, state collapse, and any other social ills afflicting states in the postcommunist world. Focusing on the ethnic dimensions of institutions, both formal and informal, can be one way of unraveling the many strands of ethnicity. Some of these ethnic strands may be analytically connected. Others may have in common no more than the adjective.

How might one go about the unraveling? In the study of migration, ground-level field work has been taken for granted by researchers as the primary method. More than in most social science fields, immigration specialists have long assumed that a perfectly reasonable way of trying to understand why people behave as they do is simply to ask them. That is a laudable assumption, of course. But other methods—from deductive theorizing to formal modeling to survey-based quantitative work—are rather more novel in this particular field. Employing them might speak not only to the relationship between ethnicity and movement but also to the relationships among the study of international migration, postcommunist studies, and comparative politics in general.

First, the systematic, statistical study of the ethnic dimensions of migration is only beginning. Numbers are notoriously difficult to acquire, largely because so much of international migration as a phenomenon takes place off the books, through extralegal channels. That is even more the case in instances in which there is a clear ethnic component to movement: when migrants are seeking to escape from a repressive government in a sending state, when they rely primarily on ethnic networks to circumvent state institutions, or when they have reason to believe that they would be targeted because of their ethnicity in the receiving state.

An important step, however, is to try to develop better ways of understanding broad patterns. The use of systematic surveys or structured interviews among immigrant or at-risk groups is one method, although survey results can overstate the willingness of people to move abroad without taking into account their ability to move. Moreover, national-level data for many postcommunist countries are unlikely to be better in the foreseeable future than they are at present. Not only are data-collecting agencies weak but also data on the flow and stock of people—on emigration, immigration, and total population—are usually highly politicized. Debates about the form and structure of censuses in the Russian Federation and elsewhere are ample testimony of the degree to which simply counting people coming in, leaving, and staying is not a purely academic enterprise.[42]

Second is the need to interrogate the concept of ethnicity and to link up ethnic politics with deductive theorizing about human behavior. In much of the literature on ethnicity, we are often asked to make certain heroic assumptions about the determinants of political behavior. We are asked to assume that most people, most of the time, are willing to sacrifice a great deal for an imagined nation or ethnic group; that they will leave home or fight to the death for a perceived transgression to their national pride; or that they would rather suffer untold hardship than spend one more hour in the company of someone of an opposing ethnic group, now deemed to be an enemy. Only recently, however, have both scholars and journalists begun to ask better questions about ethnicity and politics beyond the mysterious workings of "identity." That is surely the way forward in thinking about ethnicity and migration as well.

For example, states are critical players in the migration game but not always in obvious senses. State institutions make and implement migration policy and seek to remedy the uncontrolled movement of people across their borders; there is obviously no migration policy without the institutions that formulate it. However, states are more than policy-making engines responding to the desires of migrants who want to get in and the desires of domestic political actors who want to keep them out. As the two case studies have shown, states can actually end up influencing migration in ways that a simple reading of their policies on migration would not reveal.

If Hungary's Status Law is representative of an emerging trend, the laws on ethnic diasporas across eastern Europe and Eurasia may be a way of ensuring that the diasporas stay in their host states and not return permanently to their ostensible homelands. The rhetoric of nationalists can thus be misleading. As the Hungarian Status Law reveals, what was initially perceived by nationalists in both host and kin states as a genuine effort to either help the diaspora or interfere in host-state affairs actually turned out to be a way of limiting migration. Likewise, in the case of sex workers, the facilitating policies of some states—the relatively liberal visa regimes in transit states along the EU border, for example—can have an important impact on the routes via which traffickers move women across international frontiers.

Much of the migration literature has been helpful in charting why particular groups might choose to migrate at particular times, the impact of ethnic migrants on ethnic relations in receiving states, the power of identity issues in providing a context for violence among migrant coethnics, and the complex relationship between sending and receiving states.[43] What has been less clear, however, has been the set of ethnic linkages and social networks that might lead migrants to move in the first place and then ease their passage once on the road, or the precise effects of state policy on the ethnic affiliations of potential migrant groups. Taking ethnicity seriously means attributing less to the imponderable power of identity and exploring the actual mechanisms through which ethnic affinity really matters—or doesn't.

In an important study of patterns of global migration, Paul Massey and others argued that theories of international migration must contain at least four elements: an account of the structural forces that promote emigration, an account of the forces that attract immigration, a microtheory of the motivations and goals of individual migrants, and a theory of the social and economic structures that link regions of out- and in-migration.[44] So far, most of the literature in the social sciences has focused on the first three of these areas. A greater appreciation of the institutional dimensions of migration can help flesh out the fourth element of Massey's comprehensive theory.

I have dealt with only two things that the postcommunist cases can contribute to theory building in this regard, but there are many more. Eastern Europe and Eurasia are regions that, taken as a whole, have more weak states than strong ones. They have experienced periods of intense internal and interstate migration. They now straddle the borders of a political entity, the EU, that seeks to harmonize migration policy among its existing members and accession countries, while still admitting of an immense diversity of citizenship policies within individual states.[45] They are regions in which migration is wrapped up in fundamental questions of state and nation building, about who is a legitimate citizen and who is not, and in which these questions are still as thorny as they were in the immediate years after the collapse of communism. There are thus few more propitious areas for exploring the mutual influences of the state, ethnicity, and movement than a world that, virtually overnight, changed the way its denizens were expected to think about each.

9

Conclusion

History and the Science of Politics

Consider this account of the origins of the Second World War:

> Hitler's rise to power brought long-submerged animosities to the
> surface. Among Britons, the threat of a revived Germany sparked
> fears that the contagion of nationalism would spread from Berlin to
> London and prompt Britain's own Germanic ruling house to wipe
> away the civil liberties that the country had known since the Middle
> Ages. In the Soviet Union, there were memories of the once-powerful
> Teutonic Knights and their battles with the Slavs, a struggle that
> seemed, to many, a foreshadowing of the advent of a new Teutonic
> power in Europe. Once war came, the Americans were loath to
> defend either France or Britain. France and the United States were
> traditional allies, but in a time of crisis, the cultural crevasse between
> America's Protestant, Anglo-Saxon core and the Catholic Latins
> of Paris proved difficult to bridge. Likewise, Britain—remembered
> in the salons of Boston and New York as the former colonial
> oppressor—was initially left to fend for herself. It was an attack
> from the Shinto Japanese that finally convinced the Christian
> Americans that the devils they knew were better than the ones
> they did not.

That is history written in the ethnic mode, and it is, of course, barmy (and, in
this case, completely my own invention). But for a good part of the 1990s, it
was the standard way of writing about violence in the postcommunist world,

especially the bloody end of Yugoslavia. Today, it still informs journalistic, policy-oriented, and even scholarly writing about conflicts in that region and beyond. Substitute "Sunni" and "Shiite" or "Georgian" and "Ossetian" for some of the proper nouns in the paragraph above to see how the template of ancient hatreds and imperial legacies has lingered on after the end of the Balkan wars.

The problem with this way of seeing the world, to paraphrase Dr. Johnson, is that it isn't even wrong. Any visitor to eastern Europe and Eurasia knows that discussions with politicians and average citizens frequently involve a history lesson: about Romania's Latin heritage, about Bulgaria as a historically tolerant land, or about the Serbs' medieval defense of Christendom. Yet that fact cannot really explain why southeast Europe developed as it did in the 1990s, nor why the wars of the Yugoslav succession continued to proliferate, nor why the violence that attended some parts of Eurasia's transition from Soviet communism was absent in others. Many people in many places feel strongly about their histories and their identities. Not all of them end up like Kosovo and Nagorno-Karabakh.

Our thinking about the nature of politics, social mobilization, and political violence in the postcommunist world has been afflicted by what might be called an intensive cliophilia—an obsessive concern with finding explanations for contemporary political troubles in the distant and troubled past. Cliophilia (from Clio, the Greek muse of history) has tended to define the basic problems of interest to social scientists, the categories of analysis, and the contours of scholarly discussion. The public at large—of which scholars, too, are a part—is a history-friendly world. Readers and writers have a normal and healthy interest in the past and in ways of behaving, dressing, speaking, and thinking that seem curious and exotic today. But in the study of eastern Europe and Eurasia, we have too often relied on facile historical explanations for phenomena that are surprising, disconcerting, or otherwise difficult to explain. If those phenomena touch on neuralgic issues such as death, identity, and revenge, we seem all the more prone to believe that history, somehow, holds the key.

The essays in this book make two overall arguments that are oblique to this line of thinking. First, history is an unreliable guide to the present, even to—perhaps especially to—those social phenomena that wrap themselves in its mantle. The purveyors of nationalism and the entrepreneurs of large-scale social violence frequently use the past as a source of rhetoric and a way of marketing their cause to potential constituents and patrons. It is easy for scholars to take these entrepreneurs at their word and to uncritically incorporate their own accounts into scholarly analysis. Categories of practice—the nation or the ethnic group, for example—can too easily become categories of analysis.[1] Chapters 5 through 8 examine this tendency through an analysis of the utility of "eastern Europe" as a category, the emergence and evolution of unrecognized states in Eurasia, the politics of ethnic diasporas across the same region, and the intersection of ethnicity and population movements across the post-communist world. As these chapters showed, history matters in ways that are usually more pedestrian than we might believe. When political elites choose to manipulate the present through their own self-serving manipulation of the past, they come up against the same constraints as any other political actor: the hurdles to collective action, the scarcity of resources, and the competing interests that swirl within the communities they are seeking to mobilize. The challenge for analysts is to distinguish clever marketing—of region, religion, identity, or historical grievance—from real causation.

Second, although history may be unhelpful in making sense of some of eastern Europe and Eurasia's greatest challenges today, an appreciation for our own scholarly past is critical to seeing where we have gone right—and wrong—in understanding the extremes of political life, from nationalism to large-scale violence. Chapters 2 through 4 examine, in different ways, the relationship between the evolution of political science and some of its subfields, and the nature of real-world politics in the former communist lands. Scholars have a past, and they work within traditions that can either inspire or, as Marx put it, weigh like a nightmare on the living. Cliophilia has sometimes been a brake to comprehending real-world politics, but it can also be a boon to understanding the pitfalls and promise of our own scholarly disciplines.

What, then, of the relationship between history as a discipline and political science? There are few intellectual rivalries that are expressed with quite the same quiet derision as that between historians and political scientists. The former are often at best puzzled by their colleagues in political science, who seem overly committed to reducing the plethora of human behavior into discrete and measurable variables. At worst, they can see their work as little more than current-affairs commentary, informed by cursory readings of the New York Times mixed with considerable chutzpah. The latter frequently read and cite the work of the former, but often with little regard for the complex scholarly debates that inform that work or with little sense of the multiple interpretive traditions within which any given historian is working.[2] At worst, historians think of political scientists as slipshod journalists, pontificating on some aspect of present realities with little regard for the messy and multifaceted power of the past and even less regard for the variable realities of period and place. At worst, political scientists think of historians as antiquarian storytellers too eager to assert causal relationships instead of proving them and often corralled in their research ambitions by their profession's tendency to focus on a single period or place.

To think in a historical mode is to attempt to re-create the categories, beliefs, values, and systems of meaning that might have made sense in times and places other than our own. It is an effort to embrace the foreignness of the past without assuming that our existing mental maps and conceptual guide-books necessarily work there. The explication of meaning and the promise of interpretation are among its cardinal virtues. A wobbly sense of causality and misplaced faith in the perceptive gaze of the researcher are its chief vices.

To think in a social-scientific mode is to assume that the most intricate features of social life, like those of the natural world, are potentially knowable. It is to make falsifiable hypotheses about the social world and then test those hypotheses through the well-planned accumulation of data and evidence. It prioritizes self-conscious method and seeks precision in statements of cause and effect. Explanation and generalization are among its cardinal virtues. A persistent presentism and decontextualized argumentation are its chief vices.

Given these contrasting intellectual orientations, is it possible for these two professions to speak to each other in meaningful ways? Most important, are there elements of method that one could contribute to the other? Is the work of historians fated to remain a data mine for political scientists and that of political scientists to remain unreadably jejune to historians? Both professions periodi-cally take up these questions and, on occasion, even produce illuminating collec-tions of essays that urge scholars to extend a hand across the abyss.[3] But there are particular lessons that the study of extreme politics in the east European and Eurasian context can contribute to the bigger question of interdisciplinary and transdisciplinary research, as the essays in this volume try to show. In fact, there are at least three reasons for believing that the distance between these two disci-plines may be less monumental than is often believed.

First, the sheer depth and richness of historical experience in the postcom-munist world mean that political scientists must be unusually attuned to the manipulation and meaning of historical events. This is not to say that explana-tions for political change should rely on simplistic accounts of the power of the past, much less that current events should be read as a straightforward repeti-tion of past patterns. Rather, in contrast to societies in which historical narra-tives are either not widely shared or are generally ignored, eastern Europe and Eurasia is a place where historical experience is reified and categorized in eve-rything from school curricula to everyday parlance. Political scientists who ven-ture onto this piece of real estate must be particularly sensitive to the ways in which history-talk can be both a product of politics and its determinant.

Second, the old area studies tradition of "Communist Studies" or "Soviet-ology" encouraged multiple competencies among its practitioners. Region-specific master's degrees continue to do so today, even if, at the doctoral level, training has tended to prize diversity in a range of methods rather than diversity of disciplines. Earlier generations of Sovietologists were forced to work in data-poor and access-restricted environments, but they compensated by cross-training in several fields. Political scientists tended to know, in detail, the relevant historical nodal points in the countries they studied, along with the major works of Western scholarship in several historical subfields. Historians were able to comment knowledgably on contemporary politics. Both knew something of the literatures and languages of the places they studied. That older tradition still has something to teach us about the value of plurality in scholarly education and the ability to appreciate the alternative lenses available in different university departments.

Third, postcommunist Europe and Eurasia remain areas in which coming to terms with the past is more than an intellectual vocation. The problems of overcoming, working through, or erasing historical experience are apparent in the region's art and literature and also as a matter of high politics. Lustration laws that seek to rid government of individuals with ties to the old regime, state commissions charged with uncovering and prosecuting the crimes of the communist past, projects for new school textbooks that treat the communist period as a historical fact, the renovation of state museums to include exhibits on communism or ignore the period altogether—all have been issues of major public debate and political wrangling from the Czech Republic to Central Asia. The panoply of archival documents on this period will not be fully available until perhaps 2019, given the thirty-year rule in force in most states. There is thus a long way to go before the traumatic past of this region ceases to be a subject of widespread public and political concern. Making sense of history is itself part of the political game.

The essays in this book are dispatches from the frontier. That swath of real estate lay for much of the twentieth century on the far side of an impenetrable veil. In the early twenty-first, it is still often a byword for extremisms both political and personal. But the essays are also excursions into the interstices between historical thinking and political science theorizing. As this region—if it can still be called such a thing—moves further into the present century, historians and political scientists must take seriously the multiple perspectives that each discipline offers. The postcommunist world's unpredictable past and overdetermined present are too lush to be explored alone.

Notes

CHAPTER 1

1. Samuel Johnson, *Journey to the Western Islands* (Boston: Houghton Mifflin, 1965), 69.

2. Derek Chollet and James Goldgeier, *America between the Wars, 11/9 to 9/11* (New York: Public Affairs, 2008).

3. Lotta Harbom and Peter Wallensteen, "Armed Conflict and Its International Dimensions, 1946–2004," *Journal of Peace Research* 42, no. 5 (2005); and Harbom and Wallensteen, "Patterns of Major Armed Conflicts, 1997–2006," *SIPRI Yearbook 2007* (Stockholm: Stockholm International Peace Research Institute, 2007), 79–90.

4. Boutros Boutros-Ghali, "An Agenda for Peace: Preventive Diplomacy, Peacemaking, and Peace-keeping," available at www.un.org/Docs/SG/agpeace.html.

5. Hugh Seton-Watson, *Nationalism and Communism* (New York: Praeger, 1964).

6. Seton-Watson, *Nationalism and Communism*, 202.

CHAPTER 2

1. Hugh Seton-Watson, *Nationalism and Communism* (New York: Praeger, 1964) and *Nations and States* (Boulder, Colo.: Westview, 1977); Elie Kedourie, *Nationalism*, 4th ed. (Oxford: Blackwell, 1993); Ernest Gellner, *Thought and Change* (Chicago: University of Chicago Press, 1964), *Nations and Nationalism* (Oxford: Blackwell, 1983), *Culture, Identity, and Politics* (Cambridge: Cambridge University Press, 1987), and *Encounters with Nationalism* (Oxford: Blackwell, 1994); and Anthony D. Smith, *The Ethnic Origins and Nations* (Oxford: Blackwell, 1986), *The Ethnic Revival* (Cambridge: Cambridge University Press, 1981), *National Identity* (London: Penguin, 1991), and *Nations and Nationalism in a Global Era* (London: Polity Press, 1995).

2. Classic works by American scholars include Carlton J. H. Hayes, *Essays on Nationalism* (New York: Macmillan, 1926), *The Historical Evolution of Modern Nationalism* (New York: Richard Smith, 1931), and *Nationalism: A Religion* (New York: Macmillan, 1960); Hans Kohn, *The Idea of Nationalism* (New York: Macmillan, 1944); and Boyd C. Shafer, *Nationalism: Myth and Reality* (New York: Harcourt, Brace and World, 1955) and *Faces of Nationalism* (New York: Harcourt, Brace, Jovanovich, 1972).

3. See Karl Deutsch, *Nationalism and Social Communication*, 2nd ed. (Cambridge, Mass.: MIT Press, 1966); Louis L. Snyder, *The Meaning of Nationalism* (New Brunswick, N.J.: Rutgers University Press, 1954) and *Varieties of Nationalism: A Comparative Study* (Hinsdale, Ill.: Dryden, 1976); Donald Horowitz, *Ethnic Groups in Conflict* (Berkeley: University of California Press, 1985); Liah Greenfeld, *Nationalism: Five Roads to Modernity* (Cambridge, Mass.: Harvard University Press, 1992); Ted Robert Gurr, *Minorities at Risk: A Global View of Ethnopolitical Conflicts* (Washington, D.C.: United States Institute of Peace Press, 1993); Walker Connor, *Ethnonationalism: The Quest for Understanding* (Princeton, N.J.: Princeton University Press, 1994); and Rogers Brubaker, *Citizenship and Nationhood in France and Germany* (Cambridge, Mass: Harvard University Press, 1992), *Nationalism Reframed: Nationhood and the National Question in the New Europe* (Cambridge: Cambridge University Press, 1996), and *Ethnicity without Groups* (Cambridge, Mass.: Harvard University Press, 2005).

4. Gabriel A. Almond, *A Discipline Divided: Schools and Sects in Political Science* (London: Sage, 1990), 13.

5. Jack Hayward, "Political Science in Britain," *European Journal of Political Research* 20 (1991): 311.

6. Michael Oakeshott, "Rationalism in Politics," in his *Rationalism in Politics and Other Essays* (Indianapolis, Ind.: Liberty Fund, 1991), 23.

7. Alfred Cobban, "The Decline of Political Theory," *Political Studies Quarterly* 68 (1953): 335.

8. Harold J. Laski, *Nationalism and the Future of Civilization* (London: Watts, 1932), 5.

9. Hayes spent his entire academic career at Columbia, from his entrance as an undergraduate to his retirement as full professor in 1950. He also served as Roosevelt's ambassador to Spain during the Second World War. See Carlton J. H. Hayes, *Wartime Mission in Spain, 1942–1945* (New York: Macmillan, 1945).

10. See, for example, Deutsch, *Nationalism;* Rupert Emerson, *Government and Nationalism in Southeast Asia* (New York: Institute of Pacific Relations, 1942); Joshua A. Fishman, *Language and Nationalism* (Rowley, Mass.: Newbury House, 1973); and Leonard W. Doob, *Patriotism and Nationalism: Their Psychological Foundations* (New Haven, Conn.: Yale University Press, 1964).

11. See Laski, *Nationalism* and *A Grammar of Politics*, 3rd ed. (London: George Allen and Unwin, 1934), especially chaps. 2 and 6; G. D. H. Cole, *Europe, Russia, and the Future* (New York: Macmillan, 1942); and E. H. Carr, *Nationalism and After* (London: Macmillan, 1945). To be fair to Carr, however, his arguments on the fate of nation-states are far subtler than his title might indicate. See Ernest Gellner's charitable treatment of Carr in Gellner, *Encounters*, 20–33.

12. See, for example, Ernest Gellner, *Saints of the Atlas* (London: Weidenfeld and Nicolson, 1969), *Spectacles and Predicaments: Essays in Social Theory* (Cambridge: Cambridge University Press, 1979), *Relativism and the Social Sciences* (Cambridge: Cambridge University Press, 1985), *Plough, Sword and Book: The Structure of Human History* (London: Collins Harvill, 1988), and *Conditions of Liberty: Civil Society and Its Rivals* (New York: Penguin, 1994).

13. See the survey of the elder Seton-Watson's legacy in Hugh Seton-Watson and Christopher Seton-Watson, *The Making of a New Europe: R. W. Seton-Watson and the Last Years of Austria Hungary* (Seattle: University of Washington Press, 1981). Among the family's most important works on central and eastern Europe are R. W. Seton-Watson, *The Rise of Nationality in the Balkans* (London: Constable, 1917), *The Southern Slav Question and the Habsburg Monarchy* (New York: H. Fertig, 1969 [1911]), and *A History of the Roumanians* (Cambridge: Cambridge University Press, 1934); and Hugh Seton-Watson, *East Central Europe between the Wars, 1918–1941* (Cambridge: Cambridge University Press, 1945), *The East European Revolution* (New York: Praeger, 1956), and *The Russian Empire, 1801–1917* (Oxford: Clarendon, 1967).

14. John Plamenatz, *On Alien Rule and Self-Government* (London: Longmans, 1960); C. A. Macartney, *National States and National Minorities* (Oxford: Oxford University Press, 1934), *Hungary and Her Successors* (Oxford: Oxford University Press, 1934), and *The Habsburg Empire, 1790–1918* (New York: Macmillan, 1969).

15. As Brian Barry notes, this point extends far beyond nationalism to include also the study of autonomy and minority rights. See his "Self-Government Revisited," in David Miller and Larry Siedentop, eds., *The Nature of Political Theory* (Oxford: Clarendon, 1983), 123.

16. See, for example, Isaiah Berlin, "Benjamin Disraeli, Karl Marx and the Search for Identity," in *Against the Current* (New York: Viking, 1980), 252–286.

17. See the classic study of nationalism, domestic politics, and British foreign policy by R. W. Seton-Watson, *Disraeli, Gladstone and the Eastern Question: A Study in Diplomacy and Party Politics* (London: Frank Cass, 1962).

18. Royal Institute of International Affairs, *Nationalism* (Oxford: Oxford University Press, 1939).

19. See Ernest Gellner, "Nationalism and Politics in Eastern Europe," *New Left Review* 189 (1991), and "Homeland of the Unrevolution," *Daedalus* (Summer 1993).

20. Even the otherwise cosmopolitan A. J. P. Taylor initially found himself a supporter of Margaret Thatcher's policy in the Falklands, a view that he later rejected. See A. J. P. Taylor, *An Old Man's Diary* (London: Hamish Hamilton, 1984).

21. Rose's contribution on this and related themes is immense. See especially his *Politics in England* (Boston: Little Brown, 1964), *The Territorial Dimension in Government: Understanding the United Kingdom* (Chatham, N.J.: Chatham House, 1982), and his successive contributions to the various editions of Gabriel Almond and G. Bingham Powell, *Comparative Politics Today: A World View*, 9th ed. (New York: Longman, 2007).

22. On the question of national character, see Ernest Barker, *National Character and the Factors in Its Formation* (London: Methuen, 1927), and Hamilton Fyfe, *The*

Illusion of National Character, rev. ed. (London: Watts, 1946). The implications of racial, ethnic, and nationalist politics, both for the United Kingdom and for social science, are dealt with extensively in Tom Nairn, *The Break-Up of Britain,* 2nd ed. (London: Verso, 1981), and Bhikhu Parekh, *Rethinking Multiculturalism: Cultural Diversity and Political Theory,* 2nd ed. (New York: Palgrave Macmillan, 2006).

23. Linda Colley, *Britons: Forging the Nation, 1707–1837* (New Haven, Conn.: Yale University Press, 1992). For alternative views, see Hugh Kearney, *The British Isles: A History of Four Nations* (Cambridge: Cambridge University Press, 1989), and Greenfeld, *Nationalism,* chap. 2.

24. See Alfred Cobban, *Nationalism and National Self-Determination,* rev. ed. (New York: Thomas Crowell, 1969); Kedourie, *Nationalism;* and Isaiah Berlin, *Vico and Herder* (London: Hogarth, 1976).

25. Isaiah Berlin, "Nationalism: Past Neglect and Present Power," in *Against the Current,* 355.

26. Hugh Seton-Watson, *Language and National Consciousness,* offprint from *Proceedings of the British Academy* 67 (1981): 2–3.

27. Kedourie, *Nationalism,* 80. See also Kedourie's lengthy introduction to his edited volume *Nationalism in Africa and Asia* (New York: World, 1970).

28. Ramsay Muir, *Nationalism and Internationalism: The Culmination of Modern History* (Boston, 1916), 51, quoted in Snyder, *Meaning,* 56.

29. Kedourie, *Nationalism,* 144. For a further defense of the history of ideas and its place in political studies, see Elie Kedourie, "The History of Ideas and Guilt by Association," in his *The Crossman Confessions and Other Essays* (London: Mansell, 1984), 143–147.

30. Gellner, *Thought,* 151, fn. 1. Berlin shared Kedourie's view of the importance of Kant in the history of nationalist thought. See Berlin, *Sense,* 232–248.

31. Gellner, *Nations,* 33–34.

32. Gellner, *Encounters,* 61. The "LSE group" included Gellner, Kedourie, Anthony Smith, and Percy Cohen.

33. Classic statements of this view include Edward Shils, "Primordial, Personal, Sacred and Civil Ties," *British Journal of Sociology* 8 (1957); Harold Isaacs, *Idols of the Tribe: Group Identity and Political Change* (Cambridge, Mass.: Harvard University Press, 1975); Clifford Geertz, "The Integrative Revolution: Primordial Sentiments and Civil Politics in the New States," in *The Interpretation of Cultures* (New York: Basic Books, 1973), 255–310. For more recent books that share some of the assumptions of these earlier works, see Robert Kaplan, *Balkan Ghosts* (New York: St. Martin's, 1993); Daniel Patrick Moynihan, *Pandemonium* (Oxford: Oxford University Press, 1993); William Pfaff, *The Wrath of Nations: Civilization and the Furies of Nationalism* (New York: Simon and Schuster, 1993); Michael Ignatieff, *Blood and Belonging: Journeys into the New Nationalism* (London: Vintage, 1993); and Samuel P. Huntington, *The Clash of Civilizations and the Remaking of World Order* (New York: Simon and Schuster, 1996).

34. On this problem, see Susan Olzak, *The Dynamics of Ethnic Competition and Conflict* (Stanford, Calif.: Stanford University Press, 1992), 5–6.

35. As Barker poetically phrased the problem, scholars should investigate "the house of thought which men have made that their minds may dwell there together." Barker, *National Character*, 18. The study of communist Europe was especially important in the return of political culture, and studies of the region from the 1970s set the stage for the more wide-ranging discussions of democratization and civil society in the 1990s. Two important examples are A. H. Brown and John Gray, eds., *Political Culture and Political Change in Communist States* (London: Macmillan, 1977), and A. H. Brown, ed., *Political Culture and Communist Studies* (Armonk, N.Y.: M. E. Sharpe, 1985).

36. Gellner, *Thought*, 149.

37. The classic studies in this genre are Eric Hobsbawm and Terrence Ranger, eds., *The Invention of Tradition* (Cambridge: Cambridge University Press, 1983), and Benedict Anderson, *Imagined Communities: Reflections on the Origin and Spread of Nationalism*, rev. ed. (London: Verso, 1991).

38. Key works in these debates, in both Britain and North America, include Michael Hechter, *Containing Nationalism* (Oxford: Oxford University Press, 2000); Will Kymlicka, *Liberalism, Community and Culture* (Oxford: Clarendon, 1989), *Multicultural Citizenship: A Liberal Theory of Minority Rights* (Oxford: Oxford University Press, 1995), and *Politics in the Vernacular: Nationalism, Multiculturalism, and Citizenship* (Oxford: Oxford University Press, 2001); David Miller, *On Nationality* (Oxford: Clarendon, 1995); Yael Tamir, *Liberal Nationalism* (Princeton, N.J.: Princeton University Press, 1993); and Charles Taylor, *Multiculturalism and "The Politics of Recognition,"* edited by Amy Gutmann (Princeton, N.J.: Princeton University Press, 1992).

39. For an overview of race theories and their relationship to British politics, see Frederick Hertz, *Nationality in History and Politics* (London: Kegan Paul, Trench, Trubner, 1944), 66–68; and especially Ivan Hannaford, *Race: The History of an Idea in the West* (Washington, D.C.: Woodrow Wilson Center Press, 1996), chaps. 8–9.

40. George Orwell, "Notes on Nationalism," in *England Your England and Other Essays* (London: Secker and Warburg, 1953), 64. See also Orwell's well-known essay "England Your England," 192–224.

41. J. E. E. D. Acton, "Nationality," in *Essays in the History of Liberty* (Indianapolis, Ind.: Liberty Fund, 1985), 409–433.

42. J. S. Mill, "Vindication of the French Revolution of 1848," in *Collected Works of John Stuart Mill* (Toronto: Toronto University Press, 1974), 20:347.

43. J. S. Mill, *A System of Logic* in *Collected Works*, 8:923–924.

44. Cobban, *The Nation State*, 127–129. On the varieties of nationalism in Europe, see Gellner, *Encounters*, 20–33.

45. Bernard Crick, *In Defence of Politics*, 2nd ed. (London: Penguin, 1962), 80.

46. Cobban, *The Nation State*. This important study, a revised edition of the author's earlier *National Self-Determination* (1945), was published posthumously with the editorial assistance of E. H. Carr.

47. Hans Daalder, "Countries in Comparative European Politics," *European Journal of Political Research* 15, no. 1 (1987): 19, cited in E. C. Page, "British Political Science and Comparative Politics," *Political Studies* 38 (1990): 44.

48. James Mayall, *Nationalism and International Society* (Cambridge: Cambridge University Press, 1990), 2.

49. For early attempts at settling the typology problem, see Louis Wirth, "Types of Nationalism," *American Journal of Sociology* 41 (1936); and the extensive note on the use of words in RIIA, *Nationalism*, xvi–xx.

CHAPTER 3

1. Oscar Wilde to Julia Ward Howe, July 6, 1882, in Merlin Holland and Rupert Hart-Davis, eds., *The Complete Letters of Oscar Wilde* (London: Fourth Estate, 2000), 174.

2. Ernest Gellner, *Nations and Nationalism* (Oxford: Blackwell, 1983), 43.

3. Alfred Cobban, *The Nation State and National Self-Determination* (New York: Thomas Y. Crowell, 1970), 25. This book was a posthumously published version of Cobban's earlier *National Self-Determination* (Oxford University Press and the Royal Institute of International Affairs, 1945).

4. Hans Kohn, *The Idea of Nationalism: A Study in Its Origins and Background* (New York: Macmillan, 1956), 13.

5. Karl W. Deutsch, *Nationalism and Social Communication*, 2nd ed. (Cambridge, Mass.: MIT Press, 1966), 173.

6. Gellner, *Nations and Nationalism*, 4.

7. See Rogers Brubaker, *Nationalism Reframed* (Cambridge: Cambridge University Press, 1996) and *Ethnicity without Groups* (Cambridge, Mass.: Harvard University Press, 2004).

8. Jeremy King, *Budweisers into Czechs and Germans: A Local History of Bohemian Politics, 1848–1948* (Princeton, N.J.: Princeton University Press, 2002), 6.

9. Timothy Snyder, *The Reconstruction of Nations* (New Haven, Conn.: Yale University Press, 2003), 10.

10. C. Vann Woodward, "The Search for Southern Identity," in his *The Burden of Southern History*, 3rd ed. (Baton Rouge: Louisiana State University Press, 1993), 3–25.

11. On the "white experience" as one component of Southernness, see Jason Sokol, *There Goes My Everything: White Southerners in the Age of Civil Rights, 1945–1975* (New York: Vintage, 2007).

12. Drew Gilpin Faust, *A Sacred Circle: The Dilemma of the Intellectual in the Old South, 1840–1860* (Baltimore: Johns Hopkins University Press, 1977).

13. Chandra Manning, *What This Cruel War Was Over: Soldiers, Slavery, and the Civil War* (New York: Knopf, 2007).

14. Faust, *A Sacred Circle*, 122.

15. Andrew Marr, *The Battle for Scotland* (London: Penguin, 1995), 2.

16. J. G. Lockhart, *The Life of Sir Walter Scott* (London: J. M. Dent and Sons, 1931), 429.

17. John Prebble, *The King's Jaunt: King George IV and Scotland* (London: Collins, 1988); Robert Clyde, *From Rebel to Hero: The Image of the Highlander, 1745–1830* (East

Linton: Tuckwell Press, 1995); Hugh Trevor-Roper, *The Invention of Scotland* (New Haven: Yale University Press, 2008).

18. Hugh MacDiarmid, "Ebb and Flow," in *Collected Poems of Hugh MacDiarmid* (New York: Macmillan, 1962).

19. Donald Mackenzie Wallace, *Russia* (New York, 1877; reprint: New York: AMS Press, 1970), 377–378; William Glen, *Journal of a Tour from Astrachan to Karass* (Edinburgh: David Brown, 1822), 3; Ebenezer Henderson, *Biblical Researches and Travels in Russia* (London: James Nisbet, 1826), 446–450; and Richard Wilbraham, *Travels in the Trans-Caucasian Provinces of Russia* (London: John Murray, 1839), 154, 165.

20. Charles King, "Imagining Circassia: David Urquhart and the Making of North Caucasus Nationalism," *Russian Review* 66, no. 2 (2007).

21. Hadji Hayder Hassan and Kustan Ogli Ismael, "To the Queen from the Circassian Deputies," August 26, 1862, in Stewart E. Rolland, *Circassia: Speech of Stewart E. Rolland, at a Public Meeting Held at the Corn Exchange, Preston, October 1, 1862, to Receive the Deputies from Circassia* (London: Hardwicke, 1862), 3.

22. I. Drozdov, "Posledniaia bor'ba s gortsami na zapadnom Kavkaze," *Kavkazskii sbornik* 2 (1877): 457.

23. See Georgi Derluguian, *Bourdieu's Secret Admirer in the Caucasus* (Chicago: University of Chicago Press, 2005).

CHAPTER 4

1. Thucydides, *History of the Peloponnesian War*, trans. Rex Warner (New York: Penguin, 1972), 3.82. For an exploration of the notion of civil war in Thucydides, see Jonathan J. Price, *Thucydides and Internal War* (Cambridge: Cambridge University Press, 2001).

2. See Steven R. David, "Internal War: Causes and Cures," *World Politics* 49, no. 4 (July 1997); and Nicholas Sambanis, "A Review of Recent Advances and Future Directions in the Literature on Civil War," *Defense and Peace Economics* 13, no. 2 (2002).

3. See Roy Licklider, "The Consequences of Negotiated Settlements in Civil Wars, 1945–1993," *American Political Science Review* 89, no. 3 (1995), and "Early Returns: Results of the First Wave of Statistical Studies of Civil War Termination," *Civil Wars* 1, no. 3 (1998); Ibrahim Elbadawi and Nicholas Sambanis, "How Much War Will We See? Explaining the Prevalence of Civil War," *Journal of Conflict Resolution* 46, no. 3 (June 2002); and the special issue of the *Journal of Conflict Resolution* 46, no. 1 (February 2002), edited by Paul Collier and Nicholas Sambanis and based on the World Bank's civil war modeling project.

4. See Stephen John Stedman, *Peacemaking in Civil War: International Mediation in Zimbabwe, 1974–1980* (Boulder, Colo.: Lynne Reinner, 1991); Roy Licklider, ed., *Stopping the Killing: How Civil Wars End* (New York: New York University Press, 1993); I. William Zartman, ed., *Elusive Peace: Negotiating an End to Civil Wars* (Washington, D.C.: Brookings, 1995); Milton J. Esman and Shibley Telhami, eds., *International Organizations and Ethnic Conflict* (Ithaca, N.Y.: Cornell University Press, 1995);

Michael E. Brown, ed., *The International Dimensions of Internal Conflict* (Cambridge, Mass.: MIT Press, 1996); Barbara F. Walter and Jack Snyder, eds., *Civil Wars, Insecurity, and Intervention* (New York: Columbia University Press, 1999); Chaim Kaufmann, "Possible and Impossible Solutions to Ethnic Civil Wars," *International Security* 20, no. 4 (1996); Barbara F. Walter, *Committing to Peace: The Successful Settlement of Civil Wars* (Princeton, N.J.: Princeton University Press, 2002); Stephen John Stedman, Donald Rothchild, and Elizabeth M. Cousens, eds., *Ending Civil Wars: The Implementation of Peace Agreements* (Boulder, Colo.: Lynne Reinner, 2002); and Lise Morjé Howard, *UN Peacekeeping in Civil Wars* (Cambridge: Cambridge University Press, 2008).

5. This trend began with an influential article by Barry Posen, "The Security Dilemma and Ethnic Conflict," *Survival* 35, no. 1 (1993).

6. Several authors have questioned some of the key assumptions of the early 1990s security studies literature, such as the power of ascriptive identities in civil wars and the distinction between "old" and "new" forms of political violence. See, for example, John Mueller, "The Banality of 'Ethnic War,'" *International Security* 25, no. 1 (Summer 2000); Nicholas Sambanis, "Partition as a Solution to Ethnic War: An Empirical Critique of the Theoretical Literature," *World Politics* 52, no. 4 (July 2000); Stathis N. Kalyvas, "'New' and 'Old' Civil Wars: A Valid Distinction?" *World Politics* 54, no. 1 (2001); Mats Berdal and David M. Malone, eds., *Greed and Grievance: Economic Agendas in Civil Wars* (Boulder, Colo.: Lynne Reinner, 2000); Paul Collier and Anke Hoeffler, "Greed and Grievance in Civil War" (World Bank, January 2001); Stuart Kaufman, *Modern Hatreds: The Symbolic Politics of Ethnic War* (Ithaca, N.Y.: Cornell University Press, 2001); James D. Fearon and David D. Laitin, "Ethnicity, Insurgency, and Civil War," *American Political Science Review* 97, no. 1 (February 2003); Robert H. Bates, *When Things Fell Apart: State Failure in Late-Century Africa* (Cambridge: Cambridge University Press, 2008).

7. These are the labels used by Ashutosh Varshney in his *Ethnic Conflict and Civic Life: Hindus and Muslims in India* (New Haven, Conn.: Yale University Press, 2002), but for similar surveys, see Charles A. Kupchan, ed., *Nationalism and Nationalities in the New Europe* (Ithaca, N.Y.: Cornell University Press, 1995); Walter, *Committing to Peace;* Kaufman, *Modern Hatreds;* and Kanchan Chandra, "Introduction: Constructivist Findings and Their Non-Incorporation," *APSA-CP: Newsletter of the Organized Section in Comparative Politics of the APSA* 12, no. 1 (Winter 2001): 7–11. Other terms include primordialism (for essentialism), modernism (for instrumentalism), structuralism (for institutionalism), and postmodernism (for constructivism). The middle two are sometimes made subsets of constructivism.

8. Geertz's *Old Societies and New States* (1963) is usually given as the essentialist ur-text. Most statistical analyses of ethnic violence are implicitly essentialist in the way that data are coded. See, for example, Nicholas Sambanis, "Do Ethnic and Non-Ethnic Civil Wars Have the Same Causes? A Theoretical and Empirical Enquiry (Part 1)," *Journal of Conflict Resolution* 45, no. 3 (June 2001). For a spirited defense of the essentialist line, see Stephen Van Evera, "Primordialism Lives!" *APSA-CP: Newsletter of the Organized Section in Comparative Politics of the APSA* 12, no. 1 (Winter 2001).

9. For representative statements of the "new wars" position, see Hans Magnus Enzensberger, *Civil Wars: From L.A. to Bosnia* (New York: New Press, 1994); Samuel P. Huntington, *The Clash of Civilizations and the Remaking of World Order* (New York: Simon and Schuster, 1996); John Mueller, *The Remnants of War* (Ithaca, N.Y.: Cornell University Press, 2004); and Mary Kaldor, *New and Old Wars: Organized Violence in a Global Era*, 2nd ed. (Stanford, Calif.: Stanford University Press, 2007). For an important critique, see Kalyvas, "'New' and 'Old' Civil Wars." For a new approach to conceptualizing identity, see Rawi Abdelal, Yoshiko M. Herrera, Alastair Iain Johnston, and Rose McDermott, eds., *Measuring Identity: A Guide for Social Scientists* (Cambridge: Cambridge University Press, forthcoming).

10. Benedict Anderson, *Imagined Communities*, new ed. (London: Verso, 2006); Donald L. Horowitz, *Ethnic Groups in Conflict* (Berkeley: University of California Press, 1985).

11. For an early article that interpreted the nationalism literature for an international relations audience, see Ernst B. Haas, "What Is Nationalism and Why Should We Study It?" *International Organization* 30, no. 3 (1986). See also Charles A. Kupchan, ed., *Nationalism and Nationalities in the New Europe* (Ithaca, N.Y.: Cornell University Press, 1995).

12. For useful surveys, see Robert D. Benford, "Framing Processes and Social Movements: An Overview and Assessment," *Annual Review of Sociology* 26 (August 2000); Francesca Polletta and James M. Jasper, "Collective Identity and Social Movements," *Annual Review of Sociology* 27 (August 2001); Mark Mazower, "Violence and the State in the Twentieth Century," *American Historical Review* 107, no. 4 (May 2003); Jeff Goodwin and James M. Jasper, eds., *Rethinking Social Movements: Structure, Meaning, and Emotion* (Lanham, Md.: Rowman and Littlefield, 2004).

13. The classic text is Gustave Le Bon, *The Crowd: A Study of the Popular Mind* (reprint Atlanta: Cherokee Publishing, 1982), but for a survey of this literature, see J. S. McClelland, *The Crowd and the Mob: From Plato to Canetti* (London: Unwin Hyman, 1989). For other approaches, see William Kornhauser, *The Politics of Mass Society* (Glencoe, Ill.: Free Press, 1959); Neil J. Smelser, *Theory of Collective Behavior* (Glencoe, Ill.: Free Press, 1963); and Ted Robert Gurr, *Why Men Rebel* (Princeton, N.J.: Princeton University Press, 1970).

14. See Charles Tilly, *From Mobilization to Revolution* (Reading, Mass.: Addison-Wesley, 1978); Doug McAdam et al., eds., *Comparative Perspectives on Social Movements: Political Opportunities, Mobilizing Structures, and Cultural Framings* (Cambridge: Cambridge University Press, 1996); Sidney Tarrow, *Power in Movement: Social Movements and Contentious Politics*, 2nd ed. (Cambridge: Cambridge University Press, 1998); Doug McAdam, *Political Process and the Development of Black Insurgency, 1930–1970*, 2nd ed. (Chicago: University of Chicago Press, 1999); Steven M. Buechler, *Social Movements in Advanced Capitalism: The Political Economy and Cultural Construction of Social Activism* (Oxford: Oxford University Press, 2000); and Karen Barkey and Ronan Van Rossem, "Networks of Contention: Villages and Regional Structure in the Seventeenth-Century Ottoman Empire," *American Journal of Sociology* 102, no. 5 (March 1997).

15. See Ronald Aminzade et al., *Silence and Voice in the Study of Contentious Politics* (Cambridge: Cambridge University Press, 2001); Doug McAdam et al., *Dynamics of Contention* (Cambridge: Cambridge University Press, 2001); and Charles Tilly, *The Politics of Collective Violence* (Cambridge: Cambridge University Press, 2003).

16. Donald L. Horowitz, *The Deadly Ethnic Riot* (Berkeley: University of California Press, 2001), chap. 3.

17. Stewart E. Tolnay and E. M. Beck, *A Festival of Violence: An Analysis of Southern Lynchings, 1882–1930* (Urbana: University of Illinois Press, 1995); Robert A. Pape, *Dying to Win: The Strategic Logic of Suicide Terrorism* (New York: Random House, 2005).

18. Horowitz, *Deadly Ethnic Riot,* 266.

19. Horowitz, *Deadly Ethnic Riot,* 366.

20. On the role of violent contexts and norms, see Jan T. Gross, *Revolution from Abroad: The Soviet Conquest of Poland's Western Ukraine and Western Belorussia* (Princeton, N.Y.: Princeton University Press, 1988); Timothy Snyder, *The Reconstruction of Nations: Poland, Ukraine, Lithuania, and Belarus, 1569–1999* (New Haven, Conn.: Yale University Press, 2003), and "'To Resolve the Ukrainian Question Once and for All:' The Ethnic Cleansing of Ukrainians in Poland, 1943–1947," *Journal of Cold War Studies* 1, no. 2 (Spring 1999). Gross's widely read *Neighbors: The Destruction of the Jewish Community in Jedwabne, Poland* (Princeton, N.J.: Princeton University Press, 2001) examines the power of context in a particular instance of Holocaust-era violence.

21. Scott Straus, *The Order of Genocide: Race, Power, and War in Rwanda* (Ithaca, N.Y.: Cornell University Press, 2006); John Gledhill, "A Veil of Anarchy: Transitional Violence in Romania and the Balkans" (Ph.D. diss., Georgetown University, 2007).

22. Stanley J. Tambiah, *Leveling Crowds: Ethnonationalist Conflicts and Collective Violence in South Asia* (Berkeley: University of California Press, 1996).

23. On this point, see also Padraic Kenney, *A Carnival of Revolution: Central Europe, 1989* (Princeton, N.J.: Princeton University Press, 2002).

24. Valerie Bunce, *Subversive Institutions: The Design and Destruction of Socialism and the State* (Cambridge: Cambridge University Press, 1999); Philip G. Roeder, *Where Nation-States Come From: Institutional Change in the Age of Nationalism* (Princeton, N.J.: Princeton University Press, 2007).

25. Beissinger, *Nationalist Mobilization,* 130.

26. Beissinger, *Nationalist Mobilization,* 142.

27. Ashutosh Varshney, *Ethnic Conflict and Civic Life: Hindus and Muslims in India* (New Haven, Conn.: Yale University Press, 2002).

28. Stathis N. Kalyvas, *The Logic of Violence in Civil War* (New York: Cambridge University Press, 2006).

29. Kalyvas, *Logic of Violence,* 371.

30. David D. Laitin, "Comparative Politics: The State of the Discipline," in Ira Katznelson and Helen V. Milner, eds., *Political Science: The State of the Discipline* (New York: W. W. Norton, 2002), 630–659.

31. Elisabeth Jean Wood, *Insurgent Collective Action and Civil War in El Salvador* (New York: Oxford University Press, 2003); Steven Wilkinson, *Votes and Violence: Electoral Competition and Ethnic Riots in India* (Cambridge: Cambridge University

Press, 2004); Jeremy M. Weinstein, *Inside Rebellion: The Politics of Insurgent Violence* (Cambridge: Cambridge University Press, 2007); Abdulkader Sinno, *Organizations at War in Afghanistan and Beyond* (Ithaca, N.Y.: Cornell University Press, 2008).

32. Rogers Brubaker and David D. Laitin, "Ethnic and Nationalist Violence," *Annual Review of Sociology* 24 (1998).

33. Stathis N. Kalyvas, "The Paradox of Terrorism in Civil War," *Journal of Ethics* 8 (2004).

34. Christopher Boehm, *Blood Revenge: The Anthropology of Feuding in Montenegro and Other Tribal Societies* (Lawrence: University Press of Kansas, 1984).

35. Horowitz, *Deadly Ethnic Riot*, 56; Stathis N. Kalyvas, "The Ontology of 'Political Violence': Action and Identity in Civil Wars," *Perspectives on Politics* 1, no. 3 (September 2003).

36. The best recent application of this technique is Paul R. Brass, *Theft of an Idol: Text and Context in the Representation of Collective Violence* (Princeton, N.J.: Princeton University Press, 1997). A brilliant model—although one involving the killing of cats rather than people—is Robert Darnton's "Workers Revolt: The Great Cat Massacre of the Rue Saint-Severin," in his *The Great Cat Massacre* (New York: Vintage, 1984). See also Sudhir Kakar, *The Colors of Violence: Cultural Identities, Religion, and Conflict* (Chicago: University of Chicago Press, 1996); and Liisa H. Malkki, *Purity and Exile: Violence, Memory, and National Cosmology among Hutu Refugees in Tanzania* (Chicago: University of Chicago Press, 1995).

37. Horowitz, *Deadly Ethnic Riot*, 478.

38. For further exploration of this point, see Rogers Brubaker and Frederick Cooper, "Beyond 'Identity,'" *Theory and Society* 29, no. 1 (2000).

39. E. M. Beck and Stewart E. Tolnay, "When Race Didn't Matter: Black and White Mob Violence against Their Own Color," in W. Fitzhugh Brundage, ed., *Under Sentence of Death: Lynching in the South* (Chapel Hill: University of North Carolina Press, 1997), 132–154.

40. For an explicit statement, see Ashutosh Varshney, "Nationalism, Ethnic Conflict, and Rationality," *Perspectives on Politics* 1, no. 1 (March 2003).

41. Alexander L. George and Andrew Bennett, *Case Studies and Theory Development in the Social Sciences* (Cambridge, Mass.: MIT Press, 2004); Henry E. Brady and David Collier, eds., *Rethinking Social Inquiry: Diverse Tools, Shared Standards* (Lanham, Md.: Roman and Littlefield, 2004).

CHAPTER 5

1. See the exchanges in Robert H. Bates, Chalmers Johnson, and Ian Lustick in "Controversy in the Discipline: Area Studies and Comparative Politics," *PS: Political Science and Politics* 30, no. 3 (June 1997); Robert Bates, "Theory in Comparative Politics?" *APSA Comparative Politics Newsletter* 8 (Winter 1997); Christopher Shea, "Political Scientists Clash over the Value of Area Studies," *Chronicle of Higher Education,* January 10, 1997.

2. See the special issue of *Post-Soviet Affairs* 8, no. 3 (1992); and Jack Snyder, "Science and Sovietology: Bridging the Methods Gap in Soviet Foreign Policy Studies," *World Politics* 40, no. 2 (January 1988); Peter Zwick, "The Perestroika of Soviet Studies: Thinking and Teaching about the Soviet Union in Comparative Perspective," *PS: Political Science and Politics* 24, no. 3 (September 1991); Martin Malia, "From under the Rubble, What?" *Problems of Communism* 41, nos. 1–2 (January–April 1992); Michael Cox, "The End of the USSR and the Collapse of Soviet Studies," *Coexistence* 31 (1994); Charles King, "Post-Sovietology: Area Studies or Social Science?" *International Affairs* 70, no. 2 (1994).

3. For a summary of the "new faces" in the first generation of postcommunist studies, see Christopher Shea, "New Faces and New Methodologies Invigorate Russian Studies," *Chronicle of Higher Education*, February 20, 1998. For a sampling of the first generation of postcommunist research in fields as diverse as political economy and political anthropology, see Steven Solnick, *Stealing the State: Control and Collapse in Soviet Institutions* (Cambridge, Mass.: Harvard University Press, 1998); David M. Woodruff, *Money Unmade: Barter and the Fate of Russian Capitalism* (Ithaca, N.Y.: Cornell University Press, 1999); Andrei Shleifer and Daniel Treisman, *Without a Map: Political Tactics and Economic Reform in Russia* (Cambridge, Mass.: MIT Press, 2000). Kathryn Stoner-Weiss, *Local Heroes: The Political Economy of Russian Regional Governance* (Princeton, N.J.: Princeton University Press, 1997); Kathryn Hendley, *Trying to Make Law Matter: Legal Reform and Labor Law in the Soviet Union* (Ann Arbor: University of Michigan Press, 1996); Tone Bringa, *Being Muslim the Bosnian Way: Identity and Community in a Central Bosnian Village* (Princeton, N.J.: Princeton University Press, 1996); Anastasia N. Karakasidou, *Fields of Wheat, Hills of Blood: Passages to Nationhood in Greek Macedonia, 1870–1990* (Chicago: University of Chicago Press, 1997).

4. Sidney and Beatrice Webb, *Soviet Communism: A New Civilisation?* (London: Gollancz, 1935). Some travelers, especially Panait Istrati and Nikos Kazantzakis, were far less enthusiastic about the Soviet experiment than many of their contemporaries. See Istrati, *Russia Unveiled*, trans. R. J. S. Curtis (London: George Allen and Unwin, 1931); Kazantzakis, *Russia: A Chronicle of Three Journeys in the Aftermath of the Revolution* (Berkeley, Calif.: Creative Arts, 1989).

5. The contribution of British scholars—especially Leonard Shapiro, Hugh Seton-Watson, Alec Nove, and later, Archie Brown, Stephen White, Mary McAuley, and others—was central. For an analytical survey of British scholarship, see Archie Brown, "The Study of Totalitarianism and Authoritarianism," in Jack Hayward, Brian Barry, and Archie Brown, eds., *The British Study of Politics in the Twentieth Century* (London: Oxford University Press, 1999), 345–394.

6. For important examples of this scholarship, see Merle Fainsod, *How Russia Is Ruled* (Cambridge, Mass.: Harvard University Press, 1953); Carl J. Friedrich and Zbigniew Brzezinski, *Totalitarian Dictatorship and Autocracy* (Cambridge, Mass.: Harvard University Press, 1956); Carl J. Friedrich, ed., *Totalitarianism* (Cambridge, Mass.: Harvard University Press, 1954); and Leonard Shapiro, *Totalitarianism* (London: Pall Mall, 1972). Shapiro's *The Communist Party of the Soviet Union* (London: Eyre and Spottiswoode, 1960) was no less committed to straightforward institutional analysis,

but it did mark a shift toward trying to understand process as well as structure in the Soviet state.

7. For analyses of the role of the totalitarian model in shaping both academic debate and foreign policy, see Stephen F. Cohen, *Rethinking the Soviet Experience: Politics and History since 1917* (Oxford: Oxford University Press, 1985); and Abbott Gleason, *Totalitarianism: The Inner History of the Cold War* (New York: Oxford University Press, 1995).

8. For an overview of this literature, see Gabriel A. Almond and Laura Roselle, "Model Fitting in Communism Studies," in Frederic J. Fleron Jr. and Erik P. Hoffman, eds., *Post-Communist Studies and Political Science* (Boulder, Colo.: Westview, 1993), 27–75. For examples, see Archie Brown, *Soviet Politics and Political Science* (London: Macmillan, 1974); Archie Brown and John Gray, eds., *Political Culture and Political Change in Communist States* (London: Macmillan, 1977); Archie Brown, ed., *Political Culture and Communist Studies* (London: Macmillan, 1984); Susan Gross Solomon, ed., *Pluralism in the Soviet Union: Essays in Honour of H. Gordon Skilling* (London: Macmillan, 1983).

9. Jerry F. Hough and Merle Fainsod, *How the Soviet Union Is Governed* (Cambridge, Mass.: Harvard University Press, 1979), vii.

10. For important work, see Ronald J. Hill, *Soviet Politics, Political Science and Reform* (Oxford: Martin Robertson, 1980); T. H. Rigby and Bogdan Harasymiw, eds., *Leadership Selection and Patron-Client Relations in the USSR and Yugoslavia* (London: Allen and Unwin, 1983); Stephen White and Alex Pravda, eds., *Ideology and Soviet Politics* (London: Macmillan, 1988); Archie Brown, ed., *Political Leadership in the Soviet Union* (London: Macmillan, 1989); and T. H. Rigby, *Political Elites in the USSR: Central Leaders and Local Cadres from Lenin to Gorbachev* (Aldershot, England: Edward Elgar, 1990) and *The Changing Soviet System: Mono-Organisational Socialism from Its Origins to Gorbachev's Restructuring* (Aldershot, England: Edward Elgar, 1990).

11. The work of historians, economic historians, and political sociologists was essential in the shift from the totalitarian model to elite-conflict and modernizationist models. See Theodore H. Von Laue, *Why Lenin? Why Stalin? A Reappraisal of the Russian Revolution, 1900–1930* (Philadelphia: J. B. Lippincott, 1964); Alec Nove, *Economic Rationality and Soviet Politics, or Was Stalin Really Necessary?* (New York: Praeger, 1964); Roger Pethybridge, *The Social Prelude to Stalinism* (London: Macmillan, 1974); and Kenneth Jowitt, *Revolutionary Breakthroughs and National Development: The Case of Romania, 1944–1965* (Berkeley: University of California Press, 1971).

12. Rasma Karklins, *Ethnic Relations in the USSR: The Perspective from Below* (Boston: Unwin Hyman, 1986), which received the 1987 Ralph E. Bunche Award from the American Political Science Association. Karklins's work was followed by a flood of other books, as the ethnic dimensions of Soviet politics became increasingly evident. See Lubomyr Hajda and Mark Beissinger, eds., *The Nationalities Factor in Soviet Politics and Society* (Boulder, Colo.: Westview, 1990); Bohdan Nahaylo and Victor Swoboda, *Soviet Disunion: A History of the Nationalities Problem in the USSR* (London: Hamish Hamilton, 1990); Alexander J. Motyl, *Sovietology, Rationality, Nationality: Coming to*

Grips with Nationalism in the USSR (New York: Columbia University Press, 1990); Graham Smith, ed., *The Nationalities Question in the Soviet Union* (London: Longman, 1990); Gail W. Lapidus and Victor Zaslavsky, with Philip Goldman, eds., *From Union to Commonwealth: Nationalism and Separatism in the Soviet Republics* (Cambridge: Cambridge University Press, 1992); Hélène Carrère d'Encausse, *The Great Challenge: Nationalities and the Bolshevik State, 1917–1930*, trans. Nancy Festinger (New York: Holmes and Meier, 1992) and *The End of the Soviet Empire: The Triumph of the Nations*, trans. Franklin Philip (New York: Basic Books, 1993); and Ian Bremmer and Ray Taras, eds., *Nations and Politics in the Soviet Successor States* (Cambridge: Cambridge University Press, 1993).

13. Peter Rutland, "Sovietology: Notes for a Post-Mortem," *National Interest*, no. 31 (Spring 1993): 114–115.

14. Valerie Bunce, *Subversive Institutions: The Design and Destruction of Socialism and the State* (Cambridge: Cambridge University Press, 1999), 162–164.

15. Bunce, *Subversive Institutions*, 142.

16. Transparency International, *1999 Corruption Perceptions Index*, www.transparency.de/documents/cpi/index.html.

17. Joseph Rothschild and Nancy M. Wingfield, *Return to Diversity: A Political History of East Central Europe since World War II*, 4th ed. (Oxford: Oxford University Press, 2007).

18. Leslie Holmes, *Postcommunism: An Introduction* (Durham, N.C.: Duke University Press, 1997), 15.

19. Richard Sakwa, *Postcommunism* (Buckingham, England: Open University Press, 1999), 5–6.

20. For comparison, see Stephen White, John Gardner, George Schöpflin, and Tony Saich, *Communist and Postcommunist Political Systems: An Introduction*, 3rd ed. (New York: St. Martin's, 1990); Michael Mandelbaum, ed., *Postcommunism: Four Perspectives* (New York: Council on Foreign Relations Press, 1996); Stephen White, Judy Batt, and Paul G. Lewis, eds., *Developments in Central and East European Politics*, 4th ed. (Durham, N.C.: Duke University Press, 2007); Stephen White and Daniel N. Nelson, eds., *The Politics of the Postcommunist World: From Communist to Postcommunist Politics* (London: Ashgate, 2000); Padraic Kenney, *The Burdens of Freedom: Eastern Europe since 1989* (London: Zed, 2006).

21. Bunce, *Subversive Institutions;* Katherine Verdery, *What Was Socialism, and What Comes Next?* (Princeton, N.J.: Princeton University Press, 1996); Susan Gal and Gail Kligman, eds., *Reproducing Gender: Politics, Publics, and Everyday Life after Socialism* (Princeton, N.J.: Princeton University Press, 2000).

22. Valerie Bunce, "Can We Compare Democratization in the East versus the South?" *Journal of Democracy* 6, no. 3 (July 1995), "Should Transitologists Be Grounded?" *Slavic Review* 54, no. 1 (Spring 1995), "Paper Curtains and Paper Tigers," *Slavic Review* 54, no. 4 (Winter 1995), and "Regional Differences in Democratization," *Post-Soviet Affairs* 17, no. 3 (July 1998). See also Sarah Meiklejohn Terry, "Thinking about Post-Communist Transitions: How Different Are They?" *Slavic Review* 52, no. 2 (Summer 1993); Philippe C. Schmitter with Terry Lynn Karl, "The Conceptual Travels

of Transitologists and Consolidologists: How Far East Should They Attempt to Go?" *Slavic Review* 53, no. 1 (Spring 1994); and Karl and Schmitter, "From an Iron Curtain to a Paper Curtain: Grounding Transitologists or Students of Postcommunism?" *Slavic Review* 54, no. 4 (Winter 1995).

23. See Thomas Carothers, "The End of the Transition Paradigm," *Journal of Democracy* 13, no. 1 (2002) and *Critical Mission: Essays on Democracy Promotion* (Washington, D.C.: Carnegie Endowment for International Peace, 2004); and the special section on "Debating the Transition Paradigm," *Journal of Democracy* 13, no. 3 (2002).

24. Bunce, *Subversive Institutions*, 158–159.

25. Giuseppe Di Palma, *To Craft Democracies: An Essay on Democratic Transitions* (Berkeley: University of California Press, 1990).

26. See, for example, Deborah J. Yashar, "Democracy, Indigenous Movements, and the Postliberal Challenge in Latin America," *World Politics* 52, no. 1 (October 1999).

27. For an analysis of the problems of transition modeling in a particular case, see Valerie Bunce and Maria Csanadi, "Uncertainty in the Transition: Post-Communism in Hungary," *East European Politics and Societies* 7, no. 2 (1993) and "Rethinking Recent Democratization: Lessons from the Postcommunist Experience," *World Politics* 55, no. 2 (2003).

28. For an examination of this issue, see Gerald M. Easter, "Preference for Presidentialism: Postcommunist Regime Change in Russian and the NIS," *World Politics*, 49, no. 1 (January 1997); and Anna Seleny, "Old Political Rationalities and New Democracies: Compromise and Confrontation in Hungary and Poland," *World Politics* 51, no. 3 (July 1999).

29. Thomas Carothers, *Aiding Democracy Abroad: The Learning Curve* (Washington, D.C.: Carnegie Endowment for International Peace, 1999); Janine R. Wedel, *Collision and Collusion: The Strange Case of Western Aid to Eastern Europe*, 2nd ed. (New York: Palgrave, 2001).

30. Adam Przeworski, *Democracy and the Market: Political and Economic Reforms in Eastern Europe and Latin America* (Cambridge: Cambridge University Press, 1991), xii.

31. Bunce, *Subversive Institutions*, 131.

32. Adam Przeworski and Henry Teune, *The Logic of Comparative Social Inquiry* (New York: John Wiley, 1970), 22–23.

33. For early exceptions, see Alexander J. Motyl, *Sovietology, Rationality, Nationality: Coming to Grips with Nationalism in the USSR* (New York: Columbia University Press, 1990); Philip Roeder, "Soviet Federalism and Ethnic Mobilization," *World Politics* 43, no. 1 (January 1991); Robert Hayden, "Constitutional Nationalism in the Formerly Yugoslav Republics," *Slavic Review* 51, no. 4 (Winter 1992); V. P. Gagnon, "Ethnic Nationalism and International Conflict: The Case of Serbia," *International Security* 19, no. 3 (Winter 1994–1995). Today, the pendulum has perhaps swung too far in the opposite direction, stressing the manipulative role of unscrupulous elites.

34. Daniel Treisman, *After the Deluge: Regional Crises and Political Consolidation in Russia* (Ann Arbor: University of Michigan Press, 1999).

35. Jeffrey Kahn, *Federalism, Democratization, and the Rule of Law in Russia* (Oxford: Oxford University Press, 2002); Dmitry P. Gorenburg, *Minority Ethnic Mobilization in the Russian Federation* (Cambridge: Cambridge University Press, 2003); Henry E. Hale, "Divided We Stand: Institutional Sources of Ethnofederal State Survival and Collapse," *World Politics* 56, no. 2 (2004); Elise Giuliano, "Secessionism from the Bottom Up: Democratization, Nationalism, and Local Accountability in the Russian Transition," *World Politics* 58, no. 2 (2006).

36. Treisman, *After the Deluge*, 119.

37. Treisman, *After the Deluge*, 216–217.

38. Karen Barkey, *Bandits and Bureaucrats: The Ottoman Route to State Centralization* (Ithaca, N.Y.: Cornell University Press, 1994).

39. Susan L. Woodward, *Socialist Unemployment: The Political Economy of Yugoslavia, 1945–1990* (Princeton, N.J.: Princeton University Press, 1995), especially chap. 10. See also V. P. Gagnon, *The Myth of Ethnic War: Serbia and Croatia in the 1990s* (Ithaca, N.Y.: Cornell University Press, 2004). For a longer term structural view, see Keith Darden and Anna Maria Gryzmała-Busse, "The Great Divide: Literacy, Nationalism, and the Communist Collapse," *World Politics* 59, no. 1 (2006).

40. Ronald Grigor Suny, *The Revenge of the Past: Nationalism, Revolution, and the Collapse of the Soviet Union* (Stanford, Calif.: Stanford University Press, 1993).

41. Susan L. Woodward, *Balkan Tragedy: Chaos and Dissolution after the Cold War* (Washington, D.C.: Brookings Institution, 1995); Brubaker, *Nationalism Reframed;* and Michael Hechter, *Containing Nationalism* (Oxford: Oxford University Press, 2000).

42. Philip G. Roeder, "Peoples and States after 1989: The Political Costs of Incomplete National Revivals," *Slavic Review* 58, no. 4 (1999).

43. Bunce, *Subversive Institutions*, 143.

44. Stephen F. Jones, "Democracy from Below? Interest Groups in Georgian Society," *Slavic Review* 59, no. 1 (2000); Charles King, "Potemkin Democracy," *National Interest* (Summer 2001).

45. Timur Kuran, "Now Out of Never: The Element of Surprise in the East European Revolution of 1989," *World Politics* 44, no. 1 (October 1991): 47.

46. See Henry E. Hale, "Regime Cycles: Democracy, Autocracy, and Revolution in Post-Soviet Eurasia," *World Politics* 58, no. 1 (2005).

47. For two treatments of the old eastern Europe in a pan-European context, one by a historian and another by a political scientist, see Tony Judt, *Postwar: A History of Europe since 1945* (New York: Penguin, 2005) and Milada Vachudová, *Europe Undivided: Democracy, Leverage, and Integration after Communism* (Oxford: Oxford University Press, 2005).

48. Kenneth Jowitt, *New World Disorder: The Leninist Extinction* (Berkeley: University of California Press, 1992). See also Vladimir Tismaneanu, Marc Morjé Howard, and Rudra Sil, eds., *World Order after Leninism* (Seattle: University of Washington Press, 2006).

49. See Mark R. Beissinger and Crawford Young, eds., *Beyond State Crisis? Post-Colonial Africa and Post-Soviet Eurasia in Comparative Perspective* (Washington, D.C.: Woodrow Wilson Center Press, 2002); Vadim Volkov, *Violent Entrepreneurs: The Use of Force in the Making of Russian Capitalism* (Ithaca, N.Y.: Cornell University Press, 2002); and Georgi Derluguian, *Bourdieu's Secret Admirer in the Caucasus* (Chicago: University of Chicago Press, 2005).

50. Adam Przeworski, *Democracy and the Market: Political and Economic Reforms in Eastern Europe and Latin America* (Cambridge: Cambridge University Press, 1991), 161.

51. For discussions of the ethical dimensions of post-Soviet studies, see Robert T. Huber and Susan Bronson, "The August Revolution and Soviet Studies," in Frederic J. Fleron Jr. and Erik P. Hoffman, eds., *Post-Communist Studies and Political Science* (Boulder, Colo.: Westview, 1993), 191–202; and the discussion of the "commercialization of scholarship" in *Slavic Review* 52, no. 1 (1993).

52. Gary King, Robert O. Keohane, and Sidney Verba, *Designing Social Inquiry: Scientific Inference in Qualitative Research* (Princeton, N.J.: Princeton University Press, 1994).

53. Marc Morjé Howard, *The Weakness of Civil Society in Post-Communist Europe* (Cambridge: Cambridge University Press, 2003).

CHAPTER 6

1. See David Keen, *The Benefits of Famine: A Political Economy of Famine Relief in Southwestern Sudan, 1983–1989* (Princeton, N.J.: Princeton University Press, 1994); William Reno, *Corruption and State Politics in Sierra Leone* (Cambridge: Cambridge University Press, 1995); Stephen Ellis, *The Mask of Anarchy: The Roots of Liberia's War* (New York: New York University Press, 1999); and Scott Straus, *The Order of Genocide: Race, Power, and War in Rwanda* (Ithaca, N.Y.: Cornell University Press, 2006).

2. In deeply divided societies, even spelling bees are political events, so place names in each of these instances are controversial. I use Transnistria instead of *Pridnestrov'e* or *Transdniestria* because it is more easily pronounceable, and Abkhazia, South Ossetia, and Karabakh because few people will have heard of alternative designations such as *Apsny, Iryston,* and *Azat Artsakh*. The same rule of convenience applies to other proper nouns.

3. Paul R. Pillar, *Negotiating Peace: War Termination as a Bargaining Process* (Princeton, N.J.: Princeton University Press, 1983), 25; Stephen John Stedman, *Peacemaking in Civil War: International Mediation in Zimbabwe, 1974–1980* (Boulder, Colo.: Lynne Reinner, 1991), 9; Roy Licklider, "The Consequences of Negotiated Settlements in Civil Wars, 1945–1993," *American Political Science Review* 89 (September 1995): 686.

4. Chaim Kaufmann, "Possible and Impossible Solutions to Ethnic Civil Wars," *International Security* 20 (Spring 1996); Monica Duffy Toft, *The Geography of Ethnic Violence: Identity, Interests, and the Indivisibility of Territory* (Princeton, N.J.: Princeton University Press, 2003).

5. Rui J. de Figueiredo Jr. and Barry R. Weingast, "The Rationality of Fear: Political Opportunism and Ethnic Conflict," in Barbara F. Walter and Jack Snyder, eds., *Civil Wars, Insecurity, and Intervention* (New York: Columbia University Press, 1999).

6. I. William Zartman, *Ripe for Resolution: Conflict and Intervention in Africa* (Oxford: Oxford University Press, 1985).

7. Barry R. Posen, "The Security Dilemma and Ethnic Conflict," in Michael E. Brown, ed., *Ethnic Conflict and International Security* (Princeton, N.J.: Princeton University Press, 1993); James D. Fearon, "Commitment Problems and the Spread of Ethnic Conflict," in David A. Lake and Donald Rothchild, eds., *The International Spread of Ethnic Conflict: Fear, Diffusion, and Escalation* (Princeton, N.J.: Princeton University Press, 1998); Barbara F. Walter, "The Critical Barrier to Civil War Settlement," *International Organization* 51 (Summer 1997).

8. Chaim Kaufmann, "When All Else Fails: Ethnic Population Transfers and Partitions in the Twentieth Century," *International Security* 23 (Fall 1998); Edward N. Luttwak, "Give War a Chance," *Foreign Affairs* 78 (July–August 1999).

9. David Keen, "When War Itself Is Privatized," *Times Literary Supplement,* December 29, 1995. For a full exposition of his argument, see David Keen, *The Economic Functions of Violence in Civil Wars,* Adelphi Paper 320 (Oxford: Oxford University Press and International Institute for Strategic Studies, 1998).

10. For early statements of these issues, see William Reno, *Warlord Politics and African States* (Boulder, Colo.: Lynne Reinner, 1998); Mats Berdal and David M. Malone, eds., *Greed and Grievance: Economic Agendas in Civil Wars* (Boulder, Colo.: Lynne Reinner, 2000); and several working papers by Paul Collier and his associates at Oxford University and the Development Research Group of the World Bank. See the collection of Collier's recent papers on conflict at users.ox.ac.uk/~econpco/, as well as Collier's *The Bottom Billion* (Oxford: Oxford University Press, 2007) on the economic effects of war in the developing world.

11. For an enlightening overview of the origins and course of the Karabakh war, see David D. Laitin and Ronald Grigor Suny, "Armenia and Azerbaijan: Thinking a Way Out of Karabakh," *Middle East Policy* 7 (October 1999).

12. V. A. Zolotarev, ed., *Rossiia (SSSR) v lokal'nykh voinakh i voennykh konfliktakh vtoroi poloviny XX veka* (Moscow: Institute of Military History, Russian Ministry of Defense, 2000), 45.

13. See Charles King, *The Moldovans: Romania, Russia, and the Politics of Culture* (Stanford, Calif.: Hoover Institution Press, 2000), chap. 9.

14. *The Military Balance, 2000–2001* (London: International Institute for Strategic Studies, 2000), 100; and *The Military Balance, 2008* (London: International Institute for Strategic Studies, 2008), 463–464.

15. Economic figures are based on World Bank reports at www.worldbank.org.

16. For an overview of the economic dimensions of the Caucasus conflicts, see Diana Klein et al., eds., *Ot ekonomiki voiny k ekonomike mira na Iuzhnom Kavkaze* (London: International Alert, 2004).

17. Author's interviews in Tskhinvali, October 13, 2000.

18. Author's interview with Hans-Gjorg Heinrich, advisor to OSCE mission, Tbilisi, October 23, 2000.

19. For a comprehensive study of the economics of the unrecognized states, see Stacy Closson, "State Weakness in Perspective: Trans-Territorial Energy Networks in Georgia, 1993–2003" (Ph.D. diss., London School of Economics, 2007).

20. Author's interviews with Transnistrian steelworkers, Rîbniţa, August 1, 1997.

21. Author's interview with Valeriu Prudnicov, Moldovan police commissioner, Bender, August 1, 1997.

22. *Republic of Moldova: Economic Review of the Transnistria Region, June 1998* (Washington, D.C.: World Bank, 1998), 27. For an update, see International Crisis Group, *Moldova's Uncertain Future*, Report No. 175 (August 17, 2006), available at www.icg.org.

23. See Rogers Brubaker, *Nationalism Reframed: Nationhood and the National Question in the New Europe* (Cambridge: Cambridge University Press, 1996), especially chap. 3.

24. See Zolotarev, *Rossiia (SSSR) v lokal'nykh voinakh*, especially chap. 8.

25. *Moldova suverană*, June 11, 1991, 1; *Curierul national*, April 4, 1992, 1, 7; *România liberă*, April 4–5, 1992, 8.

26. Stephen Bowers, "The Crisis in Moldova," *Jane's Intelligence Review*, November 1992, 484.

27. *Den,'* August 9–15, 1992, and Radio Maiak, September 18, 1992, both cited in Mihai Gribincea, *Politica rusă a bazelor militare: Moldova şi Gecorgia* (Chisinau: Civitas, 1999), 15. Gribincea's book is still the most thorough study of the Russian military's role in Moldova and Georgia. See also his *Trupele ruse în Republica Moldova: factor stabilizator sau sursă de pericol?* (Chisinau: Civitas, 1998).

28. Gribincea, *Politica rusă*, 42–43.

29. Author's interview with Elena Niculina, World Bank representative, Chisinau, July 29, 1997. The same point, however, could be made even about the recognized states. Russia continues to provide what amounts to subsidized gas deliveries, since outstanding debts from the former Soviet republics are often paid in government-issued bonds, which were, as Gazprom must realize, virtually worthless throughout much of the 1990s.

30. *The Military Balance, 2008*, 222.

31. *Georgia Today*, October 6–12, 2000, 4.

32. Russian peacekeeping forces, although under a separate command from regular army personnel, have had a similar influence on the local economy. Before 2008, there were around 1,500 Russian peacekeepers in Abkhazia (formally a CIS peacekeeping mission), 500 in South Ossetia, and 500 in Transnistria.

33. *Svobodnaia Gruziia*, October 24, 2000, 3, and October 25, 2000, 1.

34. In August 2000, Moldova adopted a new citizenship law that provided for dual citizenship based on bilateral agreements. Currently, however, Moldova does not have any such agreements with foreign countries.

35. *Oxford Analytica East Europe Daily Brief,* June 29, 2000.

36. For a full analysis of the Abkhaz case, see the work of Lyndon Allin summarized in his "Passport Power: Documents, Citizenship and Russian Leverage in Abkhazia," IREX Regional Policy Symposium Paper, 2008, available at http://www. irex.org/programs/symp/08/Allin_Lyndon_Executive_Summary.pdf.

37. Author's interviews in Stepanakert, September 27–28, 2000; *Russia Journal*, October 7, 2000 (electronic version at www.russiajournal.com/weekly); *Radio Free Europe/Radio Liberty Armenia Report*, May 1, 2000. Diaspora support, however, has not been as enthusiastic as Karabakh leaders would like. In 2000, a tour through the United States by Karabakh premier Anushavan Danielian produced pledges of around $5 million. The campaign had hoped to raise four times that amount.

38. Author's interview with Igor Munteanu, director of the Viitorul Foundation, Tbilisi, October 12, 2000.

39. Aleksandr Ianovskii, *Osetiia* (Tskhinvali: Ministry of Information and Press of the Republic of South Ossetia, 1993), 3, from the editor's preface.

40. A. B. Dzadziev, Kh. V. Dzutsev, and S. M. Karaev, *Etnografiia i mifologiia osetin* (Vladikavkaz: n.p., 1994), 64.

41. N. V. Babilunga and V. G. Bomeshko, *Pagini din istoria plaiului natal* (Tiraspol: Transnistrian Institute of Continuing Education, 1997), 98.

42. See, for example, N. Babilunga, ed., *Bessarabskii vopros i obrazovanie Pridnestrovskoi Moldavskoi Respubliki* (Tiraspol: Dnestr State Cooperative University, 1993), and M. Shornikov, *Pokushenie na status* (Chisinau: Chisinau Society of Russians, 1997). For a cognate view, although by a Moldovan rather than a Transnistrian, see Vasile Stati, *Istoria Moldovei* (Chisinau: Vivar-Editor, 2002).

43. See the "Corruption Perceptions Index" at www.transparency.org.

44. Author's confidential interview with senior United Nations official, Tbilisi, October 30, 2000.

45. *Radio Free Europe/Radio Liberty Caucasus Report*, April 7, 2000.

46. Heinrich interview; author's interviews with Naira Gelashvili, director of Caucasus House, Tbilisi, October 3 and 23, 2000; *Ekho-Daidzhest*, August 1–15, 2000, 7.

47. *Georgian Lifestyle Survey*, 2000, cited in *Human Development Report, Georgia 2000* (Tbilisi: United Nations Development Program, 2000), 74.

48. *Buletinul Social-democrat*, no. 2 (2000); and author's conversations with Oazu Nantoi.

49. *Foreign Broadcast Information Service–Soviet Union*, October 24, 2000.

50. For further analysis of these trends in the Transnistrian case, see "Thawing a Frozen Conflict: Legal Aspects of the Separatist Crisis in Moldova," Report of the Association of the Bar of New York, 2006, available at http://www.abcny.org/PressRoom/PressRelease/2006_0502c.htm.

51. *Georgia Today*, August 11–17, 2000, 3.

52. Author's confidential interview with senior manager of U.S. assistance program, Stepanakert, September 28, 2000. Even the OSCE Minsk Group, the main negotiating forum, is based in Tbilisi, since basing the mission in either Baku or Yerevan would have been unacceptable to one of the sides.

53. "Memorandum ob osnovakh normalizatsii otnoshenii mezhdu Respublikoi Moldova i Pridnestrov'em," signed May 8, 1997, Moscow.

54. Author's confidential interview with senior official in the United Nations Office for the Coordination of Humanitarian Assistance (UNOCHA), Tbilisi, August 29, 2000.

55. For alternative definitions of the precedent-setting elements of the Kosovo declaration, see Nikolai Sokov, "The Political and Legal Parameters of Russian Decisionmaking on Abkhazia and South Ossetia," PONARS Eurasia Policy Memo No. 6, March 2008; and Alexander Cooley, "Kosovo's Precedents: The Politics of Sovereign Emergence and Its Alternatives," PONARS Eurasia Policy Memo No. 7, March 2008, both available at esp.sfs.georgetown.edu/ponarsmemos.

56. Assembly of Kosovo, "Kosovo Declaration of Independence," February 17, 2008, available at www.assembly-kosova.org.

57. For a small sample, see Stuart J. Kaufman, *Modern Hatreds: The Symbolic Politics of Ethnic War* (Ithaca, N.Y.: Cornell University Press, 2001); Mark R. Beissinger, *Nationalist Mobilization and the Collapse of the Soviet State* (Cambridge: Cambridge University Press, 2002); Philip G. Roeder, *Where Nation-States Come from: Institutional Change in the Age of Nationalism* (Princeton, N.J.: Princeton University Press, 2007); and Christoph Zürcher, *The Post-Soviet Wars: Rebellion, Ethnic Conflict, and Nationhood in the Caucasus* (New York: New York University Press, 2007).

58. See Richard Holbrooke, *To End a War* (New York: Random House, 1998).

59. Zolotarev, *Rossiia (SSSR) v lokal'nykh voinakh*, 395.

CHAPTER 7

1. See Stephen M. Saideman, *The Ties That Divide: Ethnic Politics, Foreign Policy, and International Conflict* (New York: Columbia University Press, 2001); Stephen M. Saideman and R. William Ayres, *For Kin or Country: Xenophobia, Nationalism, and War* (New York: Columbia University Press, 2008); V. P. Gagnon Jr., "Ethnic Nationalism and International Security: The Case of Serbia," *International Security* 19, no. 3 (Winter 1994–1995); James Fearon, "Commitment Problems and the Spread of Ethnic Conflict," in David A. Lake and Donald Rothchild, eds., *The International Spread of Ethnic Conflict* (Princeton, N.J.: Princeton University Press, 1998), 107–126; Stephen Saideman, "Explaining the International Relations of Secessionist Conflicts: Vulnerability vs. Ethnic Ties," *International Organization* 51, no. 4 (Autumn 1997); Jack Snyder, "Nationalism and the Crisis of the Post-Soviet State," in Michael E. Brown, ed., *Ethnic Conflict and International Security* (Princeton, N.J.: Princeton University Press, 1993), 79–101; David Carment and Patrick James, "Internal Constraints and Interstate Ethnic Conflict: Toward a Crisis-Based Assessment of Irredentism," *Journal of Conflict Resolution* 39, no. 1 (March 1995); David R. Davis, Keith Jaggers, and Will H. Moore, "Ethnicity, Minorities, and International Conflict Patterns," in David W. Carment and Patrick James, eds., *Wars in the Midst of Peace: The International Politics of Ethnic Conflict* (Pittsburgh, Pa.: University of Pittsburgh Press, 1997); Donald Rothchild and Alexander J. Groth, "Pathological Dimensions of Domestic and International

Ethnicity," *Political Science Quarterly* 110, no. 1 (Spring 1995); Ted Robert Gurr, "The Internationalization of Protracted Communal Conflicts since 1945: Which Groups, Where, and How?" in Manus I. Midlarsky, ed., *The Internationalization of Communal Strife* (London: Routledge, 1992); and Abram Chayes and Antonia Handler Chayes, *Preventing Conflict in the Post-Communist World: Mobilizing International and Regional Organizations* (Washington, D.C.: Brookings, 1996).

2. David D. Laitin, "Identity in Formation: The Russian-speaking Nationality in the Post-Soviet Diaspora," *Archives européenes de sociologie* 36, no. 2 (1995). For an overview and critique of the idea of a Russian diaspora as a mobilized source of opposition to local governments, which Anatol Lieven has termed the failure of "the Serbian option" in Russian politics, see Lieven, *Chechnya: Tombstone of Russian Power* (New Haven, Conn.: Yale University Press, 1998), 243–268.

3. There are a range of other cases that are significant, of course: Azerbaijanis in Azerbaijan and Iran, Uzbeks in Uzbekistan and other parts of Central Asia, Uyghurs in China and their relationship to Muslim Turkic populations in Central Asia, Han Chinese in the Russian Far East, along with eastern Europe and Eurasia's three largest archetypal diasporic peoples, the Jews, Armenians, and Roma. The three cases here have been chosen for the following reasons.

First, they all involve a newly independent state and its effort to establish ties with a territorially dispersed population whose link to the state is primarily culture, not citizenship. I am interested in examining the relationship between a state and an ethnic group outside that state. There are certainly many other issues at stake in the study of diasporas—where diasporic identities come from, what counts as a genuine diaspora, how diasporas maintain intergenerational solidarity, and so on. Although fascinating, these questions are not the core concern here.

Second, these cases represent stranded diasporas, communities that became separated from their newly defined homelands because of changes in international borders. These cases thus provide a kind of blank slate on which states and coethnic communities can rework their own conceptions of civic identity, ethnic ties, and state obligations.

Third, the states concerned have had varying levels of success in building bridges to, and varying commitment toward, their diasporas. Not all the diaspora policies covered here have been successful, and some have yielded outcomes that their originators perhaps did not intend. Accounting for these divergent developments is one of the goals of this chapter.

4. On the Russian diaspora, see Neil J. Melvin, *Russians beyond Russia: The Politics of National Identity* (London: Pinter, 1995); Vladimir Shlapentokh, Munir Sendich, and Emil Payin, eds., *The New Russian Diaspora: Russian Minorities in the Former Soviet Republics* (Armonk, N.Y.: M. E. Sharpe, 1994); Paul Kolstoe, *Russians in the Former Soviet Republics* (Bloomington: Indiana University Press, 1995); Jeff Chinn and Robert Kaiser, *Russians as the New Minority: Ethnicity and Nationalism in the Soviet Successor States* (Boulder, Colo.: Westview, 1996); David D. Laitin, *Identity in Formation: The Russian-Speaking Populations in the Near Abroad* (Ithaca, N.Y.: Cornell University Press, 1998).

5. James N. Rosenau, *Along the Domestic-Foreign Frontier: Exploring Governance in a Turbulent World* (Cambridge: Cambridge University Press, 1997).

6. Thomas Sowell, *Migrations and Cultures: A World View* (New York: Basic Books, 1996); Dimitri C. Constas and Athanasios G. Platias, eds., *Diasporas in World Politics: The Greeks in Comparative Perspective* (London: Macmillan, 1993); and Gabriel Sheffer, ed., *Modern Diasporas in International Politics* (London: Croom Helm, 1986).

7. *The Bolzano/Bozen Recommendations on National Minorities in Inter-State Relations and Explanatory Note, June 2008* (The Hague: OSCE High Commissioner on National Minorities, 2008), available at www.osce.org/hcnm/item_11_33388.html.

8. Rogers Brubaker, *Nationalism Reframed* (Cambridge: Cambridge University Press, 1996), 103. Emphasis in original.

9. For further discussion of the mutability of diaspora consciousness, see Paul Gilroy, *"There Ain't No Black in the Union Jack": The Cultural Politics of Race and Nation* (London: Hutchinson, 1987); Robin Cohen, *Global Diasporas: An Introduction* (London: UCL Press, 1997); James Clifford, "Diasporas," *Cultural Anthropology* 9, no. 3 (August 1994); and Yossi Shain, *Kinship and Diasporas in International Affairs* (Ann Arbor: University of Michigan Press, 2007).

10. Stephen Van Evera, "Hypotheses on Nationalism and the Causes of War," in Charles A. Kupchan, ed., *Nationalism and Nationalities in the New Europe* (Ithaca, N.Y.: Cornell University Press/Council on Foreign Relations, 1995): 137–138.

11. Kalevi J. Holsti, *The State, War, and the State of War* (Cambridge: Cambridge University Press, 1996), 127.

12. For overviews of the administrative system and its links with ethnic mobilization, see Robert Kaiser, *The Geography of Nationalism in Russia and the USSR* (Princeton, N.J.: Princeton University Press, 1994). On Soviet nation building, see Yuri Slezkine, "The USSR as a Communal Apartment, or How a Socialist State Promoted Ethnic Particularism," *Slavic Review* 53, no. 2 (Summer 1994); Terry Martin, *The Affirmative Action Empire: Nations and Nationalism in the Soviet Union, 1923–1939* (Ithaca, N.Y.: Cornell University Press, 2002); and Francine Hirsch, *Empire of Nations: Ethnographic Knowledge and the Making of the Soviet State* (Ithaca, N.Y.: Cornell University Press, 2005).

13. For an overview of Russian settlement at the time of the Soviet collapse, based on the 1989 census, see Chauncy Harris, "The New Russian Minorities: A Statistical Overview," *Post-Soviet Geography* 34, no. 1 (January 1993).

14. The comparison of Russians with the imperial elites of other empires can be overdrawn, but for thoughtful and careful comparisons, see Karen Dawisha and Bruce Parrott, eds., *The End of Empire? The Transformation of the USSR in Comparative Perspective* (Armonk, N.Y.: M. E. Sharpe, 1997).

15. Melvin, *Russians beyond Russia*, 10.

16. Constantine Dmitriev, "New Migration Tests Russian Immigration Policy," *Transition*, June 28, 1996, 56. Between 1992 and 1996, an estimated 3 million people migrated to Russia from the non-Russian republics.

17. "Yeltsin Gives New Year Address with Pledge to Stand by Russian Citizens Abroad," BBC *Summary of World Broadcasts–Soviet Union* (hereafter *SWB-SU*), January

3, 1994. In a shorter address at the beginning of 1995, Yeltsin again picked out the Russians outside Russia for particular mention. "Yeltsin's New Year Address," *SWB-SU*, January 3, 1995. In a series of speeches at the beginning of 1994, the foreign minister made clear his conversion to the diaspora cause. "Kozyrev Details Russian Foreign Policy Agenda," *Foreign Broadcast Information Service–Soviet Union* (hereafter *FBIS-SOV*), February 10, 1994, 12–14; "Foreign Minister Kozyrev Outlines Parliament's Role in Foreign Policy," *SWB-SU*, February 5, 1994; and "Kozyrev Warns against Violations of Rights of Russian Minorities in Former USSR," *SWB-SU*, January 21, 1994.

18. Melvin, *Russians beyond Russia*, 21. "Ob osnovnykh napravleniakh gosudarstvennoi politiki Rossiiskoi Federatsii v otnoshenii sootechestvennikov prozhivaiushchikh za rubezhom," *Rossiiskaia gazeta*, September 22, 1994.

19. See, for example, "Russia, Belarus Lecture Balts on Human Rights," *Jamestown Foundation Monitor*, November 25, 1996; and "Developments in Russian Policy Signal Intensified Pressure," *Jamestown Foundation Monitor*, February 12, 1997. Russia also pursued an active policy in relation to the future of the Russian language in Kazakhstan. "Kazakhhstan's Language Law Seeks to Equalize Native Language with Russian," *Jamestown Foundation Monitor*, November 26, 1996; and "Kazakhh Premier under Pressure in Moscow," *Jamestown Foundation Monitor*, November 27, 1996.

20. "Russia Cutting Oil Exports through Latvia," *New York Times*, April 10, 1998.

21. Graham Smith and Andrew Wilson, "Rethinking Russia's Post-Soviet Diaspora: The Potential for Political Mobilization in Eastern Ukraine and North-East Estonia," *Europe-Asia Studies* 49, no. 5 (July 1997).

22. As Pål Kolstø notes, there are a variety of "identity trajectories" that Russians might follow, depending on whether culture, language, history, territorial settlement, or other variables are seen as integral to defining Russianness. Kolstø, "The New Russian Diaspora—An Identity of Its Own? Possible Identity Trajectories for Russians in the Former Soviet Republics," *Ethnic and Racial Studies* 19, no. 3 (July 1996).

23. For examples of these terms, see: "O voprosakh zashchity prav i interesov rossiiskikh grazhdan za predelami Rossiiskoi Federatsii" (presidential decree, November 1992); "Ob osnovnykh napravleniakh gosudarstvennoi politiki Rossiiskoi Federatsii v otnoshenii sootechestvennikov prozhivaiushchikh za rubezhom," *Rossiiskaia gazeta*, September 22, 1994; "Deklaratsiia o podderzhke Rossiiskoi Federatsiei rossiiskoi diaspory i o pokrovitel'stve rossiiskim sootechestvennikam" (resolution passed by Duma on December 8, 1995); "O gosudarstvennoi politike v otnoshenii sootechestvennikov v gosudarstvakh-uchastnikakh Sodruzhestva Nezavisimykh Gosudarstv, Latvii, Litvy, Estonii i drugikh stranakh" (draft resolution of the Duma, 1997).

24. The most apocalyptic reading was Leon Aron, "The Russians Are Coming," *Policy Review*, no. 38 (Fall 1991). For a more sober assessment, see John B. Dunlop, "Will a Large-Scale Migration of Russians to the Russian Republic Take Place over the Current Decade?" *International Migration Review* 27, no. 3 (Fall 1993).

25. Statistics in this paragraph are taken from the surveys conducted by the International Organization for Migration, available at www.iom.int/iom/Publications/

books_studies_surveys/Russian_Federation.htm, along with Timothy Heleniak, "An Overview of Migration in the Post-Soviet Space," in Cynthia J. Buckley and Blair A. Ruble, with Erin Trouth Hofmann, eds., *Migration, Homeland, and Belonging in Eurasia* (Washington, D.C.: Woodrow Wilson Center Press, 2008), 29–67.

26. For an overview of these communities, see Ann Lencyk Pawliczko, ed., *Ukraine and Ukrainians throughout the World: A Demographic and Sociological Guide to the Homeland and Its Diaspora* (Toronto: University of Toronto Press, 1994); Myron B. Kuropas, *The Ukrainian Americans: Roots and Aspirations, 1884–1954* (Toronto: University of Toronto Press, 1991); and Orest Subtelny, *Ukrainians in North America: An Illustrated History* (Toronto: University of Toronto Press, 1991).

27. Similar disillusionment affected Armenians, Poles, Latvians, and other postcommunist returnees. See "Eastern Europe's Diasporas," *Economist*, December 26, 1992; and Michael Radu, "Western Diasporas in Post-Communist Transitions," *Problems of Post-Communism* (May–June 1995).

28. Andrew Wilson, "The Ukrainians: Engaging the 'Eastern Diaspora,'" in Charles King and Neil J. Melvin, eds., *Nations Abroad: Diaspora Politics and International Relations in the Former Soviet Union* (Boulder, Colo.: Westview, 1998), 106.

29. Andrew Wilson, *Ukrainian Nationalism in the 1990s: A Minority Faith* (Cambridge: Cambridge University Press, 1997), 180; and *Konstytutsiia Ukrainy* (Kyiv: Secretariat of the Supreme Council of Ukraine, 1996), 7.

30. On the travails of building a Ukrainian nation and defining the boundaries of Ukrainianness, see the special section on "Nation Building in Ukraine," *Transition*, September 6, 1996; and Mark von Hagen, "Does Ukraine Have a History?" *Slavic Review* 54, no. 3 (Fall 1995).

31. On this problem, see President Leonid Kuchma's speech before the Second International Forum of Ukrainians, August 21, 1997, reported in *FBIS-SOV*, September 15, 1997.

32. Statistics in this paragraph are taken from the surveys conducted by the International Organization for Migration, available at www.iom.int/iom/Publications/books_studies_surveys/Ukraine(1).htm; and Heleniak, "An Overview of Migration."

33. Sally N. Cummings, "The Kazakhs: Demographics, Diasporas, and 'Return,'" in King and Melvin, eds., *Nations Abroad,* 137.

34. Cummings, "The Kazakhs," 143.

35. Statistics in this paragraph are taken from the surveys conducted by the International Organization for Migration, available at www.iom.int/iom/Publications/books_studies_surveys/Kazakstan.htm.

36. Ian Bremmer, "Nazarbaev and the North: Statebuilding and Ethnic Relations in Kazakhstan," *Ethnic and Racial Studies* 17, no. 4 (October 1994).

37. Cummings, "The Kazakhs," 145; and International Organization for Migration statistics.

38. Saulesh Esenova, "The Outflow of Minorities from the Post-Soviet State: The Case of Kazakhstan," *Nationalities Papers* 24, no. 4 (December 1996).

39. Pål Kølsto, "Anticipating Demographic Superiority: Kazakh Thinking on Integration and Nation Building," *Europe-Asia Studies* 50, no. 1 (January 1998): 58.

40. See Martha Brill Olcott, *Kazakhstan: Unfulfilled Promise* (Washington, D.C.: Carnegie Endowment for International Peace, 2002).

CHAPTER 8

1. Tim Heleniak, "The Changing Nationality Composition of the Central Asian and Transcaucasian States," *Post-Soviet Geography and Economics* 38, no. 6 (1997). On Russia in particular, see Harley Balzer, "Human Capital and Russian Security in the 21st Century," in Andrew Kuchins, ed., *Russia after the Fall* (Washington, D.C.: Carnegie Endowment for International Peace, 2002), 163–184.

2. See Douglas S. Massey et al., *Worlds in Motion: Understanding International Migration at the End of the Millennium* (Oxford: Clarendon, 1998), 17–59; Douglas S. Massey and J. Edward Taylor, eds., *International Migration: Prospects and Policies in a Global Market* (Oxford: Oxford University Press, 2004).

3. Massey et al., *Worlds in Motion*, 7.

4. For examples of the literatures in these areas, see Michael S. Teitelbaum, "The Population Threat," *Foreign Affairs* (Winter 1992–1993): 63–78; Myron Weiner, *The Global Migration Crisis: Challenge to States and to Human Rights* (New York: HarperCollins, 1995); Barry R. Posen, "Military Responses to Refugee Disasters," *International Security* 21, no. 1 (1996); Rogers Brubaker, *Citizenship and Nationhood in France and Germany* (Cambridge, Mass.: Harvard University Press, 1992); Jeannette Money, *Fences and Neighbors: The Political Geography of Immigration Control* (Ithaca, N.Y.: Cornell University Press, 1999); Christian Joppke, *Immigration and the Nation-State: The United States, Germany, and Great Britain* (Oxford: Oxford University Press, 2000) and *Selecting by Origin: Ethnic Migration in the Liberal State* (Cambridge, Mass.: Harvard University Press, 2005); Stephen John Stedman and Fred Tanner, eds., *Refugee Manipulation: War, Politics, and the Abuse of Human Suffering* (Washington, D.C.: Brookings Institution Press, 2003).

5. See F. Stephen Larrabee, "Down and Out in Warsaw and Budapest: Eastern Europe and East-West Migration," *International Security* 16, no. 4 (Spring 1992); special issue of *International Migration Review* 26, no. 2 (1992); and Jeremy R. Azrael, Patricia A. Brukoff, and Vladimir D. Shkolnikov, "Prospective Migration and Emigration from the Former USSR: A Conference Report," *Slavic Review* 51, no. 2 (1992), which contains both more and less sanguine assessments about the emigration potential of former communist countries.

6. Claire Wallace and Dariusz Stola, "Introduction: Patterns of Migration in Central Europe," in Claire Wallace and Dariusz Stola, eds., *Patterns of Migration in Central Europe* (New York: Palgrave, 2001), 18.

7. Ali Mansoor and Bryce Quillin, eds., *Migration and Remittances: Eastern Europe and the Former Soviet Union* (Washington, D.C.: World Bank, 2007), available at www.worldbank.org.

8. Wallace and Stola, "Introduction," p. 32.

9. Population Division, Department of Economic and Social Affairs, United Nations Secretariat, *International Migration from Countries with Economies in Transition: 1980–1999* (New York: United Nations, 2002), 21.

10. Mansoor and Quillin, eds., *Migration and Remittances*, 115.

11. Terminology is a problem here. Some laws, such as Russia's, are known as "compatriot laws" and include relationships with citizens and coethnic noncitizens under the same legal regime. Others, such as Romania's and Bulgaria's, explicitly apply only to coethnic noncitizens abroad. Still others, such as Italy's, concern residents of a portion of the nation-state's territory that now lies in another country. I refer to all of these laws as diaspora laws, with the proviso that there are many different types beneath this rubric. Rogers Brubaker first called attention to the politics of imperfect nation-states after communism in his *Nationalism Reframed : Nationhood and the National Question in the New Europe* (Cambridge: Cambridge University Press, 1996).

12. The texts of these laws and those of other states may be found in the appendix to European Commission for Democracy through Law, *The Protection of National Minorities by Their Kin-State* (Strasbourg: Council of Europe Publishing, 2002). See also Osamu Ieda, ed., *Beyond Sovereignty: From Status Law to Transnational Citizenship?* (Sapporo: Slavic Research Center, Hokkaido University, 2006).

13. For an analysis of the Romanian and Slovak reactions, see David Adam Landau, "Identity, Institutions, and International Relations: The European Union and Hungary's Minority Abroad," unpublished paper, Georgetown University, 2003; and Ieda, ed., *Beyond Sovereignty.*

14. Zsuzsa Csergo and James M. Goldgeier, "Virtual Nationalism," *Foreign Policy* (September–October 2001).

15. However, nongovernmental organizations abroad can apply to the Hungarian government for funds for certain cultural activities deemed "beneficial to the preservation of national identity" (Act on Hungarians Living in Neighboring Countries, chap. 2, sect. 5). The law also allows the Hungarian government to engage in the "establishment, operation and development of higher education institutions" in neighboring states (chap. 2, sect. 14). But there is nothing in the law that would indicate that this is meant to be different from, say, the Greek government's funding a chair of Hellenic studies in the United States.

16. Territory is also important here. The most nationalist politicians in Hungary were particularly unwilling to see ethnic Hungarians in Slovakia and Romania move to Hungary precisely because the lands that they now inhabit were once part of the Hungarian state. Allowing unrestricted immigration would have reduced the Hungarian component of these territories' populations.

17. Brigid Fowler, "Fuzzing Citizenship, Nationalising Political Space: A Framework for Interpreting the Hungarian 'Status Law' as a New Form of Kin-State Policy in Central and Eastern Europe," Working Paper 40/02, Centre for Russian and East European Studies, University of Birmingham.

18. The immediate test case for this proposition is Romania's relationship with Moldova. In the early 1990s, Romania enthusiastically reached out to the Moldovan state, with its majority Romanian-speaking population, and allowed virtually

unrestricted movement across the international border. In time, however, further restrictions were put in place as Romania's relationship with the EU improved. Once Romania becomes an EU member, perhaps in 2007, the country might well be expected to follow the Hungarian line: making special provision for Moldovans to work in Romania but discouraging long-term migration.

19. The IOM distinguishes "alien smuggling" from "trafficking." The former is defined simply as the facilitation of an illegal crossing of an international border. The latter is alien smuggling plus the violation of the human rights of migrants.

20. The 2008 trafficking report is available at www.state.gov/g/tip/rls/ tiprpt/2008/.

21. "Russian Husband and Wife Arrested on Federal Indictment Charging Alien Smuggling for Profit and Money Laundering," press release, U.S. Attorney's Office for the Western District of Texas, August 17, 2001.

22. U.S. Department of State, "Trafficking in Persons Report 2008," available at www.state.gov/g/tip/rls/tiprpt/2008/.

23. David Binder, "In Europe, Sex Slavery Is Thriving Despite Raids," *New York Times*, October 20, 2002, 10. A subsequent multicountry raid in September 2003 netted 693 victims and 831 suspected traffickers. (The fact that raids seem to be held each year in the same month may account for the relatively low figures.) In the 2003 operation, only about 10 percent of the trafficked women accepted assistance from the IOM. David Binder, "12 Nations in Southeast Europe Pursue Traffickers in Sex Trade," *New York Times*, October 19, 2003, 6.

24. Khalid Koser, "The Smuggling of Asylum Seekers into Western Europe: Contradictions, Conundrums, and Dilemmas," in David Kyle and Rey Koslowski, eds., *Global Human Smuggling: Comparative Perspectives* (Baltimore: Johns Hopkins University Press, 2001), 59. As many tragic cases have revealed, however, human smuggling is rarely nonexploitative.

25. David Kyle and John Dale, "Smuggling the State Back In: Agents of Human Smuggling Reconsidered," in Kyle and Koslowski, eds., *Global Human Smuggling*, 33–34.

26. "New IOM Figures on the Global Scale of Trafficking," *IOM Trafficking in Migrants Quarterly Bulletin* (April 2001): 4.

27. Michael Specter, "Traffickers' New Cargo: Naïve Slavic Women," *New York Times*, January 11, 1998, A1.

28. "New IOM Figures," 5.

29. On urban-rural disparities, see *Trafficking in Women and Children from the Republic of Armenia: A Study* (Geneva: IOM, 2001), 20–21.

30. "U.S. State Department Trafficking Report a 'Mixed Bag,'" Human Rights Watch press release, July 12, 2001; "U.S. State Department Trafficking Report Missing Key Data," Human Rights Watch press release, June 6, 2002.

31. See, for example, Stephen Handelman, *Comrade Criminal: Russia's New Mafiya* (New Haven, Conn.: Yale University Press, 1995); Robert I. Friedman, *Red Mafiya: How the Russian Mob Has Invaded America* (New York: Little, Brown, 2000); David Satter, *Darkness at Dawn: The Rise of the Russian Criminal State* (New Haven,

Conn.: Yale University Press, 2003); Misha Glenny, *McMafia: A Journey through the Global Criminal Underworld* (New York: Knopf, 2008). For less sanguine assessments, see James O. Finckenauer and Elin Waring, "Russian Émigré Crime in the United States: Organized Crime or Crime That Is Organized?" *Transnational Organized Crime* 2, nos. 2–3 (1996): 139–155; and Federico Varese, *The Russian Mafia: Private Protection in a New Market Economy* (Oxford: Oxford University Press, 2001).

32. For important studies of these many other dimensions, see Susan Gal and Gail Kligman, *The Politics of Genders after Socialism* (Princeton, N.J.: Princeton University Press, 2000); Jacqui True, *Gender, Globalization, and Postsocialism* (New York: Columbia University Press, 2003); Kristen Ghodsee, *The Red Riviera: Gender, Tourism, and Postsocialism on the Black Sea* (Durham, N.C.: Duke University Press, 2005).

33. "Slavic Women Trafficked into Slavery," *Trafficking in Migrants Quarterly Bulletin*, June 1998.

34. Lejla Mavris, "Human Smugglers and Social Networks: Transit Migration through the States of the Former Yugoslavia," New Issues in Refugee Research Working Paper No. 72, UN High Commissioner for Refugees (December 2002), 2.

35. Mavris, "Human Smugglers," 5.

36. Mavris, "Human Smugglers," 6; and Human Rights Watch, *Hopes Betrayed: Trafficking of Women and Girls to Post-Conflict Bosnia and Herzegovina for Forced Prostitution* (New York: Human Rights Watch, 2002).

37. Mavris, "Human Smugglers," 3.

38. Author's interview with Joseph Limprecht, U.S. ambassador to Albania, Tirana, July 20, 2000.

39. Diego Gambetta, *The Sicilian Mafia: The Business of Private Protection* (Cambridge, Mass.: Harvard University Press, 1993).

40. Donna M. Hughes, "The 'Natasha' Trade: The Transnational Shadow Market of Trafficking in Women," *Journal of International Affairs* 53, no. 2 (Spring 2000): 6.

41. *Trafficking in Women and Children from the Republic of Armenia: A Study* (Geneva: IOM, 2001), 24.

42. See David I. Kertzer and Dominique Arel, eds., *Census and Identity: The Politics of Race, Ethnicity, and Language in National Censuses* (Cambridge: Cambridge University Press, 2001).

43. For a catalogue of these dimensions, see Milica Bookman, *Ethnic Groups in Motion: Economic Competition and Migration in Multiethnic States* (London: Frank Cass, 2002).

44. Massey et al., *Worlds in Motion*, 281.

45. See Marc Howard, *The Politics of Citizenship in the European Union* (Cambridge: Cambridge University Press, 2009).

CHAPTER 9

1. See Rogers Brubaker, *Ethnicity without Groups* (Cambridge, Mass.: Harvard University Press, 2004).

2. See Ian Lustick, "History, Historiography, and Political Science: Multiple Historical Records and the Problem of Selection Bias," *American Political Science Review* 90, no. 3 (1996).

3. See Colin Elman and Miriam Fendius Elman, eds., *Bridges and Boundaries: Historians, Political Scientists, and the Study of International Relations* (Cambridge, Mass.: MIT Press, 2001).

Bibliography

This bibliography is limited to books and journal articles. References to primary texts, news sources, and interviews may be found in the notes to each chapter.

Abdelal, Rawi, Yoshiko M. Herrera, Alastair Iain Johnston, and Rose McDermott, eds. *Measuring Identity: A Guide for Social Scientists*. Cambridge: Cambridge University Press, 2009.

Acton, J. E. E. D. *Essays in the History of Liberty*. Indianapolis: Liberty Fund, 1985.

Almond, Gabriel A. *A Discipline Divided: Schools and Sects in Political Science*. London: Sage, 1990.

Aminzade, Ronald, et al. *Silence and Voice in the Study of Contentious Politics*. Cambridge: Cambridge University Press, 2001.

Anderson, Benedict. *Imagined Communities*, new ed. London: Verso, 2006.

Azrael, Jeremy R., Patricia A. Brukoff, and Vladimir D. Shkolnikov. "Prospective Migration and Emigration from the Former USSR: A Conference Report," *Slavic Review* 51, no. 2 (1992).

Babilunga, N. V., ed. *Bessarabskii vopros i obrazovanie Pridnestrovskoi Moldavskoi Respubliki*. Tiraspol: Dnestr State Cooperative University, 1993.

Babilunga, N. V., and V. G. Bomeshko. *Pagini din istoria plaiului natal*. Tiraspol: Transnistrian Institute of Continuing Education, 1997.

Barker, Ernest. *National Character and the Factors in Its Formation*. London: Methuen, 1927.

Barkey, Karen. *Bandits and Bureaucrats: The Ottoman Route to State Centralization*. Ithaca, N.Y.: Cornell University Press, 1994.

Barkey, Karen, and Ronan Van Rossem. "Networks of Contention: Villages and Regional Structure in the Seventeenth-Century Ottoman Empire," *American Journal of Sociology* 102, no. 5 (March 1997).

Bates, Robert H. *When Things Fell Apart: State Failure in Late-Century Africa*. Cambridge: Cambridge University Press, 2008.

Beissinger, Mark R. *Nationalist Mobilization and the Collapse of the Soviet State.* Cambridge: Cambridge University Press, 2002.

Beissinger, Mark R., and Crawford Young, eds. *Beyond State Crisis? Post-Colonial Africa and Post-Soviet Eurasia in Comparative Perspective.* Washington, D.C.: Woodrow Wilson Center Press, 2002.

Benford, Robert B. "Framing Processes and Social Movements: An Overview and Assessment," *Annual Review of Sociology* 26 (August 2000).

Berdal, Mats, and David M. Malone, eds. *Greed and Grievance: Economic Agendas in Civil Wars.* Boulder, Colo.: Lynne Reinner, 2000.

Berlin, Isaiah. *Against the Current.* New York: Viking, 1980.

———. *Vico and Herder.* London: Hogarth, 1976.

Boehm, Christopher. *Blood Revenge: The Anthropology of Feuding in Montenegro and Other Tribal Societies.* Lawrence: University Press of Kansas, 1984.

Bookman, Milica. *Ethnic Groups in Motion: Economic Competition and Migration in Multiethnic States.* London: Frank Cass, 2002.

Brady, Henry E., and David Collier, eds. *Rethinking Social Inquiry: Diverse Tools, Shared Standards.* Lanham, Md.: Rowman and Littlefield, 2004.

Brass, Paul R. *Theft of an Idol: Text and Context in the Representation of Collective Violence.* Princeton, N.J.: Princeton University Press, 1997.

Bremmer, Ian. "Nazarbaev and the North: Statebuilding and Ethnic Relations in Kazakhstan," *Ethnic and Racial Studies* 17, no. 4 (October 1994).

Bremmer, Ian, and Ray Taras, eds. *Nations and Politics in the Soviet Successor States.* Cambridge: Cambridge University Press, 1993.

Bringa, Tone. *Being Muslim the Bosnian Way: Identity and Community in a Central Bosnian Village.* Princeton, N.J.: Princeton University Press, 1996.

Brown, Archie. *The Rise and Fall of Communism.* New York: Ecco, 2009.

———. *Soviet Politics and Political Science.* London: Macmillan, 1974.

Brown, Archie, ed. *Political Culture and Communist Studies.* Armonk, N.Y.: M. E. Sharpe, 1985.

Brown, Archie, ed. *Political Leadership in the Soviet Union.* London: Macmillan, 1989.

Brown, Archie, and John Gray, eds. *Political Culture and Political Change in Communist States.* London: Macmillan, 1977.

Brown, Michael E., ed. *Ethnic Conflict and International Security.* Princeton, N.J.: Princeton University Press, 1993.

Brown, Michael E., ed. *The International Dimensions of Internal Conflict.* Cambridge, Mass.: MIT Press, 1996.

Brubaker, Rogers. *Citizenship and Nationhood in France and Germany.* Cambridge, Mass.: Harvard University Press, 1992.

———. *Ethnicity without Groups.* Cambridge, Mass.: Harvard University Press, 2005.

———. *Nationalism Reframed: Nationhood and the National Question in the New Europe.* Cambridge: Cambridge University Press, 1996.

Brubaker, Rogers, and Frederick Cooper. "Beyond 'Identity,'" *Theory and Society* 29, no. 1 (2000).

Brubaker, Rogers, Margit Feischmidt, Jon Fox, and Liana Grancea. *Nationalist Politics and Everyday Ethnicity in a Transylvanian Town.* Princeton, N.J.: Princeton University Press, 2006.

Brubaker, Rogers, and David D. Laitin. "Ethnic and Nationalist Violence," *Annual Review of Sociology* 24 (1998).

Brundage, W. Fitzhugh, ed. *Under Sentence of Death: Lynching in the South.* Chapel Hill: University of North Carolina Press, 1997.

Buckley, Cynthia J., and Blair A. Ruble, with Erin Trouth Hofmann, eds. *Migration, Homeland, and Belonging in Eurasia.* Washington, D.C.: Woodrow Wilson Center Press and Johns Hopkins University Press, 2008.

Buechler, Steven M. *Social Movements in Advanced Capitalism: The Political Economy and Cultural Construction of Social Activism.* Oxford: Oxford University Press, 2000.

Bunce, Valerie. "Can We Compare Democratization in the East versus the South?" *Journal of Democracy* 6, no. 3 (July 1995).

———. "Paper Curtains and Paper Tigers," *Slavic Review* 54, no. 4 (Winter 1995).

———. "Regional Differences in Democratization," *Post-Soviet Affairs* 17, no. 3 (July 1998).

———. "Rethinking Recent Democratization: Lessons from the Postcommunist Experience," *World Politics* 55, no. 2 (2003).

———. "Should Transitologists Be Grounded?" *Slavic Review* 54, no. 1 (Spring 1995).

———. *Subversive Institutions: The Design and Destruction of Socialism and the State.* Cambridge: Cambridge University Press, 1999.

Bunce, Valerie, and Maria Csanadi. "Uncertainty in the Transition: Post-Communism in Hungary," *East European Politics and Societies* 7, no. 2 (1993).

Carment, David W., and Patrick James. "Internal Constraints and Interstate Ethnic Conflict: Toward a Crisis-Based Assessment of Irredentism," *Journal of Conflict Resolution* 39, no. 1 (March 1995).

Carment, David W., and Patrick James, eds. *Wars in the Midst of Peace: The International Politics of Ethnic Conflict.* Pittsburgh, Pa.: University of Pittsburgh Press, 1997.

Carothers, Thomas. *Aiding Democracy Abroad: The Learning Curve.* Washington, D.C.: Carnegie Endowment for International Peace, 1999.

———. *Critical Mission: Essays on Democracy Promotion.* Washington, D.C.: Carnegie Endowment for International Peace, 2004.

———. "The End of the Transition Paradigm," *Journal of Democracy* 13, no. 1 (2002).

Carr, E. H. *Nationalism and After.* London: Macmillan, 1945.

Carrère d'Encausse, Hélène. *The End of the Soviet Empire: The Triumph of the Nations.* Franklin Philip, trans. New York: Basic Books, 1993.

———. *The Great Challenge: Nationalities and the Bolshevik State, 1917–1930.* Nancy Festinger, trans. New York: Holmes and Meier, 1992.

Chayes, Abram, and Antonia Handler Chayes. *Preventing Conflict in the Post-Communist World: Mobilizing International and Regional Organizations.* Washington, D.C.: Brookings, 1996.

Chinn, Jeff, and Robert Kaiser. *Russians as the New Minority: Ethnicity and Nationalism in the Soviet Successor States.* Boulder, Colo.: Westview, 1996.

Chollet, Derek, and James Goldgeier. *America between the Wars, 11/9 to 9/11.* New York: Public Affairs, 2008.

Clifford, James. "Diasporas," *Cultural Anthropology* 9, no. 3 (August 1994).

Closson, Stacy. "State Weakness in Perspective: Trans-Territorial Energy Networks in Georgia, 1993–2003." Ph.D. dissertation. London School of Economics, 2007.

Clyde, Robert. *From Rebel to Hero: The Image of the Highlander, 1745–1830.* East Linton, Scotland: Tuckwell, 1995.

Cobban, Alfred. "The Decline of Political Theory," *Political Studies Quarterly* 68 (1953).

———. *Nationalism and National Self-Determination,* rev. ed. New York: Thomas Crowell, 1969.

———. *The Nation State and National Self-Determination.* New York: Thomas Y. Crowell, 1970.

Cohen, Robin. *Global Diasporas: An Introduction.* London: UCL Press, 1997.

Cohen, Stephen F. *Rethinking the Soviet Experience: Politics and History since 1917.* Oxford: Oxford University Press, 1985.

Cole, G. D. H. *Europe, Russia, and the Future.* New York: Macmillan, 1942.

Colley, Linda. *Britons: Forging the Nation, 1707–1837.* New Haven, Conn.: Yale University Press, 1992.

Collier, Paul. *The Bottom Billion.* Oxford: Oxford University Press, 2007.

Connor, Walker. *Ethnonationalism: The Quest for Understanding.* Princeton, N.J.: Princeton University Press, 1994.

Constas, Dimitri C., and Athanasios G. Platias, eds. *Diasporas in World Politics: The Greeks in Comparative Perspective.* London: Macmillan, 1993.

Cox, Michael. "The End of the USSR and the Collapse of Soviet Studies," *Coexistence* 31 (1994).

Crick, Bernard. *In Defence of Politics,* 2nd ed. London: Penguin, 1962.

Csergo, Zsuzsa, and James M. Goldgeier. "Virtual Nationalism," *Foreign Policy* (September–October 2001).

Darden, Keith, and Anna Maria Gryzmała-Busse. "The Great Divide: Literacy, Nationalism, and the Communist Collapse," *World Politics* 59, no. 1 (2006).

Darnton, Robert. *The Great Cat Massacre.* New York: Vintage, 1984.

David, Steven R. "Internal War: Causes and Cures," *World Politics* 49, no. 4 (July 1997).

Dawisha, Karen, and Bruce Parrott, eds. *The End of Empire? The Transformation of the USSR in Comparative Perspective.* Armonk, N.Y.: M. E. Sharpe, 1997.

Derluguian, Georgi. *Bourdieu's Secret Admirer in the Caucasus.* Chicago: University of Chicago Press, 2005.

Deutsch, Karl W. *Nationalism and Social Communication,* 2nd ed. Cambridge, Mass.: MIT Press, 1966.

Di Palma, Giuseppe. *To Craft Democracies: An Essay on Democratic Transitions.* Berkeley: University of California Press, 1990.

Doob, Leonard W. *Patriotism and Nationalism: Their Psychological Foundations.* New Haven, Conn.: Yale University Press, 1964.

Dunlop, John B. "Will a Large-Scale Migration of Russians to the Russian Republic Take Place over the Current Decade?" *International Migration Review* 27, no. 3 (Fall 1993).

Dzadziev, A. B., Kh. V. Dzutsev, and S. M. Karaev. *Etnografiia i mifologiia osetin.* Vladikavkaz: n.p., 1994.

Dzugaev, K. G., ed. *Iuzhnaia Osetiia: 10 let respublike.* Vladikavkaz: Iryston, 2000.

Easter, Gerald M. "Preference for Presidentialism: Postcommunist Regime Change in Russia and the NIS," *World Politics* 49, no. 1 (January 1997).

Elbadawi, Ibrahim, and Nicholas Sambanis. "How Much War Will We See? Explaining the Prevalence of Civil War," *Journal of Conflict Resolution* 46, no. 3 (June 2002).

Ellis, Stephen. *The Mask of Anarchy: The Roots of Liberia's War.* New York: New York University Press, 1999.

Elman, Colin, and Miriam Fendius Elman, eds. *Bridges and Boundaries: Historians, Political Scientists, and the Study of International Relations.* Cambridge, Mass.: MIT Press, 2001.

Emerson, Rupert. *Government and Nationalism in Southeast Asia.* New York: Institute of Pacific Relations, 1942.

Enzensberger, Hans Magnus. *Civil Wars: From L.A. to Bosnia.* New York: New Press, 1994.

Esenova, Saulesh. "The Outflow of Minorities from the Post-Soviet State: The Case of Kazakhstan," *Nationalities Papers* 24, no. 4 (December 1996).

Esman, Milton J., and Shibley Telhami, eds. *International Organizations and Ethnic Conflict.* Ithaca, N.Y.: Cornell University Press, 1995.

European Commission for Democracy through Law. *The Protection of National Minorities by Their Kin-State.* Strasbourg, France: Council of Europe Publishing, 2002.

Fainsod, Merle. *How Russia Is Ruled.* Cambridge, Mass.: Harvard University Press, 1953.

Faust, Drew Gilpin. *A Sacred Circle: The Dilemma of the Intellectual in the Old South, 1840–1860.* Baltimore: Johns Hopkins University Press, 1977.

Fearon, James D., and David D. Laitin. "Ethnicity, Insurgency, and Civil War," *American Political Science Review* 97, no. 1 (February 2003).

Finckenauer, James O., and Elin Waring. "Russian Émigré Crime in the United States: Organized Crime or Crime That Is Organized?" *Transnational Organized Crime* 2, nos. 2–3 (1996).

Fishman, Joshua A. *Language and Nationalism.* Rowley, Mass.: Newbury House, 1973.

Fleron, Frederic J., Jr., and Erik P. Hoffman, eds. *Post-Communist Studies and Political Science.* Boulder, Colo.: Westview, 1993.

Friedman, Robert I. *Red Mafiya: How the Russian Mob Has Invaded America.* New York: Little, Brown, 2000.

Friedrich, Carl J., ed. *Totalitarianism.* Cambridge, Mass.: Harvard University Press, 1954.

Friedrich, Carl J., and Zbigniew Brzezinski. *Totalitarian Dictatorship and Autocracy.* Cambridge, Mass.: Harvard University Press, 1956.

Fyfe, Hamilton. *The Illusion of National Character,* rev. ed. London: Watts, 1946.

Gagnon, V. P. "Ethnic Nationalism and International Conflict: The Case of Serbia," *International Security* 19, no. 3 (Winter 1994–1995).

———. *The Myth of Ethnic War: Serbia and Croatia in the 1990s.* Ithaca, N.Y.: Cornell University Press, 2004.

Gal, Susan, and Gail Kligman, eds. *Reproducing Gender: Politics, Publics, and Everyday Life after Socialism.* Princeton, N.J.: Princeton University Press, 2000.

Gambetta, Diego. *The Sicilian Mafia: The Business of Private Protection.* Cambridge: Harvard University Press, 1993.

Geertz, Clifford. *The Interpretation of Cultures.* New York: Basic Books, 1973.

Gellner, Ernest. *Conditions of Liberty: Civil Society and Its Rivals.* New York: Penguin, 1994.

———. *Culture, Identity, and Politics.* Cambridge: Cambridge University Press, 1987.

———. *Encounters with Nationalism.* Oxford: Blackwell, 1994.

———. "Homeland of the Unrevolution," *Daedalus* (Summer 1993).

———. "Nationalism and Politics in Eastern Europe," *New Left Review* 189 (1991).

———. *Nations and Nationalism.* Oxford: Blackwell, 1983.

———. *Plough, Sword and Book: The Structure of Human History.* London: Collins Harvill, 1988.

———. *Relativism and the Social Sciences.* Cambridge: Cambridge University Press, 1985.

———. *Saints of the Atlas.* London: Weidenfeld and Nicolson, 1969.

———. *Spectacles and Predicaments: Essays in Social Theory.* Cambridge: Cambridge University Press, 1979.

———. *Thought and Change.* Chicago, University of Chicago Press, 1964.

George, Alexander L., and Andrew Bennett. *Case Studies and Theory Development in the Social Sciences.* Cambridge, Mass.: MIT Press, 2004.

Ghodsee, Kristen. *The Red Riviera: Gender, Tourism, and Postsocialism on the Black Sea.* Durham, N.C.: Duke University Press, 2005.

Gilroy, Paul. *"There Ain't No Black in the Union Jack": The Cultural Politics of Race and Nation.* London: Hutchinson, 1987.

Giuliano, Elise. "Secessionism from the Bottom Up: Democratization, Nationalism, and Local Accountability in the Russian Transition," *World Politics* 58, no. 2 (2006).

Gleason, Abbott. *Totalitarianism: The Inner History of the Cold War.* New York: Oxford University Press, 1995.

Gledhill, John. "A Veil of Anarchy: Transitional Violence in Romania and the Balkans." Ph.D. dissertation, Georgetown University, 2007.

Glen, William. *Journal of a Tour from Astrachan to Karass.* Edinburgh: David Brown, 1822.

Glenny, Misha. *McMafia: A Journey through the Global Criminal Underworld.* New York: Knopf, 2008.

Goodwin, Jeff, and James M. Jasper, eds. *Rethinking Social Movements: Structure, Meaning, and Emotion.* Lanham, Md.: Rowman and Littlefield, 2004.

Gorenburg, Dmitry P. *Minority Ethnic Mobilization in the Russian Federation.* Cambridge: Cambridge University Press, 2003.

Greenfield, Liah. *Nationalism: Five Roads to Modernity.* Cambridge, Mass.: Harvard University Press, 1992.

Gribincea, Mihai. *Politica rusă a bazelor militare: Moldova și Georgia.* Chisinau: Civitas, 1999.

———. *Trupele ruse în Republica Moldova: factor stabilizator sau sursă de pericol?* Chisinau: Civitas, 1998.

Gross, Jan T. *Neighbors: The Destruction of the Jewish Community in Jedwabne, Poland.* Princeton, N.J.: Princeton University Press, 2001.

———. *Revolution from Abroad: The Soviet Conquest of Poland's Western Ukraine and Western Belorussia.* Princeton, N.J.: Princeton University Press, 1988.

Gurr, Ted Robert. *Minorities at Risk: A Global View of Ethnopolitical Conflicts.* Washington, D.C.: United States Institute of Peace Press, 1993.

———. "Peoples against States: Ethnopolitical Conflict and the Changing World System," *International Studies Quarterly* 38, no. 3 (September 1994).

———. *Why Men Rebel.* Princeton, N.J.: Princeton University Press, 1970.

Haas, Ernst B. "What Is Nationalism and Why Should We Study It?" *International Organization* 30, no. 3 (1986).

Hajda, Lubomyr, and Mark Beissinger, eds. *The Nationalities Factor in Soviet Politics and Society.* Boulder, Colo.: Westview, 1990.

Hale, Henry E. "Divided We Stand: Institutional Sources of Ethnofederal State Survival and Collapse," *World Politics* 56, no. 2 (2004).

———. "Regime Cycles: Democracy, Autocracy, and Revolution in Post-Soviet Eurasia," *World Politics* 58, no. 1 (2005).

Handelman, Stephen. *Comrade Criminal: Russia's New Mafiya.* New Haven, Conn.: Yale University Press, 1995.

Hannaford, Ivan. *Race: The History of an Idea in the West.* Washington, D.C.: Woodrow Wilson Center Press, 1996.

Harbom, Lotta, and Peter Wallensteen. "Armed Conflict and Its International Dimensions, 1946–2004," *Journal of Peace Research* 42, no. 5 (2005).

Harris, Chauncy. "The New Russian Minorities: A Statistical Overview," *Post-Soviet Geography* 34, no. 1 (January 1993).

Hayden, Robert. "Constitutional Nationalism in the Formerly Yugoslav Republics," *Slavic Review* 51, no. 4 (Winter 1992).

Hayes, Carlton J. H. *Essays on Nationalism.* New York: Macmillan, 1926.

———. *The Historical Evolution of Modern Nationalism.* New York, Richard Smith, 1931.

———. *Nationalism: A Religion.* New York, Macmillan, 1960.

———. *Wartime Mission in Spain, 1942–1945.* New York: Macmillan, 1945.

Hayward, Jack. "Political Science in Britain," *European Journal of Political Research* 20 (1991).

Hayward, Jack, Brian Barry, and Archie Brown, eds., *The British Study of Politics in the Twentieth Century.* London: British Academy and Oxford University Press, 1999.

Hechter, Michael. *Containing Nationalism.* Oxford: Oxford University Press, 2000.

Heleniak, Tim. "The Changing Nationality Composition of the Central Asian and Transcaucasian States," *Post-Soviet Geography and Economics* 38, no. 6 (1997).

Henderson, Ebenezer. *Biblical Researches and Travels in Russia*. London: James Nisbet, 1826.

Hendley, Kathryn. *Trying to Make Law Matter: Legal Reform and Labor Law in the Soviet Union*. Ann Arbor: University of Michigan Press, 1996.

Heraclides, Alexis. "Secessionist Minorities and External Involvement," *International Organization* 44, no. 3 (Summer 1990).

———. *The Self-Determination of Minorities in International Politics*. London: Frank Cass, 1991.

Hertz, Frederick. *Nationality in History and Politics*. London: Kegan Paul, Trench, Trubner, 1944.

Hill, Ronald J. *Soviet Politics, Political Science and Reform*. Oxford: Martin Robertson, 1980.

Hirsch, Francine. *Empire of Nations: Ethnographic Knowledge and the Making of the Soviet State*. Ithaca, N.Y.: Cornell University Press, 2005.

Hobsbawm, Eric, and Terrence Ranger, eds. *The Invention of Tradition*. Cambridge: Cambridge University Press, 1983.

Holbrooke, Richard. *To End a War*. New York: Random House, 1998.

Holmes, Leslie. *Postcommunism: An Introduction*. Durham, N.C.: Duke University Press, 1997.

Holsti, Kalevi J. *The State, War, and the State of War*. Cambridge: Cambridge University Press, 1996.

Horowitz, Donald L. *The Deadly Ethnic Riot*. Berkeley: University of California Press, 2001.

———. *Ethnic Groups in Conflict*. Berkeley: University of California Press, 1985.

Hough, Jerry F., and Merle Fainsod. *How the Soviet Union Is Governed*. Cambridge, Mass.: Harvard University Press, 1979.

Howard, Lise Morjé. *UN Peacekeeping in Civil Wars*. Cambridge: Cambridge University Press, 2008.

Howard, Marc Morjé. *The Politics of Citizenship in Europe*. Cambridge: Cambridge University Press, 2009.

———. *The Weakness of Civil Society in Post-Communist Europe*. Cambridge: Cambridge University Press, 2003.

Hughes, Donna M. "The 'Natasha' Trade: The Transnational Shadow Market of Trafficking in Women," *Journal of International Affairs* 53, no. 2 (Spring 2000).

Huntington, Samuel P. *The Clash of Civilizations and the Remaking of World Order*. New York: Simon and Schuster, 1996.

Ianovskii, Aleksandr. *Osetiia*. Tskhinvali: Ministry of Information and Press of the Republic of South Ossetia, 1993.

Ieda, Osamu, ed. *Beyond Sovereignty: From Status Law to Transnational Citizenship?* Sapporo: Slavic Research Center, Hokkaido University, 2006.

Ignatieff, Michael. *Blood and Belonging: Journeys into the New Nationalism*. London: Vintage, 1993.

Isaacs, Harold. *Idols of the Tribe: Group Identity and Political Change*. Cambridge, Mass.: Harvard University, 1975.

Istrati, Panait. *Russia Unveiled.* R. J. S. Curtis, trans. London: George Allen and Unwin, 1931.

Johnson, Samuel. *Journey to the Western Islands.* Boston: Houghton Mifflin, 1965.

Jones, Stephen F. "Democracy from Below? Interest Groups in Georgian Society," *Slavic Review* 59, no. 1 (2000).

Joppke, Christian. *Immigration and the Nation-State: The United States, Germany, and Great Britain.* Oxford: Oxford University Press, 2000.

———. *Selecting by Origin: Ethnic Migration in the Liberal State.* Cambridge, Mass.: Harvard University Press, 2005.

Jowitt, Kenneth. *New World Disorder: The Leninist Extinction.* Berkeley: University of California Press, 1992.

———. *Revolutionary Breakthroughs and National Development: The Case of Romania, 1944–1965.* Berkeley: University of California Press, 1971.

Judt, Tony. *Postwar: A History of Europe since 1945.* New York: Penguin, 2005.

Kahn, Jeffrey. *Federalism, Democratization, and the Rule of Law in Russia.* Oxford: Oxford University Press, 2002.

Kaiser, Robert. *The Geography of Nationalism in Russia and the USSR.* Princeton, N.J.: Princeton University Press, 1994.

Kakar, Sudhir. *The Colors of Violence: Cultural Identities, Religion, and Conflict.* Chicago: University of Chicago Press, 1996.

Kaldor, Mary. *New and Old Wars: Organized Violence in a Global Era,* 2nd ed. Stanford, Calif.: Stanford University Press, 2007.

Kalyvas, Stathis N. *The Logic of Violence in Civil War.* New York: Cambridge University Press, 2006.

———. "'New' and 'Old' Civil Wars: A Valid Distinction?" *World Politics* 54, no. 1 (2001).

———. "The Ontology of 'Political Violence': Action and Identity in Civil Wars," *Perspectives on Politics* 1, no. 3 (September 2003).

———. "The Paradox of Terrorism in Civil War," *Journal of Ethics* 8 (2004).

Kaplan, Robert. *Balkan Ghosts.* New York: St. Martin's, 1993.

Karakasidou, Anastasia N. *Fields of Wheat, Hills of Blood: Passages to Nationhood in Greek Macedonia, 1870–1990.* Chicago: University of Chicago Press, 1997.

Karklins, Rasma. *Ethnic Relations in the USSR: The Perspective from Below.* Boston: Unwin Hyman, 1986.

Karl, Terry Lynn, and Philippe C. Schmitter. "From an Iron Curtain to a Paper Curtain: Grounding Transitologists or Students of Postcommunism?" *Slavic Review* 54, no. 4 (Winter 1995).

Katznelson, Ira, and Helen V. Milner, eds. *Political Science: The State of the Discipline.* New York: W. W. Norton, 2002.

Kaufman, Stuart J. *Modern Hatreds: The Symbolic Politics of Ethnic War.* Ithaca, N.Y.: Cornell University Press, 2001.

Kaufmann, Chaim. "Possible and Impossible Solutions to Ethnic Civil Wars," *International Security* 20, no. 4 (1996).

———. "When All Else Fails: Ethnic Population Transfers and Partitions in the Twentieth Century," *International Security* 23 (Fall 1998).

Kazantzakis, Nikos. *Russia: A Chronicle of Three Journeys in the Aftermath of the Revolution*. Berkeley, Calif.: Creative Arts Book Company, 1989.

Kearney, Hugh. *The British Isles: A History of Four Nations*. Cambridge: Cambridge University Press, 1989.

Kedourie, Elie. *The Crossman Confessions and Other Essays*. London: Mansell, 1984.

———. *Nationalism*, 4th ed. Oxford: Blackwell, 1993.

Kedourie, Elie, ed. *Nationalism in Africa and Asia*. New York: World, 1970.

Keen, David. *The Benefits of Famine: A Political Economy of Famine Relief in Southwestern Sudan, 1983–1989*. Princeton, N.J.: Princeton University Press, 1994.

———. *The Economic Functions of Violence in Civil Wars*, Adelphi Paper 320. Oxford: Oxford University Press and International Institute for Strategic Studies, 1998.

Kenney, Padraic. *The Burdens of Freedom: Eastern Europe since 1989*. London: Zed, 2006.

———. *A Carnival of Revolution: Central Europe, 1989*. Princeton, N.J.: Princeton University Press, 2002.

Kertzer, David I., and Dominique Arel, eds. *Census and Identity: The Politics of Race, Ethnicity, and Language in National Censuses*. Cambridge: Cambridge University Press, 2001.

King, Charles. "Imagining Circassia: David Urquhart and the Making of North Caucasus Nationalism," *Russian Review* 66, no. 2 (2007).

———. *The Moldovans: Romania, Russia, and the Politics of Culture*. Stanford, Calif.: Hoover Institution Press, 2000.

———. "Post-Sovietology: Area Studies or Social Science?" *International Affairs* 70, no. 2 (1994).

———. "Potemkin Democracy," *The National Interest* (Summer 2001).

King, Charles, and Neil J. Melvin, eds. *Nations Abroad: Diaspora Politics and International Relations in the Former Soviet Union*. Boulder, Colo.: Westview, 1998.

King, Gary, Robert O. Keohane, and Sidney Verba. *Designing Social Inquiry: Scientific Inference in Qualitative Research*. Princeton, N.J.: Princeton University Press, 1994.

King, Jeremy. *Budweisers into Czechs and Germans: A Local History of Bohemian Politics, 1848–1948*. Princeton, N.J.: Princeton University Press, 2002.

Klein, Diana, et al., eds. *Ot ekonomiki voiny k ekonomike mira na Iuzhnom Kavkaze*. London: International Alert, 2004.

Kohn, Hans. *The Idea of Nationalism*. New York, Macmillan, 1944.

———. *The Idea of Nationalism: A Study in Its Origins and Background*. New York: Macmillan, 1956.

Kølsto, Pål. "Anticipating Demographic Superiority: Kazakh Thinking on Integration and Nation Building," *Europe-Asia Studies* 50, no. 1 (January 1998).

———. "The New Russian Diaspora—An Identity of Its Own? Possible Identity Trajectories for Russians in the Former Soviet Republics," *Ethnic and Racial Studies* 19, no. 3 (July 1996).

———. *Russians in the Former Soviet Republics*. Bloomington: Indiana University Press, 1995.

Kornhauser, William. *The Politics of Mass Society*. Glencoe, Ill.: Free Press, 1959.

Kuchins, Andrew. *Russia after the Fall*. Washington, D.C.: Carnegie Endowment for International Peace, 2002.

Kupchan, Charles A., ed. *Nationalism and Nationalities in the New Europe*. Ithaca, N.Y.: Cornell University Press, 1995.

Kuran, Timur. "Now Out of Never: The Element of Surprise in the East European Revolution of 1989," *World Politics* 44, no. 1 (October 1991).

Kuropas, Myron B. *The Ukrainian Americans: Roots and Aspirations, 1884–1954*. Toronto: University of Toronto Press, 1991.

Kyle, David, and Rey Koslowski, eds. *Global Human Smuggling: Comparative Perspectives*. Baltimore: Johns Hopkins University Press, 2001.

Kymlicka, Will. *Liberalism, Community and Culture*. Oxford: Clarendon, 1989.

———. *Multicultural Citizenship: A Liberal Theory of Minority Rights*. Oxford: Oxford University Press, 1995.

———. *Politics in the Vernacular: Nationalism, Multiculturalism, and Citizenship*. Oxford: Oxford University Press, 2001.

Laitin, David D. "Identity in Formation: The Russian-Speaking Nationality in the Post-Soviet Diaspora," *Archives européenes de sociologie* 36, no. 2 (1995).

———. *Identity in Formation: The Russian-Speaking Populations in the Near Abroad*. Ithaca, N.Y.: Cornell University Press, 1998.

Laitin, David D., and Ronald Grigor Suny. "Armenia and Azerbaijan: Thinking a Way Out of Karabakh," *Middle East Policy* 7 (October 1999).

Lake, David A., and Donald Rothchild, eds. *The International Spread of Ethnic Conflict: Fear, Diffusion, and Escalation*. Princeton, N.J.: Princeton University Press, 1998.

Lapidus, Gail W., and Victor Zaslavsky with Philip Goldman, eds. *From Union to Commonwealth: Nationalism and Separatism in the Soviet Republics*. Cambridge: Cambridge University Press, 1992.

Larrabee, F. Stephen. "Down and Out in Warsaw and Budapest: Eastern Europe and East-West Migration," *International Security* 16, no. 4 (Spring 1992).

Laski, Harold J. *A Grammar of Politics*, 3rd ed. London: George Allen and Unwin, 1934.

———. *Nationalism and the Future of Civilization*. London: Watts, 1932.

Le Bon, Gustave. *The Crowd: A Study of the Popular Mind*. Reprint ed. Atlanta: Cherokee Publishing, 1982.

Licklider, Roy. "The Consequences of Negotiated Settlements in Civil Wars, 1945–1993," *American Political Science Review* 89, no. 3 (1995).

———. "Early Returns: Results of the First Wave of Statistical Studies of Civil War Termination," *Civil Wars* 1, no. 3 (1998).

Licklider, Roy, ed. *Stopping the Killing: How Civil Wars End*. New York: New York University Press, 1993.

Lieven, Anatol. *Chechnya: Tombstone of Russian Power*. New Haven, Conn.: Yale University Press, 1998.

Lockhart, J. G. *The Life of Sir Walter Scott*. London: J. M. Dent and Sons, 1931.

Lustick, Ian. "History, Historiography, and Political Science: Multiple Historical Records and the Problem of Selection Bias," *American Political Science Review* 90, no. 3 (1996).

Luttwak, Edward N. "Give War a Chance," *Foreign Affairs* 78 (July–August 1999).

Macartney, C. A. *The Habsburg Empire, 1790–1918.* New York: Macmillan, 1969.

———. *Hungary and Her Successors.* Oxford: Oxford University Press, 1934.

———. *National States and National Minorities.* Oxford: Oxford University Press, 1934.

MacDiarmid, Hugh. *Collected Poems of Hugh MacDiarmid.* New York: Macmillan, 1962.

Malia, Martin. "From under the Rubble, What?" *Problems of Communism* 41, nos. 1–2 (January–April 1992): 89–106.

Malkki, Liisa H. *Purity and Exile: Violence, Memory, and National Cosmology among Hutu Refugees in Tanzania.* Chicago: University of Chicago Press, 1995.

Mandelbaum, Michael, ed. *Postcommunism: Four Perspectives.* New York: Council on Foreign Relations Press, 1996.

Manning, Chandra. *What This Cruel War Was Over: Soldiers, Slavery, and the Civil War.* New York: Knopf, 2007.

Mansoor, Ali, and Bryce Quillin, eds. *Migration and Remittances: Eastern Europe and the Former Soviet Union.* Washington, D.C.: World Bank, 2007.

Marr, Andrew. *The Battle for Scotland.* London: Penguin, 1995.

Martin, Terry. *The Affirmative Action Empire: Nations and Nationalism in the Soviet Union, 1923–1939.* Ithaca, N.Y.: Cornell University Press, 2002.

Massey, Douglas S., et al. *Worlds in Motion: Understanding International Migration at the End of the Millennium.* Oxford: Clarendon, 1998.

Massey, Douglas S., and J. Edward Taylor, eds. *International Migration: Prospects and Policies in a Global Market.* Oxford: Oxford University Press, 2004.

Mayall, James. *Nationalism and International Society.* Cambridge: Cambridge University Press, 1990.

Mazower, Mark. "Violence and the State in the Twentieth Century," *American Historical Review* 107, no. 4 (May 2003).

McAdam, Doug. *Political Process and the Development of Black Insurgency, 1930–1970,* 2nd ed. Chicago: Chicago University Press, 1999.

McAdam, Doug, et al. *Dynamics of Contention.* Cambridge: Cambridge University Press, 2001.

McAdam, Doug, et al., eds. *Comparative Perspectives on Social Movements: Political Opportunities, Mobilizing Structures, and Cultural Framings.* Cambridge: Cambridge University Press, 1996.

McClelland, J. S. *The Crowd and the Mob: From Plato to Canetti.* London: Unwin Hyman, 1989.

McFaul, Michael. *Russia's Unfinished Revolution.* Ithaca, N.Y.: Cornell University Press, 2001.

McFaul, Michael, and Kathryn Stoner-Weiss, eds. *After the Collapse of Communism: Comparative Lessons of Transition.* Cambridge: Cambridge University Press, 2004.

Melvin, Neil J. *Russians beyond Russia: The Politics of National Identity.* London: Pinter, 1995.

Midlarsky, Manus I., ed. *The Internationalization of Communal Strife.* London: Routledge, 1992.

Mill, J. S. *Collected Works of John Stuart Mill.* 33 vols. Toronto: Toronto University Press, 1963–1991.

Miller, David. *On Nationality.* Oxford: Clarendon, 1995.

Miller, David, and Larry Siedentop, eds. *The Nature of Political Theory.* Oxford: Clarendon, 1983.

Money, Jeannette. *Fences and Neighbors: The Political Geography of Immigration Control.* Ithaca, N.Y.: Cornell University Press, 1999.

Motyl, Alexander J. *Sovietology, Rationality, Nationality: Coming to Grips with Nationalism in the USSR.* New York: Columbia University Press, 1990.

Moynihan, Daniel Patrick. *Pandemonium.* Oxford: Oxford University Press, 1993.

Mueller, John E. "The Banality of 'Ethnic War,'" *International Security* 25, no. 1 (Summer 2000).

———. *The Remnants of War.* Ithaca, N.Y.: Cornell University Press, 2004.

Nahaylo, Bohdan, and Victor Swoboda. *Soviet Disunion: A History of the Nationalities Problem in the USSR.* London: Hamish Hamilton, 1990.

Nairn, Tom. *The Break-Up of Britain,* 2nd ed. London: Verso, 1981.

Nove, Alec. *Economic Rationality and Soviet Politics, or Was Stalin Really Necessary?* New York: Praeger, 1964.

Oakeshott, Michael. *Rationalism in Politics and Other Essays.* Indianapolis, Ind.: Liberty Fund, 1991.

Olcott, Martha Brill. *Kazakhstan: Unfulfilled Promise.* Washington, D.C.: Carnegie Endowment for International Peace, 2002.

Olzack, Susan. *The Dynamics of Ethnic Competition and Conflict.* Stanford, Calif.: Stanford University Press, 1992.

Orwell, George. *England Your England and Other Essays.* London: Secker and Warburg, 1953.

Pape, Robert A. *Dying to Win: The Strategic Logic of Suicide Terrorism.* New York: Random House, 2005.

Parekh, Bhikhu. *Rethinking Multiculturalism: Cultural Diversity and Political Theory,* 2nd ed. New York: Palgrave Macmillan, 2006.

Pawliczko, Ann Lencyk, ed. *Ukraine and Ukrainians throughout the World: A Demographic and Sociological Guide to the Homeland and Its Diaspora.* Toronto: University of Toronto Press, 1994.

Paxson, Margaret. *Solovyovo: The Story of Memory in a Russian Village.* Bloomington: Indiana University Press, 2005.

Pethybridge, Roger. *The Social Prelude to Stalinism.* London: Macmillan, 1974.

Pfaff, William. *The Wrath of Nations: Civilization and the Furies of Nationalism.* New York: Simon and Schuster, 1993.

Pillar, Paul R. *Negotiating Peace: War Termination as a Bargaining Process.* Princeton, N.J.: Princeton University Press, 1983.

Plamenatz, John. *On Alien Rule and Self-Government.* London: Longmans, 1960.

Polletta, Francesca, and James M. Jasper. "Collective Identity and Social Movements," *Annual Review of Sociology* 27 (August 2001).

Population Division, Department of Economic and Social Affairs, United Nations Secretariat. *International Migration from Countries with Economies in Transition: 1980–1999*. New York: United Nations, 2002.

Posen, Barry R. "Military Responses to Refugee Disasters," *International Security* 21, no. 1 (1996).

Prebble, John. *The King's Jaunt: King George IV and Scotland*. London: Collins, 1988.

Price, Jonathan J. *Thucydides and Internal War*. Cambridge: Cambridge University Press, 2001.

Przeworski, Adam. *Democracy and the Market: Political and Economic Reforms in Eastern Europe and Latin America*. Cambridge: Cambridge University Press, 1991.

Przeworski, Adam, and Henry Teune. *The Logic of Comparative Social Inquiry*. New York: John Wiley, 1970.

Radu, Michael. "Western Diasporas in Post-Communist Transitions," *Problems of Post-Communism* (May–June 1995).

Reno, William. *Corruption and State Politics in Sierra Leone*. Cambridge: Cambridge University Press, 1995.

———. *Warlord Politics and African States*. Boulder, Colo.: Lynne Reinner, 1998.

Rigby, T. H. *The Changing Soviet System: Mono-organisational Socialism from Its Origins to Gorbachev's Restructuring*. Aldershot, England: Edward Elgar, 1990.

———. *Political Elites in the USSR: Central Leaders and Local Cadres from Lenin to Gorbachev*. Aldershot, England: Edward Elgar, 1990.

Rigby, T. H., and Bogdan Harasymiw, eds. *Leadership Selection and Patron-Client Relations in the USSR and Yugoslavia*. London: Allen and Unwin, 1983.

Roeder, Philip G. "Peoples and States after 1989: The Political Costs of Incomplete National Revivals," *Slavic Review* 58, no. 4 (1999).

———. "Soviet Federalism and Ethnic Mobilization," *World Politics* 43, no. 1 (January 1991).

———. *Where Nation-States Come From: Institutional Change in the Age of Nationalism*. Princeton, N.J.: Princeton University Press, 2007.

Rolland, Stewart E. *Circassia: Speech of Stewart E. Rolland, at a Public Meeting Held at the Corn Exchange, Preston, October 1, 1862, to Receive the Deputies from Circassia*. London: Hardwicke, 1862.

Rose, Richard. *Politics in England*. Boston: Little Brown, 1964.

———. *The Territorial Dimension in Government: Understanding the United Kingdom*. Chatham, N.J.: Chatham House, 1982.

Rosenau, James N. *Along the Domestic-Foreign Frontier: Exploring Governance in a Turbulent World*. Cambridge: Cambridge University Press, 1997.

Roshwald, Aviel. *The Endurance of Nationalism*. Cambridge: Cambridge University Press, 2006.

Rothchild, Donald, and Alexander J. Groth. "Pathological Dimensions of Domestic and International Ethnicity," *Political Science Quarterly* 110, no. 1 (Spring 1995).

Rothschild, Joseph, and Nancy M. Wingfield. *Return to Diversity: A Political History of East Central Europe since World War II*, 4th ed. Oxford: Oxford University Press, 2007.

Royal Institute of International Affairs. *Nationalism.* Oxford: Oxford University Press, 1939.

Rutland, Peter. "Sovietology: Notes for a Post-Mortem," *National Interest*, no. 31 (Spring 1993).

Saideman, Stephen M. "Explaining the International Relations of Secessionist Conflicts: Vulnerability vs. Ethnic Ties," *International Organization* 51, no. 4 (Autumn 1997).

———. *The Ties That Divide: Ethnic Politics, Foreign Policy, and International Conflict.* New York: Columbia University Press, 2001.

Saideman, Stephen M., and R. William Ayres. *For Kin or Country: Xenophobia, Nationalism, and War.* New York: Columbia University Press, 2008.

Sakwa, Richard. *Postcommunism.* Buckingham, England: Open University Press, 1999.

Sambanis, Nicholas. "Do Ethnic and Non-Ethnic Civil Wars Have the Same Causes? A Theoretical and Empirical Enquiry (Part 1)," *Journal of Conflict Resolution* 45, no. 3 (June 2001).

———. "Partition as a Solution to Ethnic War: An Empirical Critique of the Theoretical Literature," *World Politics* 52, no. 4 (July 2000).

———. "A Review of Recent Advances and Future Directions in the Literature on Civil War," *Defense and Peace Economics* 13, no. 2 (2002).

Satter, David. *Darkness at Dawn: The Rise of the Russian Criminal State.* New Haven, Conn.: Yale University Press, 2003.

Schmitter, Philippe C., with Terry Lynn Karl. "The Conceptual Travels of Transitologists and Consolidologists: How Far East Should They Attempt to Go?" *Slavic Review* 53, no. 1 (Spring 1994).

Seleny, Anna. "Old Political Rationalities and New Democracies: Compromise and Confrontation in Hungary and Poland," *World Politics* 51, no. 3 (July 1999).

Seton-Watson, Hugh. *East Central Europe between the Wars, 1918–1941.* Cambridge: Cambridge University Press, 1945.

———. *The East European Revolution.* New York: Praeger, 1956.

———. *Nationalism and Communism.* New York: Praeger, 1964.

———. *Nations and States.* Boulder, Colo.: Westview, 1977.

———. *The Russian Empire, 1801–1917.* Oxford: Clarendon, 1967.

Seton-Watson, Hugh, and Christopher Seton-Watson. *The Making of a New Europe: R. W. Seton-Watson and the Last Years of Austria Hungary.* Seattle: University of Washington Press, 1981.

Seton-Watson, R. W. *Disraeli, Gladstone and the Eastern Question: A Study in Diplomacy and Party Politics.* London: Frank Cass, 1962.

———. *A History of the Roumanians.* Cambridge: Cambridge University Press, 1934.

———. *The Rise of Nationality in the Balkans.* London: Constable, 1917.

———. *The Southern Slav Question and the Habsburg Monarchy.* New York: H. Fertig, 1969 [1911].

Shafer, Boyd C. *Faces of Nationalism.* New York, Harcourt, Brace, Jovanovich, 1972.

———. *Nationalism: Myth and Reality.* New York, Harcourt, Brace and World, 1955.

Shain, Yossi. *Kinship and Diasporas in International Affairs*. Ann Arbor: University of Michigan Press, 2007.

———. *Marketing the American Creed Abroad: Diasporas in the U.S. and Their Homelands*. Cambridge: Cambridge University Press, 1999.

Shapiro, Leonard. *The Communist Party of the Soviet Union*. London: Eyre and Spottiswoode, 1960.

———. *Totalitarianism*. London: Pall Mall, 1972.

Sheffer, Gabriel, ed. *Modern Diasporas in International Politics*. London: Croom Helm, 1986.

Shils, Edward. "Primordial, Personal, Sacred and Civil Ties," *British Journal of Sociology* 8 (1957).

Shlapentokh, Vladimir, Munir Sendich, and Emil Payin, eds. *The New Russian Diaspora: Russian Minorities in the Former Soviet Republics*. Armonk, N.Y.: M. E. Sharpe, 1994.

Shleifer, Andrei, and Daniel Treisman. *Without a Map: Political Tactics and Economic Reform in Russia*. Cambridge, Mass.: MIT Press, 2000.

Shornikov, M. *Pokushenie na status*. Chisinau: Chisinau Society of Russians, 1997.

Sinno, Abdulkader. *Organizations at War in Afghanistan and Beyond*. Ithaca, N.Y.: Cornell University Press, 2008.

Slezkine, Yuri. "The USSR as a Communal Apartment, or How a Socialist State Promoted Ethnic Particularism," *Slavic Review* 53, no. 2 (Summer 1994).

Smelser, Neil J. *Theory of Collective Behavior*. Glencoe, Ill.: Free Press, 1963.

Smith, Anthony D. *The Ethnic Origins and Nations*. Oxford: Blackwell, 1986.

———. *The Ethnic Revival*. Cambridge: Cambridge University Press, 1981.

———. *National Identity*. London: Penguin, 1991.

———. *Nations and Nationalism in a Global Era*. London: Polity, 1995.

Smith, Graham, ed. *The Nationalities Question in the Soviet Union*. London: Longman, 1990.

Smith, Graham, and Andrew Wilson. "Rethinking Russia's Post-Soviet Diaspora: The Potential for Political Mobilization in Eastern Ukraine and North-East Estonia," *Europe-Asia Studies* 49, no. 5 (July 1997).

Snyder, Jack. "Science and Sovietology: Bridging the Methods Gap in Soviet Foreign Policy Studies," *World Politics* 40, no. 2 (January 1988).

Snyder, Louis L. *The Meaning of Nationalism*. New Brunswick, N.J.: Rutgers University Press, 1954.

———. *Varieties of Nationalism: A Comparative Study*. Hinsdale, Ill.: Dryden, 1976.

Snyder, Timothy. *The Reconstruction of Nations: Poland, Ukraine, Lithuania, and Belarus, 1569–1999*. New Haven, Conn.: Yale University Press, 2003.

———. "'To Resolve the Ukrainian Question Once and For All': The Ethnic Cleansing of Ukrainians in Poland, 1943–1947," *Journal of Cold War Studies* 1, no. 2 (Spring 1999).

Sokol, Jason. *There Goes My Everything: White Southerners in the Age of Civil Rights, 1945–1975*. New York: Vintage, 2007.

Solnick, Steven. *Stealing the State: Control and Collapse in Soviet Institutions*. Cambridge, Mass.: Harvard University Press, 1998.

Solomon, Susan Gross, ed. *Pluralism in the Soviet Union: Essays in Honour of H. Gordon Skilling*. London: Macmillan, 1983.

Sowell, Thomas. *Migrations and Cultures: A World View*. New York: Basic Books, 1996.

Stati, Vasile. *Istoria Moldovei*. Chisinau: Vivar-Editor, 2002.

Stedman, Stephen John. *Peacemaking in Civil War: International Mediation in Zimbabwe, 1974–1980*. Boulder, Colo.: Lynne Reinner, 1991.

Stedman, Stephen John, Donald Rothchild, and Elizabeth M. Cousens, eds. *Ending Civil Wars: The Implementation of Peace Agreements*. Boulder, Colo.: Lynne Reinner, 2002.

Stedman, Stephen John, and Fred Tanner, eds. *Refugee Manipulation: War, Politics, and the Abuse of Human Suffering*. Washington, D.C.: Brookings Institution Press, 2003.

Stoner-Weiss, Kathryn. *Local Heroes: The Political Economy of Russian Regional Governance*. Princeton, N.J.: Princeton University Press, 1997.

———. *Resisting the State: Reform and Retrenchment in Post-Soviet Russia*. Cambridge: Cambridge University Press, 2006.

Straus, Scott. *The Order of Genocide: Race, Power, and War in Rwanda*. Ithaca, N.Y.: Cornell University Press, 2006.

Suny, Ronald Grigor. *The Revenge of the Past: Nationalism, Revolution, and the Collapse of the Soviet Union*. Stanford, Calif.: Stanford University Press, 1993.

Tambiah, Stanley J. *Leveling Crowds: Ethnonationalist Conflicts and Collective Violence in South Asia*. Berkeley: University of California Press, 1996.

Tamir, Yael. *Liberal Nationalism*. Princeton, N.J.: Princeton University Press, 1993.

Tarrow, Sidney. *Power in Movement: Social Movements and Contentious Politics*, 2nd ed. Cambridge: Cambridge University Press, 1998.

Taylor, A. J. P. *An Old Man's Diary*. London: Hamish Hamilton, 1984).

Taylor, Charles. *Multiculturalism and "The Politics of Recognition."* Princeton, N.J.: Princeton University Press, 1992.

Teitelbaum, Michael S. "The Population Threat," *Foreign Affairs* (Winter 1992–1993).

Terry, Sarah Meiklejohn. "Thinking about Post-Communist Transitions: How Different Are They?" *Slavic Review* 52, no. 2 (Summer 1993).

Thucydides. *History of the Peloponnesian War*. Rex Warner, trans. New York: Penguin, 1972.

Tilly, Charles. *From Mobilization to Revolution*. Reading, Mass.: Addison-Wesley, 1978.

———. *The Politics of Collective Violence*. Cambridge: Cambridge University Press, 2003.

Tismaneanu, Vladimir, Marc Morjé Howard, and Rudra Sil, eds. *World Order after Leninism*. Seattle: University of Washington Press, 2006.

Toft, Monica Duffy. *The Geography of Ethnic Violence: Identity, Interests, and the Indivisibility of Territory*. Princeton, N.J.: Princeton University Press, 2003.

Tolnay, Stewart E., and E. M. Beck. *A Festival of Violence: An Analysis of Southern Lynchings, 1882–1930*. Urbana: University of Illinois Press, 1995.

Treisman, Daniel. *After the Deluge: Regional Crises and Political Consolidation in Russia*. Ann Arbor: University of Michigan Press, 1999.

Trevor-Roper, Hugh. *The Invention of Scotland*. New Haven, Conn.: Yale University Press, 2008.

True, Jacqui. *Gender, Globalization, and Postsocialism*. New York: Columbia University Press, 2003.

Urban, Michael. "The Politics of Identity in Russia's Postcommunist Transition: The Nation against Itself," *Slavic Review* 53, no. 3 (Fall 1994).

Vachudová, Milada. *Europe Undivided: Democracy, Leverage, and Integration after Communism*. Oxford: Oxford University Press, 2005.

Varese, Frederico. *The Russian Mafia: Private Protection in a New Market Economy*. Oxford: Oxford University Press, 2001.

Varshney, Ashutosh. *Ethnic Conflict and Civic Life: Hindus and Muslims in India*. New Haven, Conn.: Yale University Press, 2002.

———. "Nationalism, Ethnic Conflict, and Rationality," *Perspectives on Politics* 1, no. 1 (March 2003).

Verdery, Katherine. *What Was Socialism, and What Comes Next?* Princeton, N.J.: Princeton University Press, 1996.

Volkov, Vadim. *Violent Entrepreneurs: The Use of Force in the Making of Russian Capitalism*. Ithaca, N.Y: Cornell University Press, 2002.

Von Hagen, Mark. "Does Ukraine Have a History?" *Slavic Review* 54, no. 3 (Fall 1995).

Von Laue, Theodore H. *Why Lenin? Why Stalin? A Reappraisal of the Russian Revolution, 1900–1930*. Philadelphia: J. B. Lippincott, 1964.

Wallace, Claire, and Dariusz Stola, eds. *Patterns of Migration in Central Europe*. New York: Palgrave, 2001.

Wallace, Donald Mackenzie. *Russia*. New York: AMS, 1970 [1877].

Walter, Barbara F. *Committing to Peace: The Successful Settlement of Civil Wars*. Princeton, N.J.: Princeton University Press, 2002.

———. "The Critical Barrier to Civil War Settlement." *International Organization* 51 (Summer 1997).

Walter, Barbara F., and Jack Snyder, eds. *Civil Wars, Insecurity, and Intervention*. New York: Columbia University Press, 1999.

Webb, Sidney, and Beatrice Webb. *Soviet Communism: A New Civilisation?* London: Gollancz, 1935.

Wedel, Janine R. *Collision and Collusion: The Strange Case of Western Aid to Eastern Europe*, 2nd ed. New York: Palgrave, 2001.

Weiner, Myron. *The Global Migration Crisis: Challenge to States and to Human Rights*. New York: HarperCollins, 1995.

Weinstein, Jeremy M. *Inside Rebellion: The Politics of Insurgent Violence*. Cambridge: Cambridge University Press, 2007.

White, Stephen, Judy Batt, and Paul G. Lewis, eds. *Developments in Central and East European Politics*, 4th ed. Durham, N.C.: Duke University Press, 2007.

White, Stephen, John Gardner, George Schöpflin, and Tony Saich. *Communist and Postcommunist Political Systems: An Introduction*, 3rd ed. New York: St. Martin's, 1990.

White, Stephen, and Daniel N. Nelson, eds. *The Politics of the Postcommunist World: From Communist to Postcommunist Politics.* London: Ashgate, 2000.

White, Stephen, and Alex Pravda, eds. *Ideology and Soviet Politics.* London: Macmillan, 1988.

Wilbraham, Richard. *Travels in the Trans-Caucasian Provinces of Russia.* London: John Murray, 1839.

Wilde, Oscar. *The Complete Letters of Oscar Wilde.* Ed. Merlin Holland and Rupert Hart-Davis. London: Fourth Estate, 2000.

Wilkinson, Steven. *Votes and Violence: Electoral Competition and Ethnic Riots in India.* Cambridge: Cambridge University Press, 2004.

Wilson, Andrew. *Ukrainian Nationalism in the 1990s: A Minority Faith.* Cambridge: Cambridge University Press, 1997.

Wirth, Louis. "Types of Nationalism," *American Journal of Sociology* 41 (1936).

Wood, Elisabeth Jean. *Insurgent Collective Action and Civil War in El Salvador.* New York: Oxford University Press, 2003.

Woodruff, David M. *Money Unmade: Barter and the Fate of Russian Capitalism.* Ithaca, N.Y.: Cornell University Press, 1999.

Woodward, C. Vann. *The Burden of Southern History,* 3rd ed. Baton Rouge: Louisiana State University Press, 1993.

Woodward, Susan L. *Balkan Tragedy: Chaos and Dissolution after the Cold War.* Washington, D.C.: Brookings Institution, 1995.

———. *Socialist Unemployment: The Political Economy of Yugoslavia, 1945–1990.* Princeton, N.J.: Princeton University Press, 1995.

Yashar, Deborah J. "Democracy, Indigenous Movements, and the Postliberal Challenge in Latin America," *World Politics* 52, no. 1 (October 1999).

Zartman, I. William. *Ripe for Resolution: Conflict and Intervention in Africa.* Oxford: Oxford University Press, 1985.

Zartman, I. William, ed. *Elusive Peace: Negotiating an End to Civil Wars.* Washington, D.C.: Brookings Institution Press, 1995.

Zolotarev, V. A., ed. *Rossiia (SSSR) v lokal'nykh voinakh i voennykh konfliktakh vtoroi poloviny XX veka.* Moscow: Institute of Military History, Russian Ministry of Defense, 2000.

Zürcher, Christoph. *The Post-Soviet Wars: Rebellion, Ethnic Conflict, and Nationhood in the Caucasus.* New York: New York University Press, 2007.

Zwick, Peter. "The Perestroika of Soviet Studies: Thinking and Teaching about the Soviet Union in Comparative Perspective," *PS: Political Science and Politics* 24, no. 3 (September 1991).

Index

LaVergne, TN USA
16 October 2010
201076LV00003B/1/P